HMONG

HISTORY OF A PEOPLE

by
Keith Quincy

Eastern Washington University Press
Cheney, Washington

To my wife, Anna Moore Quincy

© 1988 Eastern Washington University Press
Cheney, Washington 99004
ISBN 0-910055-07-6

TABLE OF CONTENTS

ACKNOWLEDGMENTS

The research and writing of this book was undertaken with a great deal of trepidation. Writing it was not my own idea. This honor goes to See Vue, a former student and friend. It was his constant enthusiasm for the project that repeatedly overcame my reservations about seeing it through to the end. When I complained, as I often did, that this was no job for a political philosopher and that others were more competent to undertake the task, he simply observed that even if this were true no one else had come forward to volunteer.

See Vue also arranged numerous interviews with American Hmong, especially older Hmong knowledgeable in folklore and in many instances eye-witnesses to important events not covered in the memoirs of French colonial administrators. Without their testimony, the chapters that attempt to chronicle the lives of the Hmong in Indochina would have been very thin indeed. Those who deserve special mention are: Thao Her, Bliacher Lee, Fu Vu, Tou Vu, Neng Vu, Cher Sue Vue, Nao Yang Vue, Seng Vue, Shue Long Vue, Tong Leng Vue, Xia Ying Vue, Katoua Xiong, Terry Xiong, Nao Ying Yang, and Cher Cha Yang. Terry Xiong deserves additional credit for ferreting out unavailable material on the Hmong Chao Fa.

Obtaining most of the research material for this book would have been impossible without the expert help of Suzanne Schenk of the Kennedy Library who spent untold hours locating hard to find articles and books, many not available in the U.S. Indeed, Ms. Schenk became something of an expert on Hmong bibliography and found some material on her own that I did not know even existed.

Much time was saved by Dr. David Bell who permitted me to shamelessly pilfer his large personal library on China and Southeast Asia. His advice on reading material was always invaluable.

Dr. Khunying Suriya Ratanakul of Mahidol University, Thailand, was gracious enough to set aside time from her busy research schedule to read a rough draft of the book and save me from some embarrassing errors and to suggest additional research topics. An early draft was also read by Mr. Pao Vue who suggested additional topics for research. Dr. James Wallace read a later draft and offered valuable comments.

I owe a special debt to Professor Bill Kidd who was instrumental in obtaining additional release time from my teaching duties so that I could finish the book. The E.W.U. Research and Scholarship Committee was also gracious in granting me two sabbatical leaves to do research and conduct interviews. Grants from the E.W.U. Foundation helped defray costs for research related travel.

Most of the work for the book was undertaken during Professor James Wallace's tenure as department chairman. If it had not been for his unflagging support, including adjustments in my teaching schedule to free up time for writing, the book would still be in rough draft.

John Eldridge was given the unenviable task of serving as the book's editor. We had very different ideas about what sort of book this was to be. I wanted an academic book slanted to a general audience. He considered this a contradiction in terms. In the end, his view won out. It is now a leaner and, I trust, better book.

Finally, I must thank my wife, Anna Quincy, who not only never complained of her absentee husband holed up in his office until the early morning hours, but read every page of the many rough drafts with unfeigned interest and reminded me from time to time when my own energy flagged that the book and the Hmong were worth the effort.

INTRODUCTION

There are slightly more than six million Hmong. Most live in China. The rest are to be found in the mountain ranges of southeast Asia. In recent years, thousands of Laotian Hmong have abandoned Southeast Asia for the west. While a number have settled in France, Canada and Australia, the majority have sought refuge in the U.S.

The Hmong are montagnards, but they have not always lived in the mountains. Nor have they always lived in China. Central Siberia was their home before they migrated to northern China and later competed with the Chinese for the rich soil along the banks of the Yellow River and became, according to ancient Chinese history, the first enemies of the Chinese. Odd looking, enemies, too, for many of them were probably blond and blue eyed. Such Hmong are still to be found, though they are few in number. They are testimony to the Hmong's Caucasian ancestry, and to an original homeland in southern Russia or on the Iranian plateau.

The Chinese made war on the Hmong and drove them south into the region encompassing present day Hupeh and Hunan provinces. Relations between the Hmong and Chinese vacillated between uneasy truce and armed conflict for centuries, with the Hmong suffering many devastating defeats. The tables were turned in the fourth century A.D. when the Hmong established an independent kingdom that for a time even rivaled the power of the Empire. The Hmong kingdom survived until the tenth century when it was brutally crushed by imperial forces. While thousands of Hmong were reduced to near slavery by the Chinese, the vast majority fled the Hupeh/Hunan region for the mountain zones of Kweichow, Szechwan and Yunnan where they lived beyond the reach of the Chinese and enjoyed relative peace and independence until the eighteenth century when the emperors of the Manchu dynasty waged a war of extermination against the Hmong of Kweichow and southern Szechwan. A century later, the Yunnanese Hmong suffered a similar fate.

The depth of Chinese animosity toward the Hmong was due in part to the Hmong's refusal to embrace Chinese culture. Some Hmong did assimilate, but they were few in number. They were called the "cooked" Hmong in contrast to the "raw" Hmong who stubbornly rejected Chinese ways which the Chinese equated with civilization itself. This conceit did not impress the Hmong who took pride in their own rich culture and their shamanist religion, both of which they have preserved relatively unchanged for thousands of years. But like the Jews, the Hmong were forced to pay a heavy price for maintaining their cultural identity.

Relentless persecution forced the Hmong to become perpetual migrants, moving slowly southward from Honan to Kweichow, Szechwan, and Yunnan. Some continued the southward migration into southeast Asia. From the middle of the nineteenth century onward thousands of Hmong crossed the Chinese border into north Vietnam, Laos, Thailand and Burma in search of a new home where they might at last live in peace.

It was not to be. After World War II, southeast Asia was plunged into a state of more or less permanent war: first with the French pitted against the Vietnamese, then the Americans taking the place of the French, and finally the Vietnamese turning aggressor against their southeast Asian neighbors.

Throughout the conflict the Hmong were forced to take sides, or change allegiances, as one principal actor after another withdrew from the struggle, leaving the Hmong to fend for themselves. It was the Laotian Hmong who fought America's secret war in Laos and sacrificed nearly one third of their population to prevent the Vietnamese communists from turning Laos into a puppet state.

The following pages document the history of this remarkable people who are little known to the American public. This book looks to another audience as well: to the children of the thousands of Laotian Hmong who have sought a new life in America. They have much to be proud of. Hopefully, this admittedly incomplete account of their ancestors will help to sustain that pride until a definitive history is completed by scholars of their own race.

CHAPTER

1

CH'IEN-LUNG'S REVENGE

The year was 1776. After a three year campaign in the field, General Akoui entered Peking at the head of his victorious army with 250 prisoners in tow. Though weary, the general had good reason to be pleased that day, for among the prisoners was Sonom, the 21-year-old Hmong king of greater Kin-tchuen, as well as the young king's immediate family and the principal members of his court.

The Manchu emperor, Ch'ien-lung, had demonstrated his appreciation by traveling ten miles from the imperial capital to greet the returning general. For even though Akoui's victory was minor in comparison to many of the empire's other triumphs, it was one the emperor had relished in anticipation. Now with the Hmong king in his grasp, Ch'ien-lung would have his revenge. It would be swift and terrible.

Throughout Ch'ien-lung's reign, China had been in more or less continuous turmoil, much of it directly attributable to his expansionist foreign policy which resulted in the greatest increase of the empire in Chinese history. Burma, Nepal, and Turkestan were conquered and made protectorates while China's hold on Tibet and Mongolia was strengthened. But these successes had their cost, not only for conquered populations but for Chinese citizens who groaned under burdensome taxes and resented their Manchu rulers who were, after all, Manchurians and not Chinese. Things were even worse for the non-Chinese minorities who were treated by both the Manchu and Chinese alike as foreigners in their own land.

Rebellions were not infrequent. There were popular uprisings in Turkestan on the frontier and rebellions at home, not only in Shantung province but in Honan which had become a particular trouble spot. There the "Society of the White Lotus," organized earlier during the Ming dynasty and now unified by a common hatred of the Manchurian usurpers, encouraged and organized numerous insurrections.

Then there was the Hmong. Compared to these other uprisings the Hmong rebellion was of minor importance. Yet, for precisely this reason it was especially irritating because Ch'ien-lung was forced to use a sledgehammer to swat a fly. Discounting the casualties, including a member of the emperor's own family, the financial burden alone was staggering. In the end, the cost of suppressing the Hmong would mount to over 70 million taels (approximately $500 million), twice what it cost to conquer all of Turkestan.

General Akoui was in fact the last of a number of generals sent by the emperor to subdue the two rebellious Hmong kingdoms of lesser and greater Kin-tchuen (near present day Suichiang). In 1767, the Governor of Szechwan province, Le Tsong-tou, informed the emperor that the Hmong had come down from their mountains and behaved like "brigands and bandits," pillaging towns and villages. The governor assured the emperor that appropriate measures had been taken and no further trouble was anticipated. Almost as soon as Ch'ien-lung received this first communique, however, Le Tsong-tou was busy drafting a second. It told of the harsh measures he had taken against the Hmong, including numerous executions. It also related how this resulted in the Hmong of greater and lesser Kin-tchuen joining forces and closing the passes through their territory, effectively severing all traffic to the southwest.

Le Tsong-tou did not have to spell out the seriousness of this. With the passes closed the defense of Burma and Nepal, and indirectly all of Tibet, would be compromised. In addition, Hmong interdiction of trading caravans passing through their territory meant an inevitable decline in the revenue from the lucrative trade that had taken years to cultivate in the southwestern protectorates. The governor's letter closed with an anxious appeal for imperial troops to put down the rebellion and reopen the passes.

The expedition was a miserable failure. Not only were no passes reopened, the Chinese were unable to so much as enter Hmong territory. The commanding general was summarily executed on his return to Peking. His replacement was more cautious and from all accounts not in the least eager to engage the Hmong in battle. This left diplomacy as the only alternative. Gifts were brought to the Hmong who came down from the heights and received them with enthusiasm. Unfortunately, the General had barely cleared his throat when the Hmong disappeared into the mountains with the peace offerings. While such conduct might be subject to various interpretations, the General preferred to read it as a sign of open submission to the emperor's authority. And so it seemed until hostilities broke out five years later.

Two envoys were sent from the Peking Court to open negotiations with the Hmong and to exhort them to come to their senses and obey the emperor. Not only were the emissaries treated badly, the two Hmong princes dared in their presence to describe the emperor's rule as criminal. To attack imperial armies was one thing, but to speak of the emperor in such a way was unheard of. In theory, the authority of Chinese emperors was based on a supposed mandate from heaven. To slander an emperor was therefore equivalent to blasphemy. When informed of this Hmong sacrilege, Ch'ien-lung flew into a rage and vowed on the spot to spare no expense in suppressing the Hmong rebellion. He would do more. He would exterminate them.

Though the idea was extreme, it lacked originality. Earlier emperors, who had also grown weary of repeated Hmong uprisings, invariably gravitated toward a policy of mass extermination. This was as much a response to the underlying cause of Hmong rebellions as it was a reaction to the rebellions themselves. For a principal reason for Hmong rebelliousness was their resistance to sinicization. It was the Hmong's refusal to accept Chinese culture as their own, a culture which the Chinese had come to equate with civilization itself, that both puzzled and infuriated state authorities. It puzzled them because they could not understand why the Hmong did not want to become civilized. It also infuriated them because this persistent refusal was viewed as an assault on the sanctity of Chinese culture and construed as evidence that the Hmong were a race of incorrigible criminals who not only posed a threat to law and order but who constituted a threat to civilization itself. Such a line of reasoning not only made a policy of extermination acceptable, it turned genocide into a moral crusade.

Determined to eradicate the Hmong, Ch'ien-lung dispatched three armies under the command of General Ouen-fou. Not only did Ouen-fou carry superior arms but with nearly 120,000 infantry and cavalry under his command he enjoyed a ten-to-one advantage in numbers over the Hmong, made even greater by the sure knowledge that the rebels would not have time to join their scattered troops and face him as a united force.

Even so, it is likely the general's face reflected grim determination rather than confidence as he led his men up the narrow mountain pass that would take them to the edge of Hmong territory. His short-legged Chinese pony, unlike a sure footed Hmong stallion, was probably already stumbling for balance, head down, eyes closed to slits against the stinging wind that came howling down the pass. Nor is it difficult to imagine Ouen-fou, bent forward over his saddle, also squinting hard against the wind. If he had glanced over his shoulder he would have seen his soldiers stretching out single file for nearly a mile, by now many of them suspicious of what he had known from the start. He was leading them into an inhospitable land.

A spur of the great Tibetan plateau, the mountains of Kweichow and Szechwan slope from an average altitude of 6,000 feet in the east to 4,000 feet in the west, with scattered peaks that rise as high as 9,000 feet. Viewed from an airplane the terrain resembles the surface of a waffle iron: the peaks of the limestone mountains are flat from erosion and each mountain is ringed by deep gorges. The occasional valley is so deep and shut in on all sides by steep inclines that it can be crossed only by taking the little paths, no more than goat trails, which run along the slopes.

To this one must add the unhealthy climate. Temperatures vary greatly from one district to another and often drop or rise unpredictably in the space of a few days or even hours. At any given time it might snow or rain. Powerful winds suddenly gust and then disappear. If one had to predict the weather, rain would be the best bet since it rains nearly two hundred days out of every year; and during this protracted rainy season malaria and other fevers breed with abandon.

But General Ouen-fou had more to worry about than miserable weather and nearly impassable terrain. For he surely was aware, as many a Chinese general before him had learned firsthand, that the Hmong are unsurpassed guerrilla fighters.

Nearly thirty years earlier another Manchu general, Fu Nai, detailed the Hmong's fighting ability with unconcealed frustration. When they "approach our camps they are never together but are divided into little groups of three or five men who hide in the trees and rocks, and are so accomplished at concealment that one never sees them. Then they ambush us so suddenly that we are unable to protect ourselves and on each occasion suffer many wounded."

Yet, to Ouen-fou's surprise, and no doubt his relief, he met only light resistance. Once safely through the first mountain pass, he ordered the two other generals under his command to hold back their forces and guard against a possible assault from the rear while he advanced through the next pass with the remaining troops. Again no resistance was encountered. The pass eventually narrowed and then sloped down into a deep gorge. Ouen-fou may have paused to consider the wisdom of entering the gorge. It was an ideal spot for an ambush. He could have returned and joined his main force, or sent messengers to direct them to join him. But he did neither. Since his scouts reported no sign of the rebels the general waved his troops on.

Once all the Chinese were inside the gorge, Hmong materialized from behind rocks and from inside the crevices and fissures that ran up the face of the rock walls that hemmed the Chinese in. This time there was no weak resistance, nor were the Hmong few in

4

number. Hmong warriors stationed on cliff edges rolled boulders down on the hapless Chinese while other Hmong moved in force to close off all the escape routes.

Then as quickly and mysteriously as it had begun the fighting suddenly ceased. The Hmong withdrew to the perimeter, attacking the Chinese only when they tried to escape. These assaults were so devastating that the Chinese gave up all thought of flight. Disheartened soldiers busied themselves gathering what firewood they could find and sat clustered in knots for warmth. As the days passed, food and water grew scarce. A few desperate infantrymen tried to escape under the cover of night, scratching and clawing their way up one of the cliffs that led to freedom. Those below discerned their fate by the screams that echoed through the gorge.

When the Hmong judged the Chinese sufficiently weakened by thirst and hunger to be able to offer only weak resistance, they launched an all out attack. Not one Chinese soldier escaped. Nor did the dead Chinese receive a decent burial, for neither of the two remaining generals bothered to mount a serious search for their commander. Probably they guessed his fate and did not wish to share it. Whatever the reason, they soon left the region and returned to Peking.

The true fate of General Ouen-fou and his men would not be learned until several years later from Hmong prisoners captured in another, more successful, campaign. Meanwhile, it was as though the earth had swallowed up nearly fifty thousand men.

It is unlikely that the emperor, once informed of the mysterious disappearance of Ouen-fou and his entire army, entertained any false hopes of the General's eventual return. Other generals serving under other emperors had disappeared in much the same way after venturing into Hmong territory, and none had ever returned. This was doubly disappointing, for Ch'ien-lung would have preferred to make an example of Ouen-fou. As a substitute he vented his anger on the other two surviving generals, executing one and exiling the other.

The emperor had tasted enough of defeat. What he needed was an extraordinary general, someone not only renowned for his tactical acumen but also possessed of bulldog tenacity when leading campaigns in the field. After canvassing his officers Ch'ien-lung settled on General Akoui, a brilliant strategist who had recently distinguished himself in campaigns in Burma and was therefore no stranger to maneuvers in mountainous terrain. By one account, Akoui was also a "cold-blooded man and single-minded in his dedication to a task, fearing nothing, not even the displeasure of the emperor, if fulfilling his duty required it."

Ch'ien-lung permitted Akoui to select his own troops and granted the general full discretion in carrying out the campaign against the

Hmong. But Akoui did more than carefully select his troops, he gathered information. He did not want to repeat the mistakes of those who had gone before him.

What he learned was that while the Chinese had often defeated the Hmong in open terrain with the advantage of superior numbers and arms, these things proved a handicap in the mountains where a large army had to travel single file over narrow trails and heavy artillery could be transported with only the greatest effort.

Yet Akoui needed superior numbers and arms to defeat the Hmong, for not only were they superb soldiers, Hmong guerrillas were especially skilled in the arts of ambush and quick retreat. Against such an enemy a large force was essential, as was the willingness to suffer steady and draining casualties in numerous skirmishes. Without adequate supplies, however, a large army could not long survive in the field. And experience had shown that on the Kweichow-Szechwan frontier supply lines were difficult to keep open.

There was an additional problem. Akoui had learned from his informants that the Hmong had erected massive strongholds at strategic locations overlooking every major pass. These strongholds could only be taken by siege. And for this Akoui needed heavy artillery, cannons weighing hundreds of pounds and capable of shattering stone walls several feet thick.

Akoui's solution to the first problem was to do without supply lines entirely. His army would carry everything it needed. This required nearly as many coolies as Akoui had soldiers. His solution to the second problem was equally bold. The heavy cannon required for mounting effective sieges were left behind in Peking. In their place Akoui carried iron ingots to enable him to forge cannons on the spot when needed.

Akoui also divided his army into several divisions so that he could enter the Hmong territory from many directions at once in a coordinated assault. And to insure that the defeat of the Hmong of greater and lesser Kin-Tchuen would be final, Akoui planned to hold troops in reserve to be used in a rear guard action to prevent Hmong troops from escaping through unguarded passes.

Akoui's forces were attacked the moment they entered Hmong territory. While the Hmong were quickly forced to retreat from the open field, they offered stiff resistance once they were in their mountains. Though the seasoned general was able to secure the first pass he entered, it was only after a furious battle in which Hmong women fought alongside their men. Yet, if Akoui had become master of the pass, he had also become its prisoner, for the Hmong had him hemmed in. For the moment it was a standoff. While Akoui set up camp the Hmong kept themselves busy building stone fortresses on the surrounding crests.

Although the Manchu general enjoyed the advantage of having put the Hmong on the defensive, he nevertheless realized that he would suffer heavy losses in any attempt to scale the cliffs to assault their fortifications. Prudence dictated patience. Three long months were spent in search of an alternate route up the mountain. The search was in vain for none existed. However, in the end Akoui's patience was rewarded.

From October to February much of Kweichow is draped in a dense fog. First it fills the valleys, then the overflow rises upward until it engulfs even the mountain crests. By December the fog is so thick that the sun shines through only a few days each month. Perhaps this bit of information was among the many facts Akoui had gathered about the land and accounts for his willingness to remain locked up in the pass. In any event, once the fog materialized, Akoui was quick to make good use of it. Under the protection of this cover a large force was sent scaling up the cliffs to take the Hmong by surprise. It was the sort of strategy the Hmong themselves would have admired had it not proved so costly to them.

Realizing that they were hopelessly outnumbered, the Hmong fought in retreat, holding each fortification until the flood of Chinese soldiers became too great to be held back. One by one their fortifications fell. But not all at once, nor even overnight. While Akoui was quick to press his advantage, the ferocity of the Hmong slowed the inevitable advance.

Within a year and a half the tenacious general had penetrated no more than forty miles into Hmong territory, but that was far enough to bring him to the capital of lesser Kin-tchuen. He placed the Hmong city under siege.

The Hmong had been caught unprepared. No Chinese army had ever penetrated so far into their mountains, let alone captured the capital of lesser Kin-tchuen. Confident that Akoui would prove no exception to the rule, the Hmong had laid away no stores of food, and the principal source of water, a well, lay outside the walls of the capital. A smaller well inside the walls served for a while, but the underground stream that fed it ran slow, and even before the supply ran out the water turned green and putrid.

Disease spread quickly throughout the population. Seng-Ke-Sang, the king of lesser Kin-tchuen, was one of the first to fall ill and die. The king's death was received as a bad omen by the Hmong trapped inside the city's walls. If they did not act, and act soon, disease and starvation would claim many more lives. Surrender was an option but not an attractive one. Memories of Chinese atrocities committed against Hmong captives were still vivid, and General Akoui gave every indication of being more cold-blooded and ruthless than the average Chinese commander. If surrender was out of the question, then an attempt to break through the enemy's lines was the only alternative left to them.

The breakout was not orderly, but it was effective. Scattering in all directions, the Hmong of lesser Kin-tchuen caught the Chinese off-guard, and by the time Akoui had reestablished control over his army, the majority of the Hmong escaped to freedom. The few hundred taken captive were summarily executed. Akoui's only consolation was that after entering the deserted city he found the body of the dead Hmong king. He ordered the head of the corpse cut off and placed in a basket and sent to the Emperor to certify the death of Seng-Ke-Sang.

Akoui then set off after the remaining rebels who were headed in the direction of greater Kin-tchuen. He razed every town and village along the way, destroying forts and in general anything that might prove of any use to the retreating Hmong who, if they rallied, might attempt to return by the same route.

When Akoui finally reached the border of the second Hmong kingdom, the young Hmong king, Sonom, was there to meet him. Again, Hmong women fought alongside their husbands, fathers and brothers. Boulders crashed down on the Chinese as they marched through the pass that led to Leouei, the capital of greater Kin-tchuen. The Chinese were ambushed from all sides. Chinese soldiers vainly tried to scale the cliffs and breach the enemy's line of defense. Hundreds fell to their death at the feet of their comrades. Despite the heavy casualties, Akoui refused to retreat. The battle raged on for days. Finally the Hmong retreated with Akoui in pursuit. The Manchu general patiently secured one position after another until he reached Leouei and placed it under siege.

The siege lasted nearly eight months, and Akoui used this time well. He joined his scattered divisions into a main force and stationed troops at key passes to block all escape routes once the capital fell into his hands. He was carefully preparing for what he erroneously believed would be the final battle.

Starvation and disease eventually took its toll on the Hmong trapped inside the city's walls. Realizing the hopelessness of the situation, Sonom led the main body of his soldiers out of the capital through a secret passage. Luckily, they encountered only one of Akoui's columns on the outskirts of the city and successfully broke through the line to make their escape.

Alerted of the breakout, Akoui quickly launched an assault on the city. He met only weak resistance and by the time he breached the city's walls he found the capital nearly deserted. Furious, he set off in pursuit of Sonom and what was left of his army. Akoui kept up the chase for ten days, but no Chinese could match the pace of a Hmong in the mountains. His troops exhausted, Akoui broke off the chase and returned to Leouei where he gathered his

troops and set off at a more leisurely pace for Karai, the last remaining Hmong fortress in the region.

As Akoui had anticipated, Sonom and the last remnants of the
Hmong army were holed up in the fortress. Akoui prepared for a
long siege. The smoke of blazing forges darkened the sky as new
cannons were made. Tents were set up, fortifications erected and,
most important of all, troops dispatched to the other side of the
mountain to prevent Sonom's escape. The General intended this
siege to be the last.

Akoui used this lull before the storm to write a dispatch to the
emperor detailing the events of the past months. Sadly, he listed
the many distinguished officers who had fallen in battle, among
them the emperor's own son-in-law, Prince Mongu. Akoui described
the siege and conquest of Leouei and assured the emperor that the
destruction of what remained of the Hmong rebel force was near
at hand.

Within a few months the Hmong conceded the hopelessness of
their position. With only a few hundred soldiers left, and food and
water running out, it would only be a matter of time before they
died of starvation or disease. Sonom summoned a general council.
It was agreed by all that surrender was unthinkable. The discus-
sion therefore turned to the best way to die. The preferable course
was to insure that as many Chinese as possible would share their
fate. It was decided that at the last moment when Akoui's cannons
had battered down the fortress walls and the Chinese were stream-
ing in, Karai would be put to the torch. The remaining Hmong along
with the Chinese who had breached their defenses would be buried
in the collapsing rubble. The destroyed garrison, a massive burial
mound, would remain as a monument to Hmong resistance.

And so it might have been had not Sonom's mother begged him
to spare his younger brother and sister. The young king did not
have the heart to refuse. On the off chance that Akoui might be
inclined toward mercy, a messenger was immediately sent to the
general's camp to request that Sonom and his entire family be spared
and that the Hmong king be allowed to rule over his old kingdom.
In return, Sonom would agree to rule under the authority of the
emperor and in his name. It was a gamble at best, but Sonom knew
that in the past Chinese emperors had often settled with tribal
minorities on similar terms.

Yet, if there was precedent for the request it was ill-timed. Several
armies and a score of generals earlier the emperor might have given
the demand serious consideration. But by now the Hmong had simply cost Ch'ien-lung too much. And, of course, there was the matter of calling him a "criminal", a sacrilege Ch'ien-lung was not about
to allow to pass unpunished.

Akoui knew this, for the emperor had not sent him on a mission of pacification but on one of annihilation. Of course, Akoui had no intention of revealing this to Sonom. The final assault on Karai would likely be a bloodbath for both sides, and Akoui had lost too many men already. He therefore stalled for time.

Akoui informed Sonom that this was the sort of request only the emperor could grant and that it would therefore be necessary to send to Peking for instructions. However, to build up Sonom's hopes the general told him that he would personally recommend leniency. Apparently heartened by these words, Sonom set aside all thought of the destruction of Karai and waited expectantly for news from Peking.

When the emperor received Akoui's communique he correctly presumed that the rebellion was as good as over. His spirits raised, he took the occasion to publicly praise the general whose exploits he described as unmatched in the empire. He announced to all present at the court that, from this day on, Akoui had permission to wear the ruby button, the ceremonial badge of a foreign prince. He also made Akoui a Count of the Empire and granted him permission to wear the gold embroidered robe of four dragons which only titled princes of the emperor's own family were permitted to wear.

Having honored Akoui the emperor retired to give the general the reply he had requested. In essence, he told Akoui to promise Sonom anything so long as it would guarantee his capture.

Upon receiving the emperor's instructions Akoui pondered how best to approach Sonom so that he might be persuaded to surrender his troops and abandon Karai. Apparently he concluded that a promise to return his kingdom to him to be ruled in the name of the emperor might backfire. Sonom might simply remain in the fortress and wait for the Chinese to withdraw before attempting to return to Leouei. Whatever his reasoning, Akoui promised Sonom only this: that should he surrender the entire royal family would be spared and his court and his soldiers could expect fair treatment.

Sonom took the bait and surrendered his forces to the General who not only treated the royal family with respect on the trip to Peking but allowed Sonom the personal liberty to visit his troops and confer with his officers. Akoui did not want Sonom to realize the real fate that awaited him in Peking, for the Hmong king could always commit suicide and cheat the emperor of his final revenge.

Indeed, the scales did not fall from Sonom's eyes until he was brought to the Emperor and his chief ministers specially summoned for the occasion. While Sonom kneeled before Ch'ien-lung an official of the court detailed the high crimes the Hmong king had committed against the empire in general, and against the emperor in particular. The reading of the sentence immediately followed. Sonom and his entire family, including the young prince and princess and ten of Sonom's close advisors, were to be tied to posts, gagged and then cut into pieces. As a final insult and a standing warning to all would-be rebels, their heads were also to be cut off and exhibited in cages with their names and titles attached.

The sentence was carried out immediately. If the emperor had counted on the additional pleasure of seeing Sonom and his family beg for mercy it is likely that he was sadly disappointed. Defeat and death were no strangers to the Hmong. For hundreds of years they had resisted Chinese repression. Victories were few, defeats many. Countless thousands had died defending Hmong freedom. Hmong prisoners rendered the only homage to the sacrifices of their ancestors available to them: to the very end they never weakened, never afforded the Chinese the satisfaction of witnessing a Hmong beg for mercy or shrink from the executioners sword.

After the execution of the royal family, nineteen of the remaining Hmong were simply decapitated. The rest, slightly more than two hundred of a rebel force that had numbered ten to twelve thousand, were given to Chinese officers as slaves.

Even this was not enough to satisfy the emperor's desire for revenge. Officials accompanied by soldiers were sent to Kweichow and Szechwan to comb the countryside in search of Hmong civilians, most of whom were simple farmers who had taken no part in the rebellion. Thousands of them were impressed into labor gangs and transported to various parts of the empire as slave labor for public-works projects.

If this was meant as an object lesson for would-be Hmong rebels, it failed to do the trick. Hmong rebellions would continue. Unfortunately, so would Chinese repression. There were some Hmong, however, who had found a way to break this endless cycle.

Thirty years prior to Sonom's execution, several hundred Hmong had abandoned China forever and crossed into Vietnam to begin a new life. During the century that followed thousands of other Hmong migrated to Vietnam, Laos, Thailand, and Burma. They settled high in the mountains far away from the densely populated lowlands. Few knew of their existence, and because of this for the first time in centuries they experienced peace.

It was not to last. By the beginning of the twentieth century they were once again victims of repression. And, once again, they rebelled. For the Hmong of Laos and Vietnam, rebellion and war became a way of life. And for the first time, they were fighting as allies of western nations who promised them freedom and independence for their loyalty. They were empty promises.

CHAPTER

2

ORIGINS

The first westerners to make contact with the Hmong in China were Catholic missionaries. This occurred early in the 17th century. The missionaries quickly learned there were two groups of Hmong, the "raw" and the "cooked'. These were Chinese labels, not Hmong. The cooked Hmong were those who had accepted Chinese ways and had settled in the lowlands and lived among the Chinese. The raw Hmong lived up in the mountains away from the Chinese. They had never accepted Chinese ways. The Chinese described them as wild barbarians who would cut a stranger's throat at the slightest provocation. While this terrifying description deterred most missionaries from attempting to make contact, a few hardy souls threw caution to the wind and sought them out.

It was not easy. For one thing, the Chinese did not always know exactly where to find them. Only lowland Hmong, who sometimes traded with their highland brothers, knew their exact location, and they were reticent to guide strangers to these hidden redoubts. Then there were the hazards of the journey. The mountain routes were serviceable for montagnards accustomed to tightrope walking over mountain crests and adept at grasping vines for support while ascending nearly vertical trails that zigzagged up mountain sides. For ordinary lowlanders, however, the trip was both harrowing and exhausting.

The few missionaries who did secure guides and endured the trek were richly rewarded for the people they found were none like they had ever seen before in China. Contrary to the popular image of the raw Hmong as a race of bloodthirsty brigands, the missionaries found them to be a gentle and generous people. The Chinese were right about one thing, the raw Hmong did not follow Chinese ways. They did not even use chopsticks, but ate with spoons like Europeans. Their children played many of the same games as European children: hide-and-seek, shuttlecock, marbles, and spinning tops. And particularly striking was the fact that many of these "raw" Hmong looked like Europeans; red or blond hair was not uncommon, and more than a few had blue eyes.

While such encounters naturally invited questions about Hmong origins, the missionaries did no more than the Chinese to provide answers. This is not to say that Chinese historians had nothing whatsoever to say about the Hmong. Quite the contrary. The Hmong play a predominant role in early Chinese history where they are described as an ancient people who occupied the fertile Yellow River basin long before the Chinese themselves migrated into the area. Since the Chinese were migrants it must surely have occurred to some Chinese historians that the Hmong may have also lived somewhere else before settling in northern China. But such ruminations, if they occurred, did not find expression in print. What is emphasized instead is the traditional enmity between the Chinese and Hmong, who are identified in the ancient histories as the first enemy of the Chinese. As a result the Hmong figure most predominantly in Chinese military history, in the narrative accounts of the numerous military campaigns mounted against them over the centuries following the establishment of the first dynasty.

And so matters stood until the beginning of this century when Father F.M. Savina was sent by the Society for Foreign Missions, headquartered in Paris, to spread the word of God to the Hmong of Laos and Tonkin (north Vietnam). As a priest, Savina was naturally dedicated to the divine mission of saving Hmong souls; but Savina was a scholar as well as a priest, and it was from the scholarly side of his personality that he acquired a fascination for the culture and history of the Hmong. Of all the issues connected with his studies, the question of Hmong origins interested Savina most, so much so that discovering a solution to the riddle became for him a consuming passion.

Savina not only mastered their language he spent years developing a romanized Hmong script, for the Hmong had no written language of their own. He also studied their religion and customs and recorded their legends which had been handed down from generation to generation for thousands of years, many presumably unchanged except for minor variations. For perspective he studied anthropology, comparative religions and linguistics, constantly factoring what was known about other peoples, ancient and modern, into what he knew about the Hmong.

By 1924 he felt confident enough to publish his views on the origins of the Hmong in his *Histoire des Miao*. Savina emphasized three facts about the Hmong which he believed were the keys to their origins: their physical appearance, their language, and their legends.

BLOND HAIR AND BLUE EYES

In appearance the Hmong are, Savina writes, "pale yellow in complexion, almost white, their hair is often light or dark brown, sometimes even red" or "corn-silk blond", and a few even have "pale blue" eyes. All of this, he argues, "disbars them from belonging to any other race of China." Savina concluded that these northern European traits were not only evidence of a mixed racial background "somewhere between the white and yellow races," but, more importantly, suggested that the original homeland of the Hmong lay outside of Asia.

Modern anthropologists have also noted the presence of European traits in Hmong populations, though instead of light skin and hair they stress facial features such as the absence of an epicanthic eyelid fold, narrow faces, and aquiline noses. Recent studies of Hmong in Laos and Thailand have led some anthropologists to classify them as the most Caucasian population of southeast Asia.

While most Hmong today are light skinned, few have blond hair or blue eyes. Yet if such Hmong are now a rarity, long ago they may have been the rule rather than the exception. Vue Nao Yang, a Laotian Hmong claims that long ago most of the Hmong in China were "white', with pale skin and light hair. This was before a major Hmong uprising. "The Chinese defeated the Hmong and as punishment for their rebellion ordered the death of every male Hmong they could find, even children and infants." Because Hmong with light skin and fair hair were easy to single out from the general population, most were killed. The few surviving "white" Hmong lived a precarious existence, as did all "white" babies born to Hmong parents, for the Chinese continued to search for them even after the Hmong migrated to Indochina.

For eighty year-old Vue Cher Sue this is more than legend. He still retains a vivid memory of the time during his childhood when the Chinese crossed over the border into Sam Neua province in northeastern Laos looking for white babies. "At that time there was only one white baby in our village. The infant's parents were warned before the Chinese arrived and they carried him into the forest where they hid until the Chinese finally left."

While we can never know for sure whether most Hmong were once blond and blue-eyed, the predominance of Caucasoid features in present day Hmong populations strongly suggests they were not originally Asians. This was Savina's conclusion, and he went on to argue that it is possible to locate their original homeland prior to their migration to China by examining their language and legends.

14

Blond Hair and Blue Eyes

15

LANGUAGE

The Hmong language is monosyllabic and tonal and extremely simple in structure. There is no conjugation of verbs, no declension of nŏuns. The vast majority of words have only one vowel, and few words end in consonants. Excluding special inflections used to ask questions or express surprise, most Hmong words can be pronounced using one of eight basic tones. Despite the simplicity of Hmong syntax, the subtlety of Hmong tones makes it a difficult language for non-Hmong speakers to master.

Savina did master the language, though. And because the Hmong had no written language of their own, he developed a romanized Hmong script modeled after the simplified Vietnamese script (Quoc Ngu) developed in the seventeenth century by the French Jesuit Alexandre de Rhodes. Not only did this make it possible to preserve the legends of the Hmong in their own language, it also permitted a detailed study of the phonetic and syntactical structure of their native tongue and, as a consequence, the identification of the place of Hmong in the classification of the languages of the world.

After determining that Hmong has no affinity with any other language of China, and is not even an Asian language, Savina classified it as a form of Ural-Altaic, one of the three major language groups of the Caucasian race. Savina believed that a language similar to present day Hmong was spoken long ago by a subgroup of the Caucasians who inhabited central Asia and western Russia, the same general region, he concluded, where the ancestors of the Hmong must have lived before migrating east into Asia.

Unfortunately, modern linguists do not accept Savina's classification. Hmong is not related to Ural-Altaic or any other major language group. The only language with which it has any affinity is Yao, though there is no evidence that the two languages are actually related. In sum, the linguistic origins of Hmong are a complete mystery.

LEGENDS

This leaves us with the Hmong legends. Savina believed that the Hmong legends, even more than the Hmong language, provide near irrefutable evidence of the Hmong's non-Asian origins. These legends, he insisted, reveal an earlier homeland outside of China; they also tell of a long migration north from this homeland into Siberia where the Hmong dwelled for an indeterminate period before migrating southward into northeast China.

Selective and necessarily incomplete, Savina's account of the Hmong legends emphasizes the parallel between Hmong, Babylonian and biblical legends, from which he concludes that the Hmong "must be viewed as having had their primitive origins on the banks of the Tigris and Euphrates, from whence they left for the north, either by the Caucuses or through Turkestan, at a time undetermined."

The legends collected by Savina include a Hmong account of the creation of the world, a history of the human race, and a history of the Hmong people, both before and after they arrived in China.

Creation

According to Savina, in the Hmong creation legends God created heaven and earth in seven days. The earth was first covered with water until God created ten suns to dry it up. The process took seven years. When the first bit of land appeared God created the first man from a pinch of earth, gave him a soul and the power of speech and sight and the ability to walk on two legs.

When this first man dreamed, a woman appeared to him, and when he awoke he found her lying beside him, a gift from God. The two became man and wife and had many children.

In those days God talked directly to man, and whenever humans needed his help they simply asked for it, though at first they needed very little divine assistance because God had created plants and animals in abundance for their use. The earth was then beautiful to behold; plants grew flowers as big as baskets and yielded equally impressive fruit. This guaranteed plenty of food to eat and, over all, an easy life.

The first complaints to God were about the ten suns which had not gone away after evaporating the seas that had once covered the earth. Indeed, the suns were slowly transforming the earth from a paradise into a desert. But God refused to take the suns away.

In those days trees were gigantic and a number were cut down and fashioned into arrows that were shot at the ten suns. All but one of them was destroyed. The remaining sun fled and hid for seven years, and for these seven years the earth was plunged into darkness. Though the sun was repeatedly entreated to return, it always refused. At the end of the seventh year a rooster crowed and, at the seventh crowing, the sun was overcome with curiosity and came out of hiding. This, so the legend goes, is why roosters have combs, for it is a gift from God for bringing back the hiding sun. It is also why roosters crow before sunrise: they are calling the sun who hides at the end of every day.

Original Sin

In the beginning humans were immortal. But one day a young woman picked and ate a white strawberry which God had forbidden anyone to touch. The same young woman also drank from a spring which God had forbidden anyone to ever approach. Angered,

God condemned all humanity to an eventual death, and expelled them from their paradise to a less fertile land where they had to labor for their food.

God was not without mercy. He taught the people how to farm the land, how to hunt, and how to make clothes to wear, for until this time men and women had no need of clothes and went about naked. Though humans were no longer immortal, for a time they still lived a very long life, sometimes reaching 800 or 900 years of age; but the drain of hard work eventually shortened their lifespan.

The Flood

The loss of immortality was followed by another disaster. It began to rain, not just at one place but all over the world. It rained for forty days and nights until nearly every living thing was drowned.

Shortly before the deluge two brothers who worked the same field were angered when they discovered that someone was coming during the night and undoing all the work they had completed during the day. They found a hiding place one evening and waited for the culprit. It was an old man who wasted no time filling in the furrows they had spent all day digging. The eldest brother wanted to kill the old man on the spot, but the younger brother wanted to question him and discover the reason for this peculiar behavior.

The old man told them that he filled in the furrows because their work was futile. A flood would soon cover the earth with water and drown all living things. It was then that the two brothers realized that the old man was God in disguise, and they asked him what they might do to escape this fate. He advised the eldest brother, who had a violent temper, to build an iron boat. To the younger brother, however, he advised the construction of a wooden boat large enough to carry his sister and himself and a male and female of every species of animal along with two seeds of every kind of flower, tree, and grain.

The two brothers did as God advised, and it was shortly after this that it began to rain. When water covered the land the iron boat sank, but the younger brother's wooden boat floated and with the rising water rose toward heaven.

When the rain finally ceased God sent nine dragons, accompanied by two huge black cranes, to dry up the land. It was the task of the dragons to drill an immense hole in the earth through which all the water would drain. The two cranes were kept busy gathering up all floating trees that might plug the hole.

Even after the water finally receded the sister and brother were forced to remain in the boat because the earth was covered with a thick layer of mud that had the appearance and consistency of chicken excrement. The two survivors were rescued from this sea of mud by a giant eagle who swooped down and carried them to a narrow piece of raised land that was dry. The eagle, himself near death from starvation, was also saved from death by the two humans who, in gratitude for his help, gave him pieces of their own flesh, taken from behind the head, armpits and knees. These hollows have remained in these places ever since.

Children of Incest

As soon as the land had dried enough for the brother and sister to walk upon it, they planted seeds and tended their fields. The brother was younger than his sister, who was near womanhood. When the brother matured he indicated his desire to marry, but his sister refused for such a thing would be a grave sin. Nevertheless, he persisted, noting that she was, after all, the only woman in the world. She finally consented to allow God to decide the issue. They carried the halves of a millstone to the top of a hill and rolled them down. When they descended to the bottom they found the two halves joined. They threw a needle and thread into the air, and when they picked them up they found that they were also joined. The sister then agreed to the marriage.

The infant born of this union was formless, without arms or legs and in some versions of the legend is shaped like an egg. The perplexed parents cut it open, believing the infant was inside. When pieces of the infant's flesh touched the ground each piece was transformed into a normal child. Seeing this, the parents cut the infant into very small pieces so as to create as many new babies as possible. By this act they repopulated the world.

Tower of Babel

One legend on which Savina placed special importance was the "Tower of Babel" story. It recalls a time in the distant past when the earth had become densely populated and construction was begun on a giant stairway to heaven. According to the legend, when the structure finally rose so high it poked through the clouds hundreds of thousands crowded on the stairs in a rush to enter heaven. This angered God who struck them with lightning and reduced the stairway to rubble.

Prior to this event, all people spoke one language. After it, each family spoke a different language. Unable to communicate with each other, families began living apart. Because of this, mankind was divided into different races, each with its own language.

The Great Migration

One of these families contained the first Hmong. In time, the Hmong multiplied to the point of overpopulation. It was then that the decision was made to leave the Hmong homeland and search for more fertile land. The migration took them over a great plateau and then to a northern region which was at the opposite end of the earth from southern China and southeast Asia where they live today. In this northern place days and nights lasted six months, the water was frozen and snow covered the ground. The people who lived there were short and squat and wore furs. There were few trees, and those that did exist were small. When the ancestors of the Hmong left this region they came to Honan, which was the first home of the Hmong in China.

After the Hmong settled in China a dispute over land arose between them and neighboring races. They brought the matter before the king, and the dispute was settled in the following way: a representative of each race would set out at dusk and return at sunrise, and each race would be given title to the land covered by their representative during the night. If any representative failed to return at daybreak, he and his people, would have to remain where he stood at sunrise. When the sun rose the representative of the Hmong was on the top of a high mountain. From that time onward the Hmong have lived on the crests among the clouds.

SAVINA'S INTERPRETATION

While Savina conceded that all primitive peoples have creation legends, and many have legends of a catastrophic flood, he insisted that the "story of the Tower of Babel and the confusion of languages is unique to the inhabitants of Chaldea," a region that encompasses present day Iraq and Syria. Indeed, Savina found the parallel between Hmong and biblical accounts of creation, original sin, and the flood so striking as to rule out mere coincidence. How, he asked, could the Hmong have come by such legends unless they had once lived, or are descended from a people who once lived, in ancient Chaldea? Drawing heavily on the ancient history and archeology of his day, Savina identified these people, the ancestors of the Hmong, as the Turanians, an ancient caucasoid people who populated the Iranian plateau and who, at the first epoches of history invaded Iran and spread across the plains situated between the Tigris and Euphrates rivers and settled in ancient Chaldea. It was here in Chaldea, prior to the period when the Turanians were forced out of the region by Aryan invaders from southern Russia and Turkestan, that the flood and Tower of Babel legends were born.

Displaced by the Aryan intruders, the Turanians returned to the Iranian plateau and from there began a steady migration into Russia, Siberia, Mongolia, Manchuria and Korea. The ancestors of the Hmong, Savina concluded, were a subgroup of these migrants. They were the band of Turanians who trekked north across western Turkestan until they reached the base of the Caucus mountains and then headed northeast into the frozen land of Siberia, pushing as

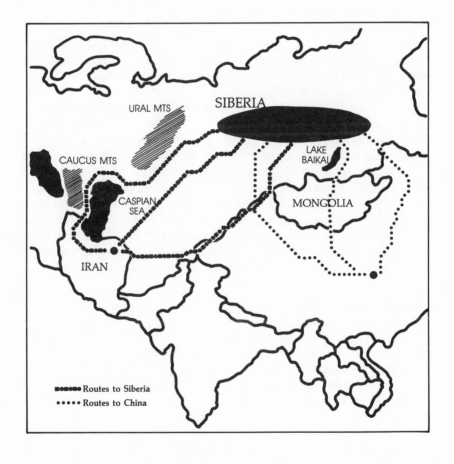

**Hmong Migrations:
Savina Account**

far north as sixty degrees latitude. After their sojourn in Siberia the ancestors of the Hmong migrated south and settled in northeast China which, according to both Hmong legend and Chinese history, placed them in Honan near the bend of the Yellow River sometime before 3000 B.C.

Actually, Savina was more confident about the location of the Hmong homeland than he was about the migration route from there to China. He conceded that it was equally likely that they crossed the Caucus mountains into Russia before heading for Siberia, or that they may have moved northeast from the Iranian plateau, over the Tyan Shan and Altai mountain chains, and then followed the Ob River into northwestern Siberia.

Savina also proposed alternative routes for the Hmong migration from Siberia to China. They may have gone directly south through Mongolia and, after reaching the Yellow River, followed it until they reached its bend in Honan. Or they may have come down through Manchuria.

However, Savina believed that the most likely route was directly south through western Siberia to the edge of Mongolia where the Hmong would have been able to pass between the Tyan Shan and Altai mountain chains, through the "pass of Dzungaria," the corridor through which so many others would later cross into Asia from the west. From there the Hmong could have easily continued east along the base of the Altai mountains until reaching the edge of the Gobi Desert. Turning south they would have quickly reached the Wei River. And by following the course of the Wei until it joins the Yellow River the Hmong would have found themselves but a short distance from upper Honan and the fertile Yellow River basin.

CAVEATS

Savina's account is fascinating, a true adventure story. But is it believable? The archeological interpretation of prehistory has changed considerably over the past sixty years. Much of what was considered valid in Savina's day is now rejected as either false or overly simplistic. The more serious problem is that the parallel between Hmong and biblical legends so crucial to Savina's interpretation of Hmong origins has not been corroborated.

No one besides Savina has identified a Hmong Tower of Babel legend, or for that matter one dealing with the confusion of languages or one depicting original sin. True, the Hmong do have a legend that refers to a stairway to the sky, but it is made up of mountains, each one taller than the previous. This mountain stairway leads not to heaven but to the home of Ndu Nyong, the god of death, an evil god who is the enemy of all mankind.

It is also true that the Hmong have legends about a golden age, a Garden of Eden if you will, but it is a disobedient wife who is described as the cause of its end, not a woman eating a forbidden fruit.

As for the loss of immortality, Hmong legend treats it as a simple fact. Vue Shue Long, a Laotian Hmong, summarizes the legend in this way: "At one time in the world there was no death, though people often got very sick. Especially as they got older. Then one day a man was turned into a tiger and when he got very old he died. This was the first death among mankind. After that no man was immortal."

Only Savina has identified a Hmong flood legend which describes the building of an ark aboard which the male and female of every species of animal and plant is placed. In the standard account it is a drum or gourd that saves the brother and sister from drowning, and the most that they carry with them on board are some seeds.

What is interesting about the Hmong flood legend is the dragon sent to dry up the land after the water had drained away. Chinese flood legends from the Shantung region, near where the Hmong are supposed to have first settled in China, relate how Pa, the lethal heat goddess who sometimes assumed the shape of a dragon, was sent by the gods to dry up the land after the flood.

The Shantung flood legends undoubtedly reflect historical fact for in ancient times the bend of the Yellow River was subject to massive flooding. This bit of history, rather than the periodic flooding of the Tigris and Euphrates rivers which gave rise to the Babylonian and biblical flood legends, is quite sufficient to account for the existence of the Hmong flood legend.

The discrepancies between the Hmong legends collected by Savina and those reported by others, and those current among the Hmong today, can probably best be explained by Savina's missionary activity. The Hmong he interviewed were also part of his flock and familiar with the standard bible stories. Wanting to please, they simply incorporated aspects of many of these stories into the telling of their own legends and inadvertently led Savina astray.

HMONG ORIGINS: ANOTHER LOOK

Yet, with all its imperfections, Savina's account of Hmong origins merits attention. If it is unlikely that the ancestors of the Hmong once made their homes on the banks of the Tigris and Euphrates rivers, it is not unreasonable to imagine they are related to a people who long ago migrated from the west into Eurasia and, later, into Siberia. This would account for the Caucasian features so prominent among the Hmong today. It would also explain the Siberian legend common to the Hmong of China and Southeast Asia, a legend so widespread among the Hmong that it is difficult to view it as mere fable.

The legend tells of a distant land once inhabited by the Hmong where days and nights were six months long, where lakes froze and people wore furs. For Hmong who have never seen snow or ice the legend tells of "rigid water" and "fine white sand'.

Then there is Hmong shamanism, which Savina underplayed since it undermines his claim that the Hmong are "primitive monotheists". The Hmong practice a pure form of shamanism. The shaman is not a witch doctor who uses rituals and magic spells to influence events. Instead, the shaman deals directly with the spirit world. After falling into a trance his soul leaves his body and enters the realm of souls, phantoms, genies and ghosts where he combats the evil spirits who cause misfortune, illness, and death. Since shamanism originated in Siberia, this is further, though not conclusive, evidence that the Hmong once lived there.

If the Hmong once lived in Siberia the probability is high that they were related to the predominantly Caucasian population that had begun to migrate to central Siberia from Eurasia in large numbers nearly 7000 years ago.

At the end of the last glaciation a warming trend set in, reaching its peak about 5000 B.C. The rise in temperature opened up northern Europe, Eurasia and Siberia to migrations from the south. By 3000 B.C., southern and central Siberia had become solidly Caucasian up to the borders of Mongolia.

The only exception to this general pattern occurred in the Minusinsk Basin, west of Lake Baikal on the northern edge of Mongolia. There, Siberian Mongoloids from the surrounding forests completely supplanted the Caucasians. It was only much later that other Mongoloids from the south moved up into central Siberia and transformed the population of the Siberian steppe from Caucasian to solidly Mongoloid by the beginning of the Christian era.

However, by this late date the Hmong had already left Siberia and were well established in China. For the consensus among experts is that the Hmong became part of Chinese history no later than 1200 B.C. and perhaps as early as 3000 B.C., which is the date given by ancient Chinese historians.

This also substantiates, though by a different route, Savina's assertion that the original homeland of the Hmong is to be found in southwestern Eurasia. For, if the Hmong formed a subgroup of the Caucasian population of Siberia before migrating to China, the location of their original homeland could quite conceivably have been somewhere on the Iranian Plateau or in southern Russia where a large portion of that population once resided before moving north into Siberia.

On the other hand, it is doubtful that the main features of Hmong culture, a culture that has survived relatively unchanged over the centuries, were fixed prior to the time the Hmong dwelt in Siberia. To the contrary, that culture reflects a life spent on the Siberian steppe and later adapted to fit the needs of a montagnard existence.

For some, the quite reasonable notion that the Hmong were once Siberians has been used as evidence for the entirely fanciful idea that they were once hard-riding Siberian nomads, and an explanation of why the Hmong of China and Indochina continue to observe a taboo against eating horse meat.

The difficulty with this view is that it places the Hmong in Siberia long after they had departed. For it was not until the first millennium B.C. that the economy of the Siberian steppe was suddenly transformed from pastoral to nomadic. It was only then, and not before, that the Siberians took to riding horses. The Siberian nomads were literally the first cowboys, riding herd on their livestock and driving them to new pasture when the old gave out from overgrazing. This made possible larger herds and, thus, a larger human population.

It was not long before these wandering nomads crossed into the territories of settled populations whose plodding infantry were no match for mounted warriors. Everywhere fortifications were erected around villages and towns as protection against the fierce Siberian horsemen. In the west, in the Ukraine, an earth rampart fifteen feet high and stretching for hundreds of miles (known as the Dragon's Wall), was constructed for just this purpose. The Great Wall of China, begun in the 4th century B.C., was meant to serve a similar function.

The Hmong, however, arrived in China on foot, for they left Siberia long before the advent of the Siberian horseman. As for the Hmong horse meat taboo, it was probably acquired long after the Hmong left Siberia, perhaps as late as the seventeenth century when the Chinese Hmong of Kweichow and Szechwan began to breed their mountain ponies for use as war horses and acquired the reputation as being among the best horsemen in the empire.

Yet if the Hmong were never Siberian horsemen, they nevertheless struck as much fear in the hearts of the Chinese as the dreaded nomads of Siberia. Indeed, at one point in time the Chinese built a scaled down version of the Great Wall to prevent Hmong on the frontier from penetrating the interior of the empire.

Over the centuries, this fear, coupled with a deep hatred, more often than not governed Chinese relations with the Hmong. The origin of this fear and its consequences for the lives of countless generations of Chinese Hmong is the focus of the next chapter.

CHAPTER

3

HMONG IN CHINA

ARCHEOLOGICAL EVIDENCE

Little is known about the earliest Hmong in China. Certainly they were not the only Siberians to migrate there. As early as 2500 B.C. groups of Siberian nomads had already penetrated most of northeastern China, gaining footholds in Manchuria as well as in present day Hopei and Shantung provinces. The Hmong were perhaps the most adventuresome of these Siberian immigrants because they continued the trek southward into the interior until they reached the bend of the Yellow River in upper Honan.

This was the home of the Yangshao Chinese who dominated the region between 4000 and 3000 B.C. Hmong culture shares some general features with the Yangshao culture. While this may be mere coincidence, it is not unreasonable to suppose that the Hmong thought it prudent to borrow liberally from the culture of their first Chinese neighbors who had mastered the tricks of survival in this new land.

The Yangshao were a mountain people, though they did not live at the dizzying heights preferred by modern Hmong. But, then, at that early date it is unlikely that the Hmong did either. Fresh from the Siberian steppes, they would have found life at the lower altitudes more tolerable than on the crests. The Yangshao practiced swidden or "slash and burn" farming where virgin land is cleared of trees and underbrush, the debris burned, and the ashes used as fertilizer. The Hmong are also swidden farmers. Like the Hmong, the Yangshao raised pigs as the principal source of their protein. And also like the Hmong, Yangshao houses had stamped earth floors, an indoor hearth, and a thatched roof supported by stout vertical posts.

The Yangshao were eventually absorbed by the Lungshan Chinese who were rice farmers. Since Chinese records indicate that some groups of Hmong practiced rice farming in the distant past, it is possible that the Hmong also borrowed from the Lungshan, though this may have been a two-way exchange because the Lungshan culture displays distinct Paleo-Siberian traits.

The Lungshan were displaced by the Shang Chinese who established the earliest Chinese dynasty identifiable by archeological records. The Shang dynasty lasted from 1500 to 1000 B.C., during which time it successfully subdued its neighbors and used many as slaves for constructing massive grave sites for Shang royalty.

Some of these burial sites excavated in the early 1930s at Anyang (200 miles northeast of the bend of the Yellow River) unearthed non-mongoloid skeletons mixed in with typically mongoloid remains. Perhaps some of the non-mongoloid skeletons belonged to Hmong slaves who manned the work gangs that built the tombs. Or, possibly some Hmong or other caucasian Siberians belonged to Shang royalty. At present, however, there is no way to know because all of the results of these finds have yet to be fully published. As one commentator has observed, the reason for this failure may be that the Chinese are embarrassed by the implication that their distant ancestors were not all Chinese.

No doubt, the Shang exercised some influence over the development of Hmong culture, but just how much is unknown. One curious fact deserves mention, however. The Shang used cowrie shells as money, and to this day the women of the Cowrie Shell Hmong still sew cowrie shells in linear or semicircular rows on the back of their blouses.

If the Hmong did borrow freely from Chinese culture when they first arrived in China, it must also noted that they vigorously opposed complete assimilation. And it is this simple fact that has made their life in China so difficult. In time the Chinese became many and the Hmong remained few. This need not have been cause for dissention between the two peoples if the Chinese had not demanded integration into the Chinese way of life as a precondition for decent treatment. The refusal of the Hmong to assimilate cost them much. Eventually they were forced to retreat to the mountain tops where the freedom to live as they pleased became the prime consolation for the hard life of the montagnard.

LEGENDARY ACCOUNTS

The near silence of the archeological evidence about the life of the first Hmong in China is a marked contrast to the prolix testimony of legend, both Hmong and Chinese. From both sources we learn that, in the beginning at least, the Hmong and Chinese enjoyed friendly relations. At the same time, the Chinese and Hmong offer different accounts of the erosion of this good will. The Hmong speak of Chinese duplicity, while the Chinese talk candidly of power politics and identify the defeat and suppression of the Hmong as the event that unified China into an empire.

Hmong Legends

One Hmong legend actually describes the Chinese and Hmong as brothers. The Hmong was the older and stronger brother. When their parents died the two brothers separated and eventually lost all trace of each other. Yet they both continued to visit their parents' graves once a year to pay their respect, though they did so at different times so that they never met. Then one day the Hmong brother noticed that someone had been worshiping at his parents' graves before him. He wondered who it might be and returned regularly to see if he could catch the culprit. The next time the Chinese brother showed up the Hmong brother grabbed him and asked what he was doing there. The Chinese brother asked him the same question. It was then that they realized they were brothers.

After this the two brothers, and their descendants, drifted apart. The legend goes on to reveal that, while the Chinese completely forgot that the Hmong and Chinese were once brothers, the Hmong did not.

Another Hmong legend tells of two great kingdoms, one Chinese, the other Hmong. The land of the Hmong lay to the north of the Yellow River, that of the Chinese to the south. The two kingdoms were constantly at war, and for some time the Hmong gained the upper hand. It was during one such period of Hmong ascendancy that the king of the Chinese contrived a diplomatic solution to the conflict.

The daughter of the Chinese king was reputed to be the most beautiful woman in China. Understandably, she had many suitors, but her father refused them all. Instead he offered her to the son of the king of the Hmong, for he concluded that only a marriage between the two royal families could bring an end to the fighting. The offer was accepted and in due course a son was born.

The old Hmong king doted on the boy, perhaps too much, for as the child grew older he became impatient to rule. But both his grandfather, the king, and his father, the next in line, showed little sign of aging and it appeared he would be an old man himself before he could ascend to the throne.

The king of the Chinese made note of the boy's ambition and waited for the appropriate time to turn it to good use. Finally, when the Hmong prince turned thirty, his Chinese grandfather invited him to spend a few months with his Chinese relatives. The grandeur of the imperial palace dazzled the Hmong prince, for in Hmong society both rulers and the ruled lived simple lives in humble surroundings. As the king expected, exposure to such opulence fanned the prince's ambition. It was then that he drew him aside and told him of a plan that would place him on the Hmong throne.

In the weeks that followed, the Hmong prince was drilled in the secrets of the martial arts, especially in the iron ball killing technique. Though they were no larger than a child's marbles, in the hands of a master these polished spheres could kill. When the prince was finally able to fling them over fifty yards with force and accuracy he was judged ready.

When he returned home no one noticed the leather pouch which he hid away for the right moment. It came one afternoon when the Hmong king was struck down as if by magic, and lay dying in a pool of his own blood.

All activity came to a standstill while the Hmong nation gathered for the funeral rites. Since they would last several days, the Hmong were easy prey for the Chinese army that had been secretly assembling on the Hmong frontier, waiting for this moment. The prearranged plan was that once the Chinese conquered the Hmong, the assassin prince would be placed on the throne, bypassing his father who was next in line.

Though the Hmong were caught by surprise and quickly defeated they were not conquered. Characteristically, they chose to abandon their kingdom rather than to be enslaved by the Chinese. Fleeing south across the Yellow River into Chinese territory, they reached the safety of the southern frontier. The assassin prince was not among them.

When it came time for the Hmong to select a new sovereign they passed over the father of the assassin and chose Mong Kao Lee, a woman, the daughter of the slain king. In her honor they henceforth called their former homeland by her name, Mongoli or Mongolia. And so it fell to Mong Kao Lee to guide the Hmong on their southern trek in search for a land where they could remain free.

The journey south led them over many mountain chains. Still accustomed to life in the lowlands, the Hmong were ill prepared for the rigors of the life of the montagnard. Then there were the mountain tribesmen, many of whom turned hostile when the Hmong crossed their territory. As in many Hmong legends, when things seemed hopeless something magical occurred to set them straight.

One day, Vu Chang Leng went into the forest to look for herbs. He was startled by a voice coming from above, in a tree. When he looked up he saw a chicken with one of its legs trapped in a tangle of branches. Much to his surprise, when the chicken saw him looking up it spoke. "If you release me from these branches," the chicken said, "I will grant you any wish." Vu Chang Leng climbed the tree and released the chicken who immediately flew away, his flapping wings cracking the air like thunder. A few minutes later the chicken returned, but in the form of a man. He had returned to reward the Hmong for helping him.

Vu Chang Leng did not want to waste his one wish foolishly. After pondering the matter he asked for the following. "I want only a souvenir to memorialize the remarkable event of coming upon a talking chicken who could also turn himself into a man, a souvenir from you which, when I am in trouble, will enable me to call upon you to grant my one wish." The request was granted and Vu Chang Leng received a small metal coin. It was a magical coin which, when waved three times, would glow and send a message to the magic chicken to come and help whomever possessed it.

Armed with the magic coin, Vu Chang Leng persuaded the Hmong to migrate across hostile territory. They had not gone very far before they were set upon by bandits. This caused some to lose faith in Vu Chang Leng. To regain the trust of his people, Vu Chang Leng marched up to the stronghold of the bandits and warned them that should they harm the Hmong again they would pay with their lives. As proof of this he waved the magic coin three times. It glowed bright red, shooting shafts of light wherever he pointed it. The bandits retreated into their fortress, trembling with fear as the sky darkened and the sounds of thunder rolled over them. Then it began to rain. The wind howled and grew in force until trees were yanked up by their roots and houses blown down and a number of the bandits sucked up screaming into the dark sky. All the while, Vu Chang Leng stood before the gate of the bandits' stronghold, the wind and rain whirling around him, and shouted repeatedly to all who would hear: "Allow the Hmong to pass unmolested or you will suffer more storms, more calamities." It was by means of Vu Chang Leng's magic coin that the Hmong were able to migrate southward deep into the Chinese frontier where, for many centuries, they lived in peace and beyond the reach of the Chinese.

Other Hmong legends expand on this account and relate that the Hmong migrated south from Honan to the lake zone of Hupeh and Hunan and from there spread out into Kweichow and Szechwan.

Chinese Legends

Chinese legends tell the story from a different perspective. It begins in the distant past, around 2700 B.C., during the reign of the legendary Emperor U-Wang who ruled as a tyrant. At this early date the Hmong (called the "Miao", or the savages, by the Chinese) were sufficiently powerful to merit a voice in government. Indeed, one of their nobles, Tche-you, served as a minister to the emperor. Though he had served the emperor well, the day came when he could no longer stomach the way U-Wang mistreated the Hmong. He unified the scattered Hmong tribes into a rebel army and engaged

U-Wang's troops near Peking and routed them. Fearing for his life, U-Wang withdrew to a stronghold south of the capital.

The emperor's defeat was welcome news to the Chinese nobility who had also suffered under his reign. They selected a popular young nobleman and renowned warrior, Huan-yuan, as their leader. Huan-yuan led their combined armies and defeated U-Wang in successive engagements. The emperor was captured and executed.

The nobility were eager to reunify China under imperial rule, and the only obstacle that stood in their way was the Hmong, whose easy victory over U-Wang had led them to envisage even greater things. Talk of an independent Hmong nation was a frequent topic of conversation in the Hmong tribal councils. If something was not done quickly, the Hmong might turn from talk to action. Other tribal minorities chaffing under Chinese rule might easily be whipped into a rebellious mood and join the Hmong in a bloody, and perhaps even successful, revolt.

The nobles therefore urged Huan-yuan not to disband his forces but to continue the campaign on Hmong territory. The fighting was fierce, and losses were heavy on both sides, but Huan-yuan was a brilliant general. The Hmong were defeated and Huan-yuan made emperor. He was also given a new name — Hoang-ti, the Yellow Emperor.

According to the legend, Hoang-ti's battlefield experience with the Hmong convinced him that they were a ferocious and savage people, too primitive to be effectively administered by ordinary laws. He therefore established a separate criminal code for the Hmong. Mutilations and executions were to replace imprisonment as the principal form of punishment. Depending on the severity of the crime, a Hmong offender was either executed, or just had his nose cut off, or perhaps both ears, or he might be castrated, or receive a more lenient sentence like being branded on the face with a hot iron.

While this legend no doubt reflects actual conflicts which occurred very early between the Hmong and the Chinese, as well as Chinese suppression of the Hmong at an early date, Hoang-ti never existed. He was a convenient fiction created by wandering Chinese scholars providing a much sought after service to Chinese nobility.

Beginning in the 5th century B.C., Chinese feudalism began to come apart at the seams. One emperor after another proved incapable of maintaining order or of controlling errant nobles who ruled as they wished in the face of vain protests from Peking. Although the emperors had lost *de facto* power, they nevertheless continued to exercise considerable authority; in the eyes of nobility and peasant alike, the emperor alone, with or without power, was still the only legitimate ruler of the realm. Hence, while many a noble longed for the crown, which seemed ripe for the plucking, most could not claim rightful succession to the throne. They had power, but lacked legitimacy. It was in the attempt to rectify this problem that noble families began to employ wandering scholars who presented themselves as experts on royal genealogy. For the right price, an ambitious governor or lord could acquire a most impressive family tree that proved he was descended from an earlier imperial family. And should he be lucky enough to capture the throne and unify China under imperial rule he could claim legitimacy through descent from an earlier dynasty.

Hoang-ti had up to that time been only a lowly agrarian god in southern Shansi. But with the stroke of a calligrapher's brush, he was transformed into the forefather of nearly every noble family who had the misfortune of not being related to either the present or past dynastic families.

In an effort to add luster to the concocted lineages, and to indirectly diminish the significance of existing royal families, Hoang-ti was passed off as the first emperor of China, a true patriot who not only unified the Chinese but routed the Hmong barbarians, their traditional enemy.

HISTORICAL ACCOUNTS: SHANG TO HAN

The events described in the Hoang-ti legend probably occurred sometime between 1600 and 800 B.C., for part of the legend is that Hoang-ti, in an effort to maintain control over the Hmong, reorganized their tribes into settlements of "eight families around a common well." The eight-family, common well system of land tenure became a prominent feature of feudal land organization during the Shang dynasty and was continued, with some modifications, through the subsequent Chou dynasty.

Shang Dynasty (1600-1028 B.C.)

The Shang were more or less at continuous war with their tribal neighbors, including the Hmong. Defeat at the hands of the Shang, and forced integration into the eight-family system, compelled large numbers of Hmong to abandon their traditional lifestyle as migrant swidden (slash-and-burn) farmers for the sedentary life of the feudal peasant.

The Shang dynasty was centered in Honan, but toward its close its territory extended all the way to western Shantung, southern Hopei, central and south Shansi, east Shensi, and parts of Kiangsu and Anhwei. The Hmong, either as peasant farmers or as free living tribes dwelling on the periphery of the Shang empire, must have participated in this expansion because by the beginning of the Chou dynasty they are to be found in nearly every area of the old Shang empire.

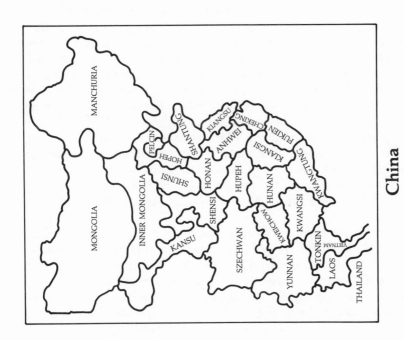

Hmong Migration in China
1600-257 B.C.

●●●● 1600-1028 B.C.
■■■■ 1029-257 B.C.

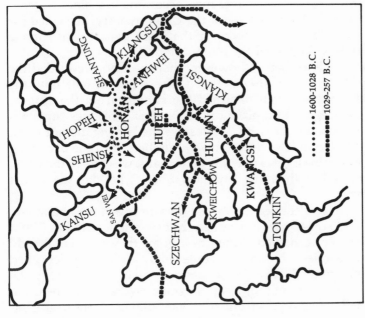

China

33

Chou Dynasty (1028-257 B.C.)

Given the oppression of the Hmong under the Shang it should come as no surprise to discover that, according to Chinese legend, when King Wu, the first king of the Chou dynasty, struggled for dominance with the last Emperor of the Shang dynasty, the Hmong immediately volunteered their support.

There is little evidence, however, that the Chou rewarded the Hmong for this help, for another Chinese legend tells how the mythical Emperor Shun banished the Hmong from the Hupeh-Hunan lake region to a place called San-wei. This was supposed to have occurred in 2250 B.C., but since the Hmong did not reach the Hupeh-Hunan lake region in any numbers until the beginning of the Chou dynasty, we may presume that it was one of the Chou Emperors rather than the mythical Shun who did the actual banishing.

Scholars have identified the ancient domain of San-wei as a mountainous area somewhere in southern Kansu, and legend has it that when the Hmong arrived at their new home they found it already occupied by a fierce mountain people led by a warrior chief called "The White Wolf." This also suggests a possible reason why the Hmong were singled out for forced migration to San-wei. The Chou maintained power on the frontier by garrisoning troops near trouble spots. To guarantee adequate food supplies, peasants from controlled areas were forced to resettle near frontier garrisons. Perhaps the Chou recalled Hmong courage and military prowess in battles with the old Shang armies and decided that only tough Hmong farmers could be expected to survive in the land of The White Wolf. If this was the intent it backfired, for once the Hmong reached San-wei they drifted up into the mountains out of the reach of the Chou garrisons. Fearing that the Hmong might eventually organize an insurrection, or join other mountain tribes in a revolt, the Chinese sought ways to control them. Mandarins were sent to live among the Hmong and learn their ways, to discover how they might be more easily governed. Few of these mandarins penetrated very far into Hmong territory, for the timid scholars feared the Hmong whom they believed to be more ferocious than the wild beasts of the region.

Having learned nothing useful about the Hmong, Chou authorities adopted the tried and true course of material rewards. The Hmong were offered choice farm land in the valleys and entire villages were constructed for their convenience, all in an effort to draw them out of their mountains. But the Hmong so valued their new won freedom that none accepted the offer and the fields and villages remained empty. What was worse, at least from the perspective of Chinese authorities, by the seventh century B.C. these same Hmong were joining forces with the Turks, Mongols and semi-nomadic Tibetan tribes of the Wei River basin in attacks on Chou garrisons.

The fate of these Kansu Hmong remains a mystery. For after a hundred years they are never again mentioned by Chinese historians. Possibly the majority were absorbed by the expanding Chinese population well before the beginning of the Christian era. There is, however, one Chinese legend which relates that the Kansu Hmong eventually abandoned the area, followed the course of the Wei River into northern Szechwan and from there entered Tibet where, presumably, they continue to live today hidden away in some distant mountain retreat.

Though a large number of the Hmong from the lake region were exempted from the forced migration to San-wei, they were hardly to be envied. Chou oppression continued unabated. The Hmong did not take it lying down, though. Revolts were frequent, frequent enough it would seem to tax the tolerance of Imperial officials who responded by intensifying the repression of the Hmong. Indeed, the level of oppression was geared up to such a pitch that it assumed the dimensions of an extermination campaign.

For a time the Hmong held their own against the Chou, and even enjoyed some early victories. But these were soon followed by a string of devastating defeats. In 826 B.C., General Fang-chou engaged the Hmong with three hundred thousand troops and three thousand war chariots. The Hmong did not have a chance. They held the field as long as possible and then retreated for their lives. Additional, though not so crushing defeats, followed. Not long after this the Hmong began to migrate from the area *en masse*.

If the Chinese commentaries are to be trusted, some fled west and reached the ocean and then sailed to the South Seas while others migrated east into Kiangsi or south through Hunan and into Kwangsi, establishing settlements along the way. But the great majority moved west into the mountain regions of Szechwan and Kweichow where they were not always welcomed by existing mountain tribes. In particular, the Keh-Lao montagnards of western Kweichow did their best to drive the Hmong back across the Hunan-Kweichow border. While we do not know the details of these battles, the outcome is known: the Keh-Lao were decimated.

Ch'in Dynasty (256-207 B.C.)

Once they reached the mountains the Hmong were beyond the reach of the Chou Emperors and their armies. For several centuries after this the Hmong lived in peace. This was in part due to events beyond their control. In 256 B.C. the last Chou emperor bowed to the military might of the powerful feudal state of Ch'in, centered in Shensi and Kansu provinces, and abdicated the throne. The lords of Ch'in quickly brought all of China under their rule by pursuing a course of extensive militarization. After neutralizing all opposition in the interior, the Ch'in concentrated their forces in the north to hold back the warrior nomads who periodically invaded the empire. Just how seriously the Ch'in took this threat is evidenced by the enormous resources they devoted to the construction of The Great Wall of China.

Because of the efforts of the Ch'in in pacifying the northern frontier, the Han dynasty was able to direct its attention south. It was not until the beginning of the Christian era, however, that his southern pacification policy posed a serious threat to the Hmong.

Han Dynasty (206 B.C.-220 A.D.)

In 25 A.D. the Han Emperor Kuang-wu Ti sent General Ma-yuan to pacify the southern kingdom of Chiao-Chih Chun (later named An-Nam and then Tonkin), which then encompassed the province of Kwangsi and northern Vietnam. General Ma-yuan first engaged the Hmong in Kwangsi and easily defeated them. He pushed on to north Vietnam, where he enjoyed equal success against the Tonkinese and a number of Kwangsi Hmong who had migrated into Tonkin some years earlier. In fact, Ma- yuan struck such fear in the hearts of the Tonkinese that before leaving the pacified region in the hands of several officers he erected a bronze column on the Tonkin border that bore the inscription: "All Tonkinese who pass this column will be known." Later, superstitious tribesmen who had not the slightest idea of the meaning of the inscription took the monument to be a material manifestation of one of their guardian spirits and promptly surrounded it with boulders to protect it from the ravages of wind and rain on the presumption that as long as the column stood their people would flourish.

Toward the end of his career, General Ma-yuan had occasion to once again engage the Hmong on the battlefield, but this time things did not go any better for him than for the general he replaced.

In 47 A.D., Emperor Kuang-wu Ti sent General Liu-Shang to quell a Hmong uprising in southern Hunan. Liu-Shang drafted troops on the coast near the mouth of the Yangtze and sailed upstream to the lake region where he disembarked and set off for southern Hunan, "full of contempt" for the Hmong whom Ma-yuan had so easily defeated in Kwangsi. However, after encountering enormous difficulty penetrating their territory he and all his men disappeared from the face of the earth. It was then that the Emperor called in the old battle-hardened Ma-yuan who, it was presumed, knew how to deal with the upstart Hmong.

In the beginning the campaign had all the earmarks of a veritable rout. The Hmong were defeated in the open field and forced to retreat with the old general in hot pursuit. Then Ma-yuan made the mistake of allowing himself to be closed up in a gorge, where

**Hmong Migration in China
256 B.C.-400 A.D.**

20,000 of his men were lost to sickness and he died himself. In retaliation, General Tou-chang was sent, not to engage the Hmong in battle, but to attack defenseless towns and villages. Unarmed civilians were killed, homes burned to the ground, and everything of any value was pillaged. This unbridled terrorism continued on and off for another three years until the emperor deemed the territory finally pacified.

Subsequent acts of suppression were small-scale and few in number. The Hmong made good use of this welcome calm in their stormy relations with the Chinese to reoccupy much lost territory. By the second century A.D., not only did they command the territory encompassing Hunan, Kweichow and southern Hupeh, but they had also moved north along the banks of the Han River deep into northern Hupeh to pose a serious threat to the Han regime. This threat was further aggravated by the pressures of Tibetan nomads moving into western Szechwan and forcing the Hmong in the area to move northeast toward their brothers who had gained control of upper Hupeh. Soon Hmong were filtering into their former Honan homeland and from there moving north into Shensi and east into Anhwei.

Between 403 and 561 there were forty Hmong uprisings in areas formerly under Chinese control. These were not bandit raids typical of other tribes. They were genuine attempts to capture and exercise political power in Hmong occupied territory.

Hmong Kingdom (400-900 A.D.)

By the middle of the sixth century even the Chinese were forced to concede the existence of a Hmong kingdom which, in one form or another, had been functioning since the beginning of the fifth century. The kingdom had evolved from a loose federation of Tribes into a hereditary monarchy. The king of the Hmong was not an absolute monarch. The independent spirited Hmong would never tolerate anyone, and especially a Hmong, exercising absolute power over them. In fact, the office of king was to some degree elective. On the death of the Hmong monarch a successor was chosen from among his sons by all men capable of bearing arms. Nor was this a hollow election, with few candidates to chose from. Then, as now, the Hmong practiced polygamy and the king was expected to have many wives and, thus, many sons from whom to choose.

There was another, more pervasive, way in which Hmong politics displayed democratic or, more correctly, republican features. The Hmong monarchy functioned very much like a federated state in which most of the real power devolved to local units.

Villages were organized into districts, with each district containing twenty villages. Every district had its own chief who was elected by all men capable of bearing arms and who could be removed

Hmong Kingdom
400-900 A.D.

through special election should he prove incompetent or corrupt. The district chief appointed a village headman for each village under his jurisdiction, the wisdom of the appointments standing as an indication of his capacity to rule.

Though a headman was appointed rather than elected, unhappy villagers could, and apparently quite often did, complain to the district chief when they felt their village headman ruled badly, for the district chief's power of appointment included the power to remove appointees for misconduct or incompetence.

Popular assemblies were another check on misconduct. They occurred both at the village and district level. Headmen were expected to call such an assembly when any important decision was to be made, such as cooperative work projects involving the laying out of new fields or the construction of roads and waterworks. Again, all men capable of bearing arms voted, and the majority vote decided the issue. Villagers could also convene the assembly on their own to deal with charges of malfeasance lodged against their headman. In such instances, if the majority agreed misconduct had occurred, it became a formal complaint that had to be presented to the district chief.

Popular assemblies were also convened at the district level for deciding important issues affecting the welfare of the district. As at the village level, this might involve issues like the building and maintenance of roads and waterworks, but it might also include issues left off the village agenda, such as the time and place of the most important Hmong communal religious celebration, the New Year festival.

This high level of participation in politics meant that most important political issues were decided at the local level. Not only did districts and villages make policy, they provided the funds and administration to implement it. While issues of national defence were decided by the king, his power to decide was severely limited by the need for consensus at the local level for implementing decisions once they were made. For it was the right of each district to determine through its popular assembly the extent of its contribution in soldiers, arms, and supplies to the enterprise.

The king's dependence on the voluntary support of hundreds of popular assemblies functioned as a serious constraint on military adventurism. For despite the ill-deserved reputation for bellicosity the Chinese have given the Hmong, they were then, as they are now, a peace loving people, slow to anger and even slower to fight unless forced to do so out of desperation. If, however, their lives or freedom are in danger they will quickly rally around a leader to defeat their enemies. The Hmong king could therefore count on popular support if the realm was truly threatened, but not otherwise.

The Hmong legal system was also administered at the local level. While custom governed crimes and their penalties, the determination of guilt or innocence was left to the village. Should any party find the decision wanting in wisdom, the verdict could always be appealed to the district chief, or even a popular assembly, though to prevent frivolous meetings the person who requested such an assembly had to provide food and lodging for all who attended.

Though the Hmong kingdom survived for nearly five hundred years, it reached the zenith of its power and prestige in the last half of the sixth century. It was during this period that China collapsed into an uneasy feudalism with different factions struggling to gain control and reunify the empire. Because the Hmong exercised *de facto* control over much of Hupeh, Hunan and Kwangsi they enjoyed considerable bargaining power with the rival factions. Hmong were appointed to high positions in the courts of competing dynasties, each seeking the Hmong as military allies in their struggles with their rivals.

This infighting continued until 618 when Li Yuan captured the throne and established the T'ang dynasty. One of the first orders of business of the new dynasty was to launch a campaign to reconquer all territories China had lost to the Hmong. Though T'ang generals proved unequal to the task, they were successful in bringing a great deal of Hmong territory under administrative control, leading to a dual system of government. Local matters were left for the Hmong to decide as they wished. However, Chinese living in Hmong territory were subject only to Chinese law. And, of course, taxes had to be paid to the empire.

It was not until 907, when the Chinese adventurer Ma Yin led a rebel army and annexed most of Hunan as the independent state of Ch'u that the Hmong kingdom was threatened with total annihilation. The Hmong rose up against Ma Yin and were defeated. Fortunately for the Hmong, Ma Yin's army was soon routed by imperial forces. But within fifty years the Sung dynasty began a series of campaigns to bring Hupeh and Hunan under tight control. During the fierce combat the Hmong king was killed as were all his generals.

The Hmong have a legend detailing these last days of their kingdom. Tchu Kyou Toua Hang was then king. He was very old, and very weary of war. Nevertheless, when the Chinese invaded Hmong territory he was in the field with his armies to meet them. The Hmong put up a fierce resistance against insurmountable odds. If it had not been for the king's only daughter, Ngao Shing, the Sung would have had an easy victory.

Ngao Shing was not only incredibly beautiful, she was endowed with supernatural powers which she exercised through the medium of a magic flag. When the Hmong were being assaulted from all

41

sides, it was she who marched forward, waved her magical flag, and called forth a terrible storm that forced the Chinese to retreat.

Ty Ching, the Commanding General of the Chinese army, feared Ngao Shing's powers and instead of resuming the war he called a truce. A messenger was sent from the Chinese's camp to the Hmong front lines to inform the Hmong king that if the magic flag were surrendered the Chinese would withdraw from Hmong territory.

Tchu Kyou Toua Hang and his advisors met to consider the offer. All present concurred that the Chinese general was laying a trap. Once he had the magic flag the Hmong would be powerless and the Chinese would slaughter them. The decision was to hand over a fake flag instead, black and white with the emblem of a dragon surrounded by flying birds: an exact duplicate of the original in every detail except that it lacked magical powers. The flag was delivered to the Chinese general who then took it to the emperor who was overjoyed with the prize.

However, one of the emperor's advisors suggested he control his enthusiasm until its authenticity had been verified. Since it was reputed that Ngao Shing's magic flag could not be burned, its authenticity could be easily determined. The flag was thrown onto a fire, and as it blazed so did the emperor's rage. General Ty Ching was placed under arrest and condemned to death. After much pleading by relatives, the general's sentence was first commuted to life imprisonment and then to a full pardon.

Ty Ching was free but disgraced. To regain his honor he asked the Emperor for permission to lead a new expedition against the Hmong. The request was granted. Despite his hatred for the Hmong, Ty Ching did not rush headlong against them. After all, Ngao Shing still possessed the magic flag. Perhaps equally important, victory over the Hmong would be sweeter were it to be gained by guile rather than force. Ty Ching meant to trick them as they had tricked him.

Ty Ching entered Hmong territory under a flag of truce, passing himself off as an emissary from the Emperor who now sought the Hmong as allies. The old king was flattered, so much so that he even consented to the provisions of the alliance which included the marriage of Ngao Shing to the Emperor's son, the next in line to the throne.

The only problem was that Ngao Shing refused to cooperate. Tchu Kyou Toua Hang was a father, but he was also a king, and it was his duty to place the welfare of his people above his own personal feelings and the happiness of his only daughter. With a heavy heart he handed Ngao Shing over to Ty Ching.

Ngao Shing was not so cooperative. She objected to the arrangement and refused to go through with the marriage. When Ty Ching learned of this he placed Ngao Shing in prison and had her tortured. But even under torture she would not consent to the marriage. As the weeks passed she grew weak and finally died.

The Hmong were still in possession of Ngao Shing's magic flag, but without Ngao Shing it was useless. Ty Ching led his army against the Hmong. Not only did he defeat them in battle and kill their king, he pursued the retreating Hmong until they were driven out of their kingdom.

Preserved in legend, the fall of the Great Hmong kingdom is viewed by the Hmong as a major turning point in their history. Politically, it was their golden age. There would be other Hmong kings, called "Kiatongs" or little kings, but none would exercise substantial power or rule over all the Hmong. This only made the glow of the golden age all that brighter and sustained a form of messianism that has lent an intensity to rebellions that mystifies outsiders. After the fall of their kingdom, the Hmong began to talk of a Hmong Messiah who would deliver them from the Chinese and restore their ancient kingdom. This Messiah would not only be a great political leader, for the Hmong never wanted for such men, he would be divinely inspired, a man with magical powers who could not be defeated by the enemy of the Hmong, no matter how numerous nor how strong.

The survivors of the fallen kingdom had more immediate problems to worry about, however. For the continued existence of the Hmong as a people was being jeopardized by the Sung dynasty's policy toward ethnic minorities, a policy that anticipated the early American policy toward the Indians. Chinese settlers were moved into Hmong territory under military escort. Garrisons were established to protect the farmers who tilled Hmong soil. Without land for their crops the Hmong faced starvation. This left them basically two choices: fight and die, or leave. Most chose the last option and migrated west into Kweichow and Szechwan. A smaller number marched southeast into Kwangsi and Kwangtung.

Dispersed and powerless, the Hmong were once again a tribal people. Though the historical origin of the Hmong tribes is unknown, there is a Hmong legend that claims the present day Hmong tribes were invented by the Chinese after the collapse of the Hmong kingdom. According to the legend the Chinese ordered the Hmong to wear clothes of different colors. Some were required to wear clothes made of black cloth and were called the Black Hmong, those who used white cloth were called the White Hmong, etc. This, so the story goes, is the origin of the five major Hmong groups in China today: White, Black, Flowery, Red and Blue. The explanation for this strange policy is that the Chinese hoped such distinctions would eventually lead to actual divisions among the Hmong, making unified action difficult.

It never came to pass. For even after the fall of the Hmong kingdom tribal affiliation was never as important to the Hmong as clan membership. As with the tribes, the origin of Hmong clans is something of a mystery, though legend attests there were originally between eight and twelve Hmong clans bearing Chinese names. Whatever their origin, from the tenth century on clan affiliation grew in importance, creating mutual rights and obligations enjoyed or owed only to members of the same clan. While this created divided loyalties, it never seriously inhibited joint action against a common enemy or put an end to Hmong rebellions.

Ming Dynasty (1368-1644)

After their flight into the mountains the majority of the Hmong lived in comparative peace until the end of the 13th century when the forces of Kublai Khan occupied Kweichow. The Mongols did not stay for long, however, nor did they penetrate very far into the mountainous regions where most of the Hmong were located. A more serious threat occurred with China's conquest of Burma, which commenced under the Mongols in 1282 and was completed by the time the Ming rose to power. Because the Ming wished to expand trade with southeast Asia, the territory of Yunnan was annexed to the empire to provide a passage to Burma. This, in turn, created the need for a more direct route to Yunnan. The old passage ran through Szechwan, but a new road through Kweichow would be even shorter. Of course, before construction could begin the region would have to be "pacified." First military zones were created and then administrative districts. Local tribal chiefs were incorporated into the administrative hierarchy with the title of "Tu Si." Once appointed, they held the position for life, and could pass it on to their heirs. And so long as the Tu Si collected taxes and preserved order, the Chinese did not interfere in tribal affairs.

Under the Ming this system was expanded and the authority of the Tu Si strengthened. In Kweichow, however, only Lolo (another tribal minority) were granted the title of Tu Si, though Lolo lords often appointed Hmong as sub-officials charged with maintaining peace among their own people. The increased autonomy granted to the Tu Si led to abuses and often tyrannical rule. The Hmong in particular were much oppressed by Lolo lords and revolts against their authority were frequent. With each revolt the Hmong grew more bold, much to the alarm of the imperial court. In 1459, General Fang-Yn was sent to Kweichow to restore order. He enjoyed an early victory, but the defeated Hmong carried out numerous raids against isolated military posts before Fang-Yn could gather enough troops from Szechwan to mount a massive campaign against them. Fang-Yn established over two thousand garrisons in the Kweichow-Szechwan region from which he launched repeated raids on Hmong

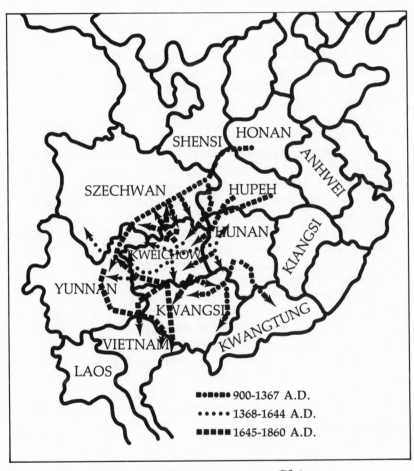

Hmong Migration in China
900-1860 A.D.

villages and military strongholds. In the end he succeeded in capturing or killing over forty thousand Hmong.

Yet within fifty years the Hmong were again attempting to reassert their independence, and revolts and rebellions continued sporadically until, by the end of the 16th century, not a year passed without the Hmong engaging in some kind of armed uprising. Not only were the Hmong exercising greater boldness, they were occupying new land across the Kweichow border into Hunan. In response, the Ming set about constructing a scaled down version of The Great Wall on the Hunan-Kweichow border. The "Hmong Wall" was ten feet high and stretched a hundred miles. Military posts were placed at intervals along the wall on the Chinese side, and no Hmong were permitted to cross over, even to trade with Chinese villagers on the other side.

Manchu Dynasty (1644-1911)

By 1640, the Ming dynasty was in serious decline. A confederation of Manchu and Mongol tribes sent one invading army after another across the northern frontier, each time coming closer to the capital. To make matters worse, the government in Peking had lost political control over much of the empire so that revenue could no longer be counted on from the provinces. This crippled efforts to raise an adequate army to repulse and destroy the invaders. Sensing the imminent collapse of the Peking government, various notables in the provinces jockeyed for political power with hopes of eventually ascending to the throne.

In 1644 Li Tzu-ch'eng, who several years earlier had taken control of all of Shensi province and declared himself emperor, led an army east and captured Peking. The last Ming emperor committed suicide before Li Tzu-ch'eng got to him. Once in power, Li Tzu-ch'eng discovered that he could not count on sufficient cooperation from either Peking officials or provincial governors to restore order to the empire. This failure merely whetted the appetites of others who were eager to follow Li Tzu-ch'eng's example and take the throne by force of arms.

General Wu San-kui was at this time commanding imperial troops on the northern frontier where he faced the army of the Manchu prince, Dorgon. The general harbored political as well as military ambitions and realized that with sufficient troops he could easily march back to Peking, take the capital and declare himself emperor. The problem was that the troops under his command were not sufficient to the task. Wu San-kui entered into secret negotiations with Prince Dorgon to see what might be arranged. A deal was struck and the general, along with his Manchu allies, entered Peking in early June of 1644.

The Manchu were not about to share power with Wu San-Kui. They would rule China on their own. Wu San-Kui had to settle for his old job as general, though he now enjoyed increased responsibility. His task was to bring all of western China under Manchu rule, which he accomplished by 1661.

As a general Wu San-kui had achieved much, but it was nothing compared with being emperor. Nearly twenty years of collaboration with the Manchu had taught him that Manchu power was really nothing more than Chinese weakness. It was only because of the inability of the Chinese to cooperate and mount a united offence that the Manchu continued to rule over China. Wu San-kui intended to turn things around, rally the Chinese, and drive the Manchu from Chinese soil.

Unfortunately, since he had devoted nearly two decades of his distinguished military career to the suppression of the western provinces he could hardly count on them for support. He therefore moved his troops further inland, traveling westward along the Yangtze, and sought patronage from the gentry, which he received. Wu San-kui declared himself emperor and immediately launched the most important military campaign of his career. What he had failed to foresee was that once the real fighting began his supporters among the gentry got cold feet. Denied the necessary manpower and supplies to defeat the Manchu forces, Wu San-kui was forced to retreat further south, setting himself up in Kwangsi near the southern border of Kweichow. He held out against the Manchu until his death when his grandson, Wu Shih-fan, took over the leadership of the resistance which effectively came to an end in 1681 when Wu Shih-fan's army was soundly defeated by the Manchu.

One of Wu Shih-fan's generals, Hwang Ming, fled from Kwangsi to Kweichow with a hundred soldiers. They were given refuge by the Hmong of Lip'ing on the eastern border of Kweichow. The following year another defeated general, Ma Bao, fled with his troops to Kweichow where he passed through Hmong territory on his way to Yunnan. Ma Bao and his men were forced to leave their weapons with the Hmong before continuing their journey. These included not only rifles, gunpowder, and armor, but also cannon.

In gratitude for their hospitality, Hwang Ming and his soldiers not only instructed the Lip'ing Hmong in the use of these weapons, but taught them how to manufacture them on their own. This is the origin of the famous Hmong Blunderbuss, or flintlock rifle, which until very recently was used by the Hmong throughout Indochina.

Prior to Hwang Ming's arrival the arsenal of Hmong weaponry consisted of crossbows, swords, knives and spears. While these weapons were crude compared to those of the Chinese, Hmong warriors often terrorized better equipped Chinese soldiers. Hmong poisoned arrows were particularly feared, for to be struck by one meant instant death. The Hmong were also ferocious in battle. Probably the most savage of all were the Jiu-Gu Hmong of central Kweichow who wore armor into combat. This included a metal helmet and chest armor made of thick buffalo hide covered with copper plates. The Jiu-Gu also covered their arms and legs with iron mail and thick iron bands. They fought with a shield in one hand, a spear in the other, and a knife between their teeth. The arrows from their crossbows were also quite deadly, not because they were dipped in poison but because they struck with such force. Jiu-Gu archers sometimes used crossbows so large that it required three men to operate them.

If Hmong poison arrows and Jiu-Gu warriors struck fear in the hearts of Chinese infantrymen, imagine the alarm when it was discovered the Hmong had acquired firearms and were venturing into territory occupied by Chinese, terrifying the inhabitants and defeating all who opposed them.

The arming of the Hmong coincided with a major change in Manchu policy toward tribal minorities which made war between the Hmong and Chinese inevitable. The Tu Si system which had placed administration of tribal territories in the hands of tribal chiefs was abandoned and tribal territories placed under the centralized control of the Chinese civil bureaucracy. As for Kweichow and Szechwan, there were additional reasons for taking immediate control of tribal territory. The land is rich in coal, silver, copper and timber which, according to official reports, the tribal minorities had failed to exploit. Then there was the question of culture. Prince Ortai, who would eventually take charge of the pacification of the Hmong, noted that "the Miao (Hmong) are really an admirable people and deserve civilization and good government. We ought to give it to them and become their rulers." Chinese farmers were brought into the region and, under military protection, allowed to take possession of the best land. Taxes were increased to the point where most Hmong were unable to pay them. To avoid the forfeiture of their land in lieu of unpaid taxes, many turned to Chinese merchants who lent them the necessary funds at an exorbitant rate of 5% per month. In no time at all thousands of Hmong lost their homes and land to their Chinese creditors.

Insurrections were frequent and in 1727 Prince Ortai used one of them as a pretext for an all out war against the Hmong. He sent General Zhang Kwang Si into central Kweichow to capture a Hmong town near the provincial capital of Kueiyang. His next attack was delayed several months while he fortified the captured town. This completed he then set out for Kueiyang itself which stands on the northern bank of the Lien river. Since he was approaching from the south he had to cross the river to assault the capital. He did so during the night, seizing Hmong boats and slaughtering Hmong boatmen who refused to ferry his men across the river. After taking Kueiyang, Zhang Kwang Si established posts along the river to control water traffic and, more particulary, to interdict a possible attempt by the Hmong to use the river as a route to recapture the city. The following year he led his army southwest toward present day Lip'ing where he encountered a Hmong army of ten thousand men, fully armed with rifle and canon. Losses were heavy on both sides, but the Chinese prevailed. Prince Ortai ordered the captured weapons melted down and cast into an iron pillar eleven feet high and placed on an island in a river the ran just south of the scene of battle as a monument to the Chinese victory over the Hmong.

Having pacified southwest Kweichow, Prince Ortai turned his attention to the southeast corner of the province. His soldiers captured four towns in quick succession, killing over one thousand Hmong in the process. Unfortunately for Ortai this did not secure the desired effect. Instead of intimidating the Hmong, Chinese ruthlessness stiffened their resolve. Scattered Hmong tribes joined forces. Stone signal towers were constructed at one mile intervals along the ridges of the mountains in which fires could be set to warn of advancing Chinese. The remains of these towers still stand today.

When the Hmong enjoyed success in some minor engagements, Peking ordered Prince Ortai to call up all the troops of Kweichow, Szechwan and Yunnan to attack the Hmong from three fronts. The fighting was furious and the Hmong suffered heavy casualties. But the Chinese sometimes suffered heavy losses as well. On one such occasion the Hmong drew the Chinese into a pass, both sides of which were ringed with rock falls. Each rock fall consisted of a wood platform braced at a forty-five degree angle against the cliff side, forming a "V" shaped cradle that was filled with rocks and small boulders. Ropes tied to the top edge of the platform held the rockfall in place. When the enemy troops were well inside the pass the order was given to cut the rope supports. The Chinese were crushed below, the survivors fleeing whence they came before the Hmong could descend from the cliffs and finish them off.

Despite the temporary advantage this gave them, the Hmong were eventually forced to concede the hopelessness of their situation. Some, sensing the fate that awaited them in defeat took a blood oath to fight to the death. They killed their wives and children and faced the imperial army as men with nothing to lose and whose only thought was to kill as many of the enemy as possible. These Hmong, fighting like demons, captured several passes and, for a time, cut all Chinese supply routes.

News of these heroics infuriated the Manchu Emperor, Shih Tsung, who dismissed Prince Ortai and replaced him with General Zhang Kwang Si. The new commander reopened the passes and cornered the remaining rebels on a high plateau where they soon found themselves without supplies. After a few months they were near starvation. When they tried to fight their way out they found the Chinese armies assembled and waiting. They were assaulted on all sides. Nearly twenty thousand Hmong fell in battle that day; another 27,000 were taken prisoner, and half of these were executed. Yet, even after killing over 30,000 Hmong soldiers, the Chinese were far from finished. Following this victory they destroyed over 12,000 Hmong villages. When it was all over the Chinese counted the Hmong rifles that had fallen into their hands. There were nearly 50,000 in all. The Hmong had obviously applied what they had learned from General Hwang Ming who fifty years earlier repaid their hospitality by instructing them in the manufacture of Chinese fire arms.

The region remained pacified until the rebellion of the two kingdoms of greater and lesser Kin-Tchuen. Following the defeat of Sonom and his people by General Akoui in 1776, another twenty years passed before the Hmong appeared in force on the Kweichow-Hunan frontier and occupied several villages. A rumor circulated that the leaders of this rebellion had taken a blood oath to drive the Chinese from Kweichow. Peking meant to nip the uprising in the bud. Troops were brought in from the neighboring provinces and a general state of war ensued.

For a time, Hmong soldiers under the leadership of Wu Ba Yue enjoyed one victory after another. Flushed with these successes Wu Ba Yue urged his troops to follow him to Peking to dethrone the emperor. Unfortunately, he did not have the slightest idea of the distance that would have to be travelled to reach Peking, or the direction one would have to take to get there. Wu Ba Yue therefore dispatched scouts to discover the route to Peking, but they never returned. Shortly after their departure Wu Ba Yue was captured and executed.

The Hmong rebelled again in Kweichow in 1801 and 1804. In response, the old Hmong "Great Wall" was rebuilt and over a thousand military posts constructed. The Hmong suffered disastrous defeats. In a final effort to fully pacify the province, the Hmong of Kweichow were forced to surrender all weapons: rifles, crossbows, spears, and armor.

Exploitation followed close on the heels of pacification. Chinese were encouraged to migrate to the province, with the result that Hmong either lost their farms to squatters who enjoyed military protection, or to creditors who confiscated their land as payment for unpaid debts. The majority of the Kweichow Hmong were reduced to dire poverty.

The final insult was a concerted effort by the civil authorities to sinicize the Hmong, forcing their children to attend Chinese schools, and prohibiting their traditional celebrations. In addition, pressure was brought to bear on Hmong villages to permit Chinese men to take Hmong women for wives.

Many Hmong found such conditions intolerable and migrated from Kweichow to the mountain areas of neighboring provinces. Some Black Hmong settled in southern Hunan and northern Kwangsi. White Hmong migrated north into Szechwan, and numbers of Flowery Hmong made the trek west to Yunnan to link up with existing Hmong communities in the province.

HMONG AND HAW

As it turned out, Yunnan was not a good choice. A large proportion of the Yunnanese were Muslims, descendants of Chinese converted to Islam by Arab traders who first entered Yunnan with their caravans over a thousand years earlier. Known as the "Haw" in Yunnan and as the "Panthays" in Burma, they were mostly merchants and traders. Though prosperous, they were excluded from polite society and much discriminated against by the non-Muslim Chinese. Ill-feeling toward them sometimes sparked riots. Haw were dragged from their homes and killed or beaten and their shops looted. Any appeal to Yunnanese authorities for protection was futile since government officials were as prejudiced and hostile toward the Haw as the general population.

In 1818 the Haw rebelled. They did so again in 1826 and 1834. Each time they were defeated. The worst, and last, Haw rebellion, the Great Panthay Rebellion, began in 1855 and lasted until 1873. Because of Peking's preoccupation with the more serious and widespread Taiping Rebellion, and the ability of the Haw to purchase modern European weapons from the British in Burma, the Haw were eventually able to take control of the entire province. Their leader, Tu Wen-hsiu, declared Yunnan an independent Muslim state. And so it remained until 1872 when Peking sent sufficient troops to regain control of the province.

Through it all the majority of Yunnan's Hmong sided with the Haw. And like the Haw they paid dearly for their rebellion. Once the Imperial army cut the supply routes to Yunnan, the rebels had to contend with starvation as well as an invading army. Then there was disease. At various times bubonic plague devastated the population.

Once the tide turned against the rebels the Chinese responded with the kind of savagery they had previously reserved for the Hmong alone. In 1871, the rebel city of Chengkiang in southern Yunnan capitulated after being subjected to a long siege. Part of the capitulation agreement was that the inhabitants of the city would be treated with mercy once the gates were opened and the Chinese let in. But once the city gates were unlocked the Chinese, under the command of Shao Ta-jen, rushed in and began to slaughter the inhabitants. Haw soldiers resisted and then retreated. Many Haw soldiers escaped, but the women, children, and elderly left behind were cut down without mercy. When night fell, the streets of Chengkiang were strewn with the bodies of nearly six thousand victims.

By the time the Chinese finally regained control of Yunnan, the population of the province had been reduced by one million. The majority of the casualties were Haw but Hmong losses were also heavy. Persecution of both Hmong and Haw followed. The Haw had all their property confiscated and were prohibited from opening shops or engaging in trade. Repeating the atrocities at Chengkiang, Chinese soldiers attacked Hmong villages and slaughtered men, women, and children indiscriminately. While many Hmong and Haw had already left the region, large numbers now formed a river of migrants, flowing southward toward Indochina.

But they were not the first Hmong to migrate to Indochina. Since the late 1700s, Hmong fed up with Manchu oppression had begun to migrate southward following the mountain chains across the border into north Vietnam.

CONTINUED SUPPRESSION

In 1855, the Hmong of Kweichow, no doubt inspired by the Taiping Rebellion, revolted one last time. Troops from four neighboring provinces were brought in to defeat the rebel force headquartered at Lungli only a short distance from the provincial capital. Approximately 3,000 Hmong were killed during the campaign, one fact among many described in a book entitled *Plans to Pacify the [Hmong] Bandits*, a work commissioned by the Manchu court to commemorate the suppression of the Hmong.

Some of the survivors packed up their worldly belongings and left the province. They too eventually reached North Vietnam. Indeed, during the last half of the 19th century thousands of Hmong from Kweichow, Szechwan, Kwangsi and Yunnan migrated from China into Indochina. For the Hmong who stayed behind, discrimination and even repression remained a fact of life.

In 1911, in western Hunan, a Chinese secret society planned the takeover of the military headquarters at Feng-huang. Hmong were recruited from the countryside to provide the cannon fodder for the major assault on the garrison. Hundreds of Hmong were cut down by rifle fire before they could scale the garrison walls. The next day their heads were piled up in front of the garrison for all to see. The Chinese who escaped were taken in by Hmong villagers and hidden from the authorities. Not unexpectedly, the Hmong were made the scapegoats for the abortive insurrection. Instead of confronting the troublesome fact that this had all the earmarks of an anti-dynastic conspiracy, local officials preferred to describe it as a Hmong rebellion. Troops were dispatched to Hmong villages to teach the rebels a lesson. Each day a hundred villagers were decapitated and their bodies dumped on the side of the road. The mass executions continued for a month until the provincial governor ordered them halted.

In 1940, a group of Hmong in southwest Kweichow attacked and killed the local official, a Chung-chia (Tai ethnic minority) who had been illegally impressing Hmong into the military, making them take the place of Chung-chia. In retaliation, the district government mounted an expedition against the Hmong villages in the area, executing villagers and burning their homes to the ground.

Three years later, the national government legalized Chinese prejudice against the Hmong by prohibiting the use of the Hmong language and urging local officials to attempt to suppress the wearing of Hmong costumes.

HMONG UNDER MAO

It was only with the victory of Mao Tse-tung over the Kuomintang regime that things improved for the Hmong of China. This dramatic reversal in policy was not without precedent. In 1912, with the inauguration of the new Chinese republic, the need to improve the lot of China's minorities was placed on the national agenda. The five colors of the new national flag symbolized what was then termed the five races of China: Han Chinese, Manchurian, Muslim, Mongol, and Tibetan. The father of the new republic, Sun Yat-Sen, was influential for a time in setting the tone for the nation's minority policy, which vacillated between assimilation into the majority culture and ethnic autonomy.

The Soviet experiment with autonomous republics for ethnic minorities provided inspiration for the second alternative, and it seemed to be gaining ground until 1927 when the special ministry for minority affairs, established in 1914, was unceremoniously reduced to a minor commission and the five color national flag was replaced by one that clearly symbolized the Nationalist Party.

Assimilation was now the goal, and to smooth the way the old method of flooding minority areas with Chinese was resumed, the principal target being Sinkiang province. However, as the Nationalists were unable to control many areas with minority populations the new policy had little effect on most minorities, including the Hmong.

In the 1920s, the fledgling Chinese communist party also raised the minority issue, favoring in the end autonomous regions that would ultimately be linked, with the Chinese majority, into a federated republic. Nothing much came of the idea until 1938 when Mao Tse-tung announced the official party position, which was that all national minorities should enjoy equal rights with the Han Chinese, that they should be accorded complete freedom to develop their own cultures, and that they should be allowed to use their own language or special dialects. Autonomous areas were also to be encouraged, with the right of self-rule limited only by the requisites of a unified Chinese Communist state.

This had become the standard communist line in ethnically complex nations as an effective means of building a united front against their political opponents. And this was precisely what Mao needed in his war with the Nationalists; if nothing else, the minorities (especially the montagnards) were able to provide his harried communist soldiers sanctuary from the superior military forces of the Kuomintang.

According to one of his comrades on the famous Long March, Mao's position on the national minorities was very much influenced by the help his troops received from the Hmong of Kwangsi in 1934. At one point during the long march the retreating Red army crossed through Hmong territory in Kwangsi. When they happened upon a Hmong village, Mao cautioned his soldiers to treat the villagers with respect and to leave their goods untouched. Because of this decent treatment, several Hmong volunteered to serve as guides for the Red Army and led them safely through the mountain passes in the region.

It is doubtful that this incident alone explains Mao's concern for the national minorities once he assumed power, but it is true that the working paper of 1949 Peking Consultative Conference devotes an entire chapter to the Hmong, and that by 1952 the communist government had established 130 autonomous areas for national minorities. While this hardly constituted self-government for minorities like the Hmong, it nevertheless meant greater respect for their culture and traditions.

One indication of this new respect was a nation-wide tour of Hmong who performed folk dances in traditional costume for millions of Han Chinese. The government also created a romanized Hmong script which was used, along with Chinese, in the instruction of the children in the many new schools that were established in their villages. In addition a serious attempt was made to improve the economy of minority regions. For the Hmong this meant not only wider markets for their traditional handicrafts but also new economic opportunities. A farm implement factory was built in the Hmong autonomous zone in Hunan. Hmong not only worked in the factory they helped manage it. Elsewhere Hmong worked in and helped run new iron and coal mines as well as lumber mills. Hmong farmers who had long ago been reduced to impoverished share croppers also benefited from the land redistribution that was also part of the new economic reforms. On the negative side, the Hmong were subjected to the same indoctrination program as the Han Chinese which included, among other things, mandatory accusation meetings where they were forced to give false testimony about the sins of their neighbors. Renowned for their truthfulness, and often blushing beet red when caught in a lie, the Hmong suffered much embarrassment at these meetings.

Nor did the Hmong escape the collectivization movement imposed on the nation by the Mao regime. But due to the remoteness of many of their villages, the pace of collectivization was much slower than what was experienced by the general population.

An even greater threat to the traditional Hmong lifestyle occurred in 1956, when the government launched a program to force millions of Han Chinese to migrate to minority regions in order to alter the demographic imbalance in favor of the Han. Today there are few areas where ethnic minorities make up a majority of the population. Intermarriage between Chinese and members of national minorities has also been encouraged. And despite the preservation of minority languages and costumes, the government has made every effort to absorb ethnic minorities into the predominant Han Chinese culture.

While there have been dramatic improvements in education for national minorities, few if any have been allowed to assume positions of authority outside their own ethnic communities. There are exceptions, of course, like Wu Chilian, a forty-three year old Hmong woman from Kiangsi province who climbed the ranks of the provincial party hierarchy and, in 1983, became head of a major subdistrict. But this is the glaring exception and not the rule. Unlike the Soviet Union where it is not uncommon for ethnic minorities to work their way up through the party hierarchy and achieve positions of power and prestige, real power in China is still exercised only by the Chinese.

It is not difficult to see that the trend toward greater assimilation of all national minorities to the dominant Chinese culture poses a serious threat to the continued existence of a distinctively Hmong way of life in China. Perhaps this is the price that must be paid for the Hmong to enjoy full citizenship and equal rights with the Chinese.

4

SETTLING IN INDOCHINA

EARLY CROSSINGS

In the late 1740s a small number of Kweichow Hmong, refugees of the massive military campaign waged against the Hmong in that province between 1727 and 1740, crossed over the Chinese border and entered Indochina. They settled in two places about 150 miles apart on the north Vietnamese border. One was at Dong Quan, a village fifty miles inland from the Gulf of Tonkin. The other was located near the limestone mountain region of Hoang-Su-Phi.

Fifty years later more Hmong entered Vietnam, but this time they were a much larger group of around six thousand. They crossed the border and occupied the mountains above the Tai village of Dong Van, just a few miles from the point where the three borders of Yunnan, Kwangsi, and Vietnam intersect. For a time, relations between the Hmong and the Tai lowlanders were strained, occasionally erupting into violence. But as the Hmong seldom ventured from their highland villages into the fertile Tai valleys below, apprehensions over claim jumping subsided and the Tai accorded the newcomers a grudging tolerance.

LAOS

Sometime between 1815 and 1818 another Hmong settlement sprang up west of Dong Van on the northern tip of the Fan Si Pan mountain range. The settlers were probably a splinter group from the Hmong community near Dong Van who left their comrades to search for better land. When they arrived at the Fan Si Pans they marked out their villages, built homes, cleared fields and planted their first crops, and generally gave every indication they meant to stay. But within a few years the homes were empty, the fields choked with weeds and the Hmong nowhere in sight.

It was all the doing of one man, a Chinese opium merchant named Ton Ma. On one of his stops to collect opium from the new Hmong community he told them of the lush, uninhabited mountains of Xieng Khouang province in eastern Laos. He also offered to lead a contingent of the Fan Si Pan Hmong to this promised land on his next trip to Xieng Khouang. Ton Ma's motives were not entirely altruistic for Xieng Khouang province contains some of the world's best opium growing areas. But, then, the Hmong were opium growers, so there was profit to be made on both sides.

Lo Pa See*, the recognized leader of the Fan Si Pan Hmong, quickly assembled the village chiefs and elders to discuss how best to proceed. The decision was that a small party under the leadership of Kue Vue would undertake an exploratory expedition to Laos. If all was as Ton Ma had described, others would follow.

The place Ton Ma led them to was just a few miles inside Laos near a town the Laotians called Nong Het. Kue Vue and his men explored other areas nearby but none impressed them as much as the terrain near Nong Het. Ton Ma had not deceived them. The mountains and high plateaus were nearly uninhabited and densely forested. The thick vegetation would mean extra work when fields had to be cleared for planting, but after it was burned the cut timber and thick underbrush would provide abundant fertilizer for the already rich soil.

After Kue Vue and his men returned to north Vietnam and informed their comrades of what they had found, the question was no longer whether a portion of the village should migrate to Laos, but whether the entire community should do so. It was decided that one large group, again led by Kue Vue, would first settle in Nong Het and, if all went well, the rest would follow.

These homesteaders traveled as the Hmong have always traveled, carrying everything they owned on their backs, driving their livestock before them, walking the crests of the mountains until they reached their destination.

Within a few years they established ten villages around Nong Het, and in honor of the Chinese trader who had made it all possible, they named one of the rivers that flowed nearby the Ton Ma. This no doubt pleased their sponsor who was a frequent visitor to Nong Het during the opium harvest. In later years when the harvests were large and his visits correspondingly longer he built a winter residence close to the river that bears his name.

---

*Traditionally, Hmong first and middle names follow the clan name (surname). Thus, Pa See Lo becomes Lo Pa See.

The success of the Hmong at Nong Het, coupled with Ton Ma's prodding, convinced Lo Pa See to lead the remaining Fan Si Pan Hmong to the area. Lo Pa See had an additional reason for the final evacuation of the remaining Hmong from the Fan Si Pan mountains. Ton Ma promised him that he would be made kiatong ("little king") of the Nong Het Hmong when he resettled.

Everything would have been perfect if it had not been for the tigers. The increase in the size of the Hmong community required the clearing of land for new fields and villages. Some of the sites chosen happened to fall well within the hunting grounds of tigers unfamiliar with and therefore unafraid of man. By one account the tigers were so numerous that guards had to be placed around workers clearing new fields to forestall attacks. A few of the tigers regularly raided villages, carrying away not only livestock but old women and young children. The Hmong were at a loss to deal with this threat until, spurred by a fatal tiger attack on an elderly woman, they devised tiger traps so effective that the problem was eliminated within a matter of months.

With the threat of tigers removed, the Nong Het Hmong enjoyed several years of uninterrupted peace until their kiatong, Lo Pa See, was murdered by Chinese bandits during an abortive raid on his village's opium cache. The death of Lo Pa See necessitated the selection of a new kiatong and the vote went to another member of the Lo clan, Lo Xia Sue.

Recruiting new kiatongs from the Lo clan became something of a precedent that remained unchallenged for several decades. But by the early 1850s this political consensus was strained by two events. New migrants, mostly members of the Ly and Moua clans, demanded more representative politics. Then there was the matter of the arrival of a Ly kiatong from China who refused to renounce authority over his own clansmen.

The Ly kiatong came from southern Szechwan where the Panthay rebellion had claimed thousands of Hmong lives. For many of the Szechwan Ly the choice was migrate or die. The old Patriarch of the Szechwan Ly had remained behind to hold off the Chinese while his four sons led a southern retreat toward Indochina. Before they departed, their father transferred his authority as kiatong of the Ly clan to one of them, Ly Nghia Vue. A full year passed before Ly Nghia Vue and the remnants of his clan finally reached Nong Het. The arrival of another kiatong posed obvious political problems for the Nong Het Hmong. Which of the two possessed ultimate authority? A compromise was reached. Ly Nghia Vue would exercise authority over the Ly, and the Lo kiatong would represent the remaining Hmong. But it was not long before the Moua clan objected to the arrangement and soon they, too, had their own kiatong, Moua Chong Kai. Though authority was divided, the Lo kiatongs continued to enjoy greater prestige and influence than either the Ly or Moua kiatongs.

Word of the success of the Nong Het Hmong attracted other Chinese Hmong to Indochina. Not all chose Laos, however. A large number headed for north Vietnam. As the Vietnamese would later characterize the event, they entered Vietnam like an invading army.

VIETNAM

In 1860, toward the end of the Taiping Rebellion in China, more Hmong crossed the border in the company of Chinese, probably Haw muslims from Yunnan and possibly even a number of defeated Taiping rebels. The group was first sighted in the frontier region of Dong Van, Yen Minh and Quan Ba. Organized as a military force, they easily routed the Vietnamese soldiers guarding the border passes and then headed south, following the course of the Song Chay River toward Hanoi.

The Vietnamese Mandarins in districts near the river town of Tuyen Quang sent troops to block the Hmong advance, but they were quickly overwhelmed and relentlessly pursued all the way to Tuyen Quang where they rallied the support of the local citizens and attempted to repel their pursuers. The Hmong launched two major assaults before the city fell into their hands. Flushed with their victories, the Hmong continued south and entered the delta region.

A mountain people, the Hmong do not do well in tropical climates. Illness, probably malaria, began to take its toll and slow their advance. This provided officials in Hanoi the breathing space to organize a resistance. All troops in the Red River delta were called up and placed under the command of Governor Son Tay. The hastily assembled army, including a unit of war elephants, intercepted the Hmong at Yen Binh, just sixty miles north of Hanoi. The Hmong held their own until the war elephants were brought forward. They had never seen such beasts and were properly terrified. The Hmong hastily retreated into the mountains where the elephants were unable to follow. They then traveled east until they reached the Clear River. From there they journeyed north to the high plateau region of Quan Ba near the Chinese border where they established several villages and remained undisturbed for years.

Other Hmong continued to cross over the Chinese border into Indochina. Like moths drawn to the glow of Nong Het, many chose to settle in Laos, but others, undaunted by the earlier Hmong defeat at Yen Binh, headed for the established Hmong settlement of Quan Ba in north Vietnam.

It was near Quan Ba on Mount Phuoc that a mysterious Hmong named Sioung began each day with sacrifices to the genies and spirits of the forest, after which he spent several grueling hours in gymnastic exercises. After months of hard practice he was able to jump incredibly high off the ground, a feat which convinced him he was at last ready to fulfill what he believed to be his destiny, to become the long awaited new king of the Hmong.

Sioung descended Mount Phouc and entered a Hmong village. The curious villages watched as he piled up benches until they formed a makeshift tower. To their amazement, the stranger reached the top bench in one leap. Sioung announced to the astonished villagers below that he was the king of the Hmong, and that the genies who gave him the power to perform such an incredible feat had also insured his success by planting magic beans which would grow into men instead of plants and that they would be his soldiers and help him defeat his enemies.

News of this remarkable event spread rapidly throughout the hill tribes in the area. Many of the Hmong, longing for a messiah, were taken in by Sioung's gymnastics and hailed him as their king. But other montagnards, like the Nung and Man, were also impressed. It was not long before Hmong, Nung and Man began showing up at the village, some bearing gifts, others simply wishing to show their respect and others just eager to have a look at the mysterious Hmong whose leaping ability was even more impressive now since he had replaced the makeshift tower of benches with a taller one made out of stones.

Many of the Hmong who acknowledged his sovereignty eagerly awaited his instructions. Sioung's first royal proclamation was the announcement of his new name. It was to be Choen-Tien. And his first command was that his subjects were to build him a palace. Much to the consternation of the Buddhists at Dong Van, the gold inlays and carved wood for Sioung's palace was obtained from raids on their pagodas. When the palace was completed, Sioung ordered his subjects to construct a tower on the palace roof. The tower's name was to be "Long-Wei', the "Seat of the Dragon'. Its principal function was to enable Sioung to be closer to heaven so that he could more easily converse with the genies and other spirits.

His residence completed, Sioung directed his attention to the problem of establishing his authority over the border region around Quan Ba. This necessitated an army, which he raised from the villages of the Hmong, Nung and Man. He recruited Hmong blacksmiths to forge flintlocks. Others collected the necessary saltpeter, sulfur and charcoal to make gunpowder. The arms and ammunition were distributed to his troops whose only special item of uniform was a white turban. One hundred flags representing Sioung's new kingdom were made and dispatched to the military posts Sioung had established throughout his realm.

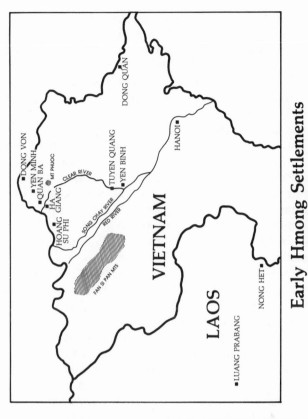

Early Hmong Settlements
North Vietnam and Laos

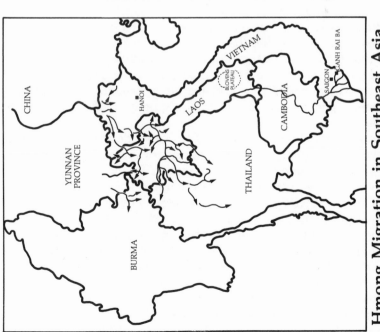

Hmong Migration in Southeast Asia
1800-1950

Soon Sioung's authority was recognized by all the tribesmen in the area, save for the Tho who would not submit. Furious at their refusal to recognize his divine right to rule, Sioung led a military expedition against them. His first assault was on the Tho village of Lang Dan. The Tho put up a weak resistance and were driven off, watching from the hills as their village was pillaged and then destroyed.

A much larger Tho village near Quan Ba was the next target. There Sioung met with greater resistance. This did not save the Tho village. It merely cost the Tho more lives. After razing the town, Sioung sent a band of his men to intercept the fleeing Tho before they could reach the provincial capital of Ha Giang and appeal to the Vietnamese Mandarin for help. When his soldiers caught up with them the terrified Tho scattered in all directions. Some escaped but most, over a thousand, were killed. Sioung's repression of the Tho continued for twelve more years.

The victories at Lang Dan and Quan Ba so increased the Hmong king's reputation among the various tribes that he no longer felt there was any need to direct his troops in the field. This task he assigned to his officers. For his part, he remained in his palace, coming out only in the morning, afternoon and at sunset to stand on his tower so that his subjects could venerate him.

Out of simple prudence, Vietnamese officials from neighboring districts paid their respects to the Hmong king. They had no desire invite his anger. It was a small price to pay to keep his troops out of their districts.

Sioung took as his wife the youngest daughter of a tribesmen named Tao Yao. Shortly after the marriage, Sioung killed his bride. Tao Yao was furious but dared not complain out of fear for his own life. He was forced into action, however, when Sioung informed him that he intended to marry his other daughter. Tao Yao immediately packed up his family and quietly made his escape to China.

Once in safer surroundings, Tao Yao's desire for vengeance quickened. He found ten men renowned for their courage, strength, and guile and employed them as assassins. In due time they arrived at Sioung's palace and presented themselves as skilled artisans in need of work. They spent several weeks doing odd jobs inside the palace until some trouble with the Tho led Sioung to dispatch most of his troops, including the majority of the palace guards, to put down the rebellion. When the few remaining guards took a break for dinner, the assassins entered the king's inner chambers and killed him.

Sioung's kingdom dissolved with his death. Among the Hmong, political authority once again returned to their freely chosen village chiefs. The Tho were no longer persecuted, though long before

Sioung's death, most had already migrated to the lowlands where they were beyond the reach of the Hmong king, and where tropical disease, like malaria, which had decimated the Hmong in their 1860 invasion of the Red River delta, provided additional insurance against Hmong attacks.

In 1911, another Hmong, bent on reviving the fallen kingdom, passed himself off as another Sioung. He even took his name. Trading on the reputation of the real Sioung, he whipped the Hmong into a rebellious mood. Now, however, the Hmong had to contend with the French as well as the Vietnamese. The second Sioung was captured and imprisoned. He died in jail, disillusioned.

The political vacuum created by the death of the first Sioung was partially filled by Shue Cha, chief of a Hmong village in the limestone mountain region near Hoang-Su-Phi. His rise to power was not as dramatic as Sioung's but it was steady. Within forty years he controlled most of the territory around Hoang-Su-Phi as well as an area of equal extent on the other side of the Chinese border. In 1894 the Chinese formally recognized his authority by granting him the title of Tu Si, a provincial administrator with full power over the tribal minorities in his district.

Without opposition from either the French or Vietnamese, Shue Cha applied his new found authority in the Vietnamese as well as the China portion of his kingdom.

The French in particular did not interfere because Shue Cha's support was crucial to the maintenance of a French monopoly in coffin wood. Hmong lumberjacks harvested the abundant coffin wood trees and, under Shue Cha's orders, delivered the timber only to the French. For the first time since their entry into Indochina some Hmong were enjoying a modest degree of affluence. Also for the first time, they were taxing the French. Shue Cha levied a duty on every stick of lumber the French purchased from the Hmong.

The renown of Shue Cha spread all the way to Laos where the Hmong began to invest him with magical powers. It was claimed that he could change himself or others into different forms. Following his death stories began to circulate that he had not actually perished but had only changed his form.

In one such tale Shue Cha changed himself into a tiger to obtain meat for some hungry Hmong. He told them that when he returned with the meat they would have to hit him or he would remain a tiger forever. But on his return he so frightened them that they ran away. After that he roamed the forests, a legendary and feared creature, a Hmong bogeyman, who occasionally raided Hmong communities and carried off the most beautiful young woman of the village.

RELATIONS WITH OTHER TRIBAL MINORITIES

In general the Hmong who settled in Laos and Vietnam maintained friendly relations with their montagnard neighbors, but there were exceptions. As we have seen, Sioung nearly exterminated the Tho tribesmen who refused to acknowledge his authority. And in Laos during the latter half of the 19th century the Hmong of Xieng Khouang province engaged in a bloody war with the Kha (also known as the Khmu), montagnards like themselves who considered the Hmong interlopers and unwisely demanded tribute from them as a condition of settlement in Kha occupied territory.

Descendants of the first inhabitants of Indochina, the Kha were driven from the fertile lowlands into the mountains by repeated waves of conquering invaders. In Laos, shortly after the establishment of the kingdom of Luang Prabang, the Kha were actually enslaved by the Lao Tai, the descendants of Tai invaders from southern China. If by the end of the nineteenth century the Kha were no longer officially slaves, they nevertheless occupied the bottom rung of the Laotian social ladder.

The arrival of Hmong offered the Kha hope of improving their social status, for the Hmong gave early evidence of a gentility bordering on servility. Here, or so it seemed at the time, was a people who could be abused with relative impunity. The Kha immediately informed the Hmong that they were trespassing on Kha land and if they wished to remain tribute would have to be paid. Though the Hmong consider all unoccupied land free for the taking, they nevertheless acquiesced to Kha demands. The Hmong did not want trouble. This concession went to the Kha's heads and they began to treat the Hmong as they themselves had been treated — with contempt.

Things went from bad to worse when the Kha discovered the delights of Hmong opium. For nearly two centuries, opium has been the Hmong's only cash crop, and it is the principal reason they cultivate the poppy. While the Hmong appreciate the medicinal benefits of opium, they consider the recreational use of the drug a bad habit and view addiction as a serious character flaw. And it was for this very reason that the Hmong reacted to the growing number of Kha opium addicts with disgust and also with alarm because the Kha began demanding tribute in opium rather than in agricultural produce and livestock. Threatened with a loss of their only source of income the pliant Hmong suddenly stiffened their backs and refused to pay. The Kha responded with violence. The Hmong gathered up their flintlocks and crossbows and went to war.

The Kha had made the mistake of equating Hmong amiability with weakness. After suffering devastating defeats, many Kha fled Xieng Khouang province and settled in the mountain region near Luang Prabang. Those who remained behind found that the Hmong were quick to forgive past injuries and eager to maintain friendly relations with any group, provided it was willing to do the same.

If peaceful relations between the Hmong and neighboring montagnards was the rule, relations between the Hmong and lowlanders were often strained. For this very reason the Hmong tried to reduce their contact with the lowlanders to a bare minimum. French colonialism changed this, especially in Laos.

FRENCH COLONIAL POLICY

French Catholic missionaries were already active in Vietnam by the early 1600s. Success in gaining converts was slow at first, then picked up by the mid 1600s. In 1664 the effort to Christianize the Vietnamese was given a shot in the arm by financial backing from the French business community.

The funds were funnelled through the new French East India Company which had been created for the express purpose of expanding trade with Vietnam. As one might surmise, East India Company funding of missionary activity in Vietnam was not altogether an expression of altruism. A network of missionaries, fluent in Vietnamese and familiar with the country, was an invaluable asset in establishing trade relations with the Vietnamese; even more so when the missionaries did double duty and worked as bookkeepers and sales agents for the company in return for transportation to Vietnam.

Though Vietnamese rulers did not respond warmly to either French traders or French missionaries, gunboat diplomacy usually brought them around to the French view of what was in their best interests. In fact, the French often used Vietnamese resistance as an excuse for expanding their presence.

In 1859, under the pretext of retaliating for the persecution of French Catholic missionaries, Admiral Rigault de Genouilly guided his nine warships into Ganh Rai Bay, and then followed the river channels inland until he reached Saigon. Troops were sent ashore and the village easily captured. Only a sleepy fishing village at the time, Saigon held promise as an excellent deep water port, and as a beachhead for later operations in the Delta region.

The French also had a larger plan. It was to use the Mekong River as a navigable route into southwest China where French goods could be marketed to millions of potential consumers, and China's natural resources such as timber, tin, coal, silver and iron ferried downstream and shipped to European markets. Then, too, there were the opium fields of Yunnan. This cheap source of raw opium could place the French on a competitive footing with the British in the international drug market.

Of course, to gain control of the Mekong required not only the colonization of Vietnam, but also Cambodia and Laos. Cambodia was made a protectorate in 1863, and all of Vietnam fell to the French in 1884. Laos followed in 1893.

Though an 1886 expedition up the Mekong revealed that the river's upper reaches were so treacherous as to prove unnavigable, it was not until 1895, when invested capital from a Parisian syndicate failed to turn a profit from an upriver trading venture, that all thought of the Mekong's use as a back door to China was abandoned. But, by then, the momentum of French colonialism had gathered such force that the issue of the navigability of the Mekong was rendered moot.

Because Vietnam offered greater potential for economic development than either Laos or Cambodia, the lion's share of French investment in economic development went to Vietnam. Enormous sums were borrowed to construct roads, canals, and railroads. One of these projects, with a price tag in excess of $60 million, was the construction of a rail line from northern Vietnam across the Chinese border into Yunnan. The project was not only expensive, it was also extremely hazardous for the Vietnamese rail gangs who hacked through jungle and carved railbeds out of the stone walls of mountain passes. One out of every three laborers who toiled on the project died before it was completed. But the French finally had their back door to China.

Ironically, the long dreamed of profits never materialized. Trade with China was barely profitable, and the railroad itself turned out to be a commercial failure. On the other hand, an elaborate system of canals for the Mekong delta transformed the river basin into one of the most productive rice producing areas of the world. Unhappily for the peasants working the paddies, the increased productivity did not translate into a higher standard of living. The surplus rice was siphoned off for export to rice hungry China and the additional revenue pocketed by the colonial administration.

The French increased Vietnamese taxes to amortize the loans for these projects, and continued to increase them until they were the highest among the colonial powers in Southeast Asia and India. The effect on the Vietnamese peasant class was devastating. Prior to the French takeover most Vietnamese peasants were landowners. Within fifty years the vast majority were landless.

Vietnamese tradition wisely forbade the confiscation of land for the payment of debts. The French ignored this tradition. A peasant's land was treated like any other real asset that could be seized for the payment of debts. Fearing the confiscation of their land for non-payment of taxes, many peasants turned to wealthy Vietnamese for loans (at interest rates that often exceeded 100% per annum) to meet their tax obligation in a futile attempt to stall off the inevitable. Slowly but surely Vietnam was transformed into a land of huge estates on which approximately 70% of the population toiled as sharecroppers. French tax policy was not only exploitative, it was shortsighted. Within two generations it created the social and economic conditions for revolution.

This might have been remedied if the French had also encouraged Vietnamese commerce and industry, creating a source of alternative employment for an impoverished peasantry. They did quite the opposite, however. Industry and banking, and any other economic activity that might result in competition with imported French goods, was prohibited.

The Bank of Indochina, established in 1875 and controlled by the Bank of Paris, exercised virtual monopolistic control over all banking in Indochina and was an effective instrument in regulating the direction of economic development. French control over the flow of capital guaranteed that even ventures which did not threaten French imports would be owned and managed by Frenchmen and not Vietnamese. The bank provided the capital for French coal mines in Tonkin and in Khammouane province, Laos; it also floated the loans for the French rubber plantations in southern and central Vietnam and on the Blovens Plateau in southern Laos (on the eve of World War II, 50% of U.S. rubber was imported from French Indochina), and bankrolled French coffee plantations in central Vietnam and southern Laos.

Following the lead of the financiers, the colonial administration established government monopolies controlling the production and sale of opium, alcohol and salt. Monopoly pricing naturally followed and provided the French with an additional, though hidden, tax on Vietnamese, Laotians and Cambodians. On the other hand, French taxes did not hit Laotians and Cambodians as hard as did the Vietnamese. Because neither country had much to exploit, as little as possible was spent to administer them.

In Laos, for example, the entire administrative bureaucracy at the turn of the century amounted to no more than 72 French officials. It was impossible for so few officials to directly oversee the administration of the country. French educated Vietnamese were therefore used to fill the middle levels of the bureaucracy. In turn, the Vietnamese employed Laotians as clerks and translators. This still left the French understaffed and forced them to rely on the traditional Laotian political system to carry out their edicts and to collect taxes. One consequence of this arrangement was that tax evasion among the ethnic Lao was commonplace. As the French returned almost no benefits for taxes levied, Laotian politicians had little incentive to alienate large segments of the population by prosecuting tax evaders.

Non-Lao ethnic minorities were another matter. Viewed as barbarians and denied political representation, they were regularly exploited by Laotian officials. This was particularly true for the hill tribes. Because of their isolation and distance from centers of power, the hill tribes had no effective means to protest unjust treatment by local authorities. Their only recourse, once the level of exploitation became intolerable, was either to rebel or to migrate.

Because of their vulnerability the hill tribes were often forced to bear the full burden of French taxes, though only a fraction of these revenues were passed on to the French. The rest was pocketed by tax collectors and local officials: an additional reason why tax evasion by Laotian montagnards was treated more harshly than tax evasion by ethnic Lao.

The Hmong not only objected to a double standard that punished tax evasion by montagnards and yet tolerated it among the ethnic Lao who enjoyed a higher standard of living and were better able to pay, they resented the contemptuous way they were treated by the very Laotian officials who were exploiting them. The Hmong in particular, were not permitted to stand in their company, and if they approached an official they had to literally crawl, head down, and wait patiently until he saw fit to recognize their presence.

Nevertheless, the Hmong did not want trouble, especially as the Laotians repeatedly reminded them of the military might of the French whom the Hmong now called the Fabkis (pronounced"Fah Key"), a word derived from the Chinese expression"Fa Kouie"— French Devils. Even though the Hmong were intimidated by such threats, they would stand for only so much abuse. For the moment, however, the Hmong of Indochina were preoccupied with getting on, with living their daily lives, observing their traditions and practicing their religion, all of which is the subject of the next chapter.

CHAPTER
5

HMONG SOCIETY

By the beginning of the twentieth century the number of Hmong in southeast Asia had grown from a few thousand to between forty and sixty thousand. The majority lived in the highlands of northern Vietnam and Laos. The remainder, only a few thousand, lived in isolated villages in northern Thailand. They were late comers from Yunnan who reached Thailand by way of Burma no earlier than 1880 and whose numbers were periodically augmented by westward migrating Laotian Hmong.

Whether in Vietnam, Laos or Thailand, Hmong villages were invariably to be found above 3,000 feet and, on occasion, as high as 5,000 feet. At this altitude the Hmong could be assured of few competitors for the available land; it also placed them beyond the reach of the tropical climate and lowland diseases that so often devastate montagnard populations. There, in the isolated mountain regions of southeast Asia, the Hmong put down roots and enjoyed generations of relative peace and prosperity in which their culture flourished.

PART I: DAILY LIFE

Most of what is known about Hmong culture and society in southeast Asia comes from the observations of anthropologists, missionaries and colonial administrators, as well as the reminiscences of living Hmong. Together, these accounts provide a colorful, if sometimes sketchy, portrait of these unique people and their daily lives which, save for the absence of constant persecution, was not unlike the lives lived by countless Chinese Hmong for the past thousand years.

The Hmong Village

At the turn of the century, Hmong villages in southeast Asia varied in size from a few families to twenty or thirty and were usually constructed along the same plan. Houses were built on slopes surrounded by high mountains. The purpose of this was entirely practical. It placed the village near a stream and guaranteed an adequate water supply. If a stream was not nearby, a bamboo aqueduct was erected to carry upstream water to the village. The slopes also provided much needed drainage to reduce the chance of flash floods during monsoons. And the surrounding mountains served as a buffer against monsoon winds and rain.

Homes were simple affairs built on whatever flat surface a chosen slope provided or, if none existed, on a terraced plot carved out of the slope. The frame of the square Hmong house consisted of stout poles driven into the ground. Split rail planking (or in some cases split bamboo) was used for siding. Since the Hmong lacked the proper tools, tight fits between adjoining planks were uncommon and finished walls showed many gaps and cracks through which cold winter winds could blow. Clusters of palm leaves fastened to a lattice work of bamboo poles served as the roof.

The only improvement made to the earthen floor inside the house was a thorough stamping to make it firm and to keep dust down to a minimum. Planks fastened to the rafters provided storage space for pots and pans, dry goods, clothes and blankets. Simple partition walls were used to separate bedrooms from the living room and cooking area. Furnishings were equally Spartan: a bench or two and a few stools for sitting. A small stove near the front door was used for cooking family meals; a larger stove toward the back of the house was used for boiling corn to be used as mash for pigs or for cooking large meals for ceremonial occasions. And no house was without its altar, usually erected against the back wall so that it faced the front door.

The size of the house depended on the size of the family, which might vary from three or four to over twenty individuals. If the family was just getting started the basic plan described above would suffice. However, more often than not, several generations lived together under one roof necessitating the addition of extra rooms and extending the floor plan to accommodate them.

Shelters for livestock were built close by, and in many cases were direct extensions of the house. This included stables for horses and cattle, sties for pigs, and coops for chickens. While the inevitable accumulation of animal waste was usually washed away with the first monsoon, in the interim between monsoons it caused serious health problems and gave Hmong villages a very distinctive odor. Infant mortality was understandably high, as were outbreaks of communicable diseases such as typhoid fever, amoebic dysentery and bubonic plague. Nor was it uncommon for entire villages to pack up and move when this occurred.

Despite the unsanitary conditions there was a strong interest in certain aspects of personal hygiene. A clean face and white teeth were much admired, so much so that when the French introduced the Indochinese to toothbrushes the Hmong were among the first to use them. And on ceremonial occasions when Hmong dressed in their finest, one could be assured that elaborate tribal costumes covered bathed skin. Paying hygiene any greater respect than this, however, required considerable effort which, from Hmong's perspective, did not justify the benefit, especially since they had almost no grasp of the connection between poor hygiene and disease — a fact which may have been partially due to the incredible physical vitality of the average Hmong. Excluding tropical diseases to which centuries of mountain living had made them particularly susceptible, unsanitary conditions that would inevitably lead to sickness and death for most people took less of a toll on the hardy Hmong. Moreover, as we shall see, the Hmong held very definite ideas about the causes of illness and death, and poor hygiene did not figure in. Of equal importance was the simple fact that Hmong villages were always temporary. There was little incentive to invest the time and energy in building better homes or constructing sewage systems when it was understood that whatever was built would invariably be abandoned, often within three years.

Things were different three hundred years ago when the Hmong of Kweichow and Szechwan lived in permanent villages. Then there was an incentive to construct fine houses, at least as far as one's income allowed. The Black Hmong of eastern Kweichow were among the wealthiest Hmong in the region, and their homes reflected it. They were not ramshackle affairs but sturdy wooden structures with sawed timber siding and heavy beam frames fitted to a base that sat on ten foot high pilings. In some villages the Hmong constructed kilns in which they fired decorative tiles for their roofs. One entered these houses up a broad staircase and through a veranda that ran along three sides of the dwelling. In the main room stood a large stone fireplace where the cooking was done. There were always benches placed in front of the fireplace to warm guests or for family gatherings at the end of the day.

In more recent times, Southeast Asian Hmong have occasionally built homes that rival those of the Black Hmong of Kweichow. But this was only in settled villages where housing was meant to be permanent. Lo Bliayao, the leader of the Lo clan in northeastern Laos until his death in 1935, lived in a large two-story stone house. At one time it accommodated over fifty people. Constructed near the turn of the century, it was still in good condition fifty years later. Unlike most of the other Hmong in the area, Lo Bliayao was not a migrant farmer. He was a wealthy rancher with nearly a thousand head of cattle.

Yang Nao Ying, a Hmong from the same region, grew up in an equally impressive home built by his grandfather, and rebuilt by his father in 1954-1955. Like Lo Bliayao, Yang Nao Ying's father was a prosperous rancher. He was also a successful farmer, whose bumper harvests (the result of using the manure from his 400 head of cattle as fertilizer for his corn fields) justified the construction of a huge storage barn. The two-story, twenty room Yang home was constructed from sawed timber. It was eighty feet long and twenty-five feet wide, large enough to house over seventy people.

After World War II, when an increasing number of Laotian Hmong either switched from swidden to paddy farming or found employment in the civil service, the establishment of a permanent residence became more common and created an incentive for a number of Hmong to improve their housing. Some even constructed their homes in the Lao fashion, on stilts. And a few of the wealthier Hmong built European style houses.

Farming

While livestock was housed near the home, fields were cultivated away from the village, the exact distance being limited by two considerations. First, they could not be too close else livestock would likely graze on them. Second, they could not be too far because precious time would be lost in traveling between village and field and the transportation of produce during the harvest would become costly and time consuming. Generally, fields were seldom closer than a half-mile and no farther away than a two-hour walk. When all arable land within this radius became exhausted the entire village abandoned the area and moved on to a new site.

Since the Hmong practiced swidden (slash and burn) farming, these moves were quite frequent. Swidden farming is both one of the oldest and least productive forms of agriculture. Except for the ashes left by burn-off, cleared fields are never fertilized, nor are they irrigated. Consequently, extended use of the same piece of land quickly exhausts the soil. When productivity drops below a certain level the land is simply abandoned. Because it may take twenty or thirty years for the soil to regenerate, when a swidden farmer abandons a field he effectively abandons it forever. By necessity, then, swidden farmers lead a migratory existence. If the available soil is rich and plentiful the distance traveled over a lifetime is short. If the soil is of a poor grade and in short supply, migration is correspondingly longer distance.

There are advantages to swidden farming, mostly born out of necessity. It does not require altering the existing landscape. Hills

Harvest Time

do not have to be terraced, canals and aqueducts do not have to be dug. It requires few tools. Axes, hoes, and planting sticks are enough to allow one to get by. What it does require, however, is hard work.

The preparation of fields for planting began in February and continued into April. Old fields were simply cleared of brush and weeded. New sites required more work. Once selected, the new site was cleared of trees and underbrush. This refuse was collected into piles and left to dry. By March the piles were ready to be burned. The ashes were then spread over the cleared fields for fertilizer.

The planting began in April. The main crop was corn. Unlike many crops, corn thrives in the mountain regions. While a portion of the corn harvest would wind up as cornbread, most of it would go to feed livestock, especially pigs. In addition to corn, the Hmong planted yams, cucumbers, pumpkins, radishes, beans, ginger, sugar cane, bananas, peaches, eggplant, melons, and tobacco.

Opium Cultivation

After the corn was harvested in August, opium poppies were planted in the same fields. The opium sap from the poppies was the only real cash crop and was normally harvested the following January. This was the most labor intensive activity of the Hmong farmer. It required the participation of the entire family, including children as young as seven. It took an adult a full month to cut and scrape just one-half acre of poppies.

A triple-blade knife was used to tap the poppy pod. The tapping occurred in the morning. By afternoon, the milky white sap from the tapping had solidified into a rubbery amber mass and the scraping could begin. The scrapings were either placed in containers or wrapped in leaves and later kneaded and then pounded into bricks of raw opium and stored until they could be sold to middleman. These middlemen were invariably Chinese, some of whom actually lived in or near a Hmong village while others were itinerant merchants who made the rounds of Hmong villages after the opium harvest.

The Hmong were always paid in silver, for they would accept nothing else. They had good reason to doubt the value of paper currency; their migratory lifestyle could land them in a different country where the currency might be greatly devalued or become completely worthless.

Prior to the arrival of the French, Hmong opium was purchased with silver bars. After the French took over, the Hmong accepted silver piasters as a substitute, though they quickly melted most of them into bars, setting aside the remainder for use as jewelry on necklaces or as decorations for ceremonial clothing.

The Hmong did not sell all of their opium. A small amount, perhaps five or ten percent of the total harvest, was processed into smoking opium for medicinal use. This involved boiling raw opium in a pot, the ratio of water to raw opium being about ten to one. The mixture was then filtered and reboiled several times until the opium became quite hard. Small pieces could then be cut off, heated over a flame until soft, and then placed in a pipe for smoking.

Income from the sale of opium was never very large. The markup for narcotics is always highest at the street level. If all went well, a hardworking family might equal the income of a lowland peasant who earned cash by selling produce in local markets. On the other hand, since the Hmong were isolated from the general population and therefore from stores and markets, they had few opportunities to spend their earnings. The rate of savings was therefore very high and over a lifetime the head of a household might accumulate a small fortune in silver. Since there were no banks, silver bars were buried in some hidden place in the forest, a particular tree or boulder marking the location. As visits to the hidden cache were infrequent it sometimes happened that its exact location was forgotten. Embarrassed Hmong who returned after a day of turning over a ton or two of earth before finally locating their savings sometimes covered their lapse of memory with the excuse that the cache had been moved by forest genies, a rationalization that provided fellow villagers considerable amusement.

There were other reasons besides the long distance from markets that accounted for the high rate of Hmong savings. At any moment a family could fall on hard times. This could happen if land gave out and the family had to migrate some distance to a new site. In such instances, a year or two might pass before new land produced enough to make a family self-sufficient. In the interim, food and clothing had to be purchased from merchants or other Hmong. Then there was always the possibility that the political climate might change and the Hmong would be driven from their land.

And, of course, there were normal outlays, such as the purchase of a horse or an ox or other livestock, though these never drained savings as much as a bride price which varied from a few to over ten bars of silver. For a man with many sons and no daughters (who would fetch a bride price and augment his savings) a large savings was part of his obligations as a father; without it the future welfare of his sons was placed in jeopardy.

Land Use

In the highlands of southeast Asia swidden fields seldom remain productive for more than a few years, and even after the first year productivity declined sharply making it necessary to continuously bring virgin land under cultivation. For the Hmong this meant that the distance between the village and planted fields continued to grow until it finally became necessary to move the village closer to the fields or simply abandon the area for a new mountain and begin the whole process over again.

Pressure on arable land was also increased by Hmong generosity. New groups of Hmong, especially if they belonged to the same clan, were welcomed into the community and granted access to unused land. The Hmong attitude toward land tenure was simple. Land became property only when it was used. Unoccupied land was therefore free for the taking. Nor was it uncommon for news of the discovery of choice land to attract entire villages to the site, turning what would have been productive land for a few into exhausted fields for the many.

Opium growing was another factor. The opium poppy takes much from the soil and gives little back. Where corn might grow lush and tall for years, the opium poppy will thrive for only a couple of seasons. And since the Hmong devoted much of their planting to opium, this accelerated the inevitable depletion of the soil.

Generally, when it came time to move, a new village was established no farther than a day's walk away. But, if a number of villages existed in the area and most of the nearby arable land had already been exhausted, there was no other choice than to seek out virgin land on the slopes of another mountain. When this was necessary a few families were sent on ahead with provisions to hold them until their first crop. If all went well these scouts would report back and the remainder of the village would join them.

Numerous small moves added up. In Thailand, for example, the pace of Hmong migration averaged about six miles per year. At that rate, between birth and death an individual might live in twenty different villages and cover several hundred miles, all by foot carrying everything he or she owned on their back. It was difficult under such circumstances for the Hmong to call any particular place their home or to develop loyalties to a particular country, especially as some may have been born in China, migrated into Vietnam and spent their later years in Laos or Thailand. If they developed loyalties they were the same loyalties the Hmong had maintained for centuries, to their family, clan and race.

The Hmong did not complain, however. They had been migrants for centuries and had come to accept this not only as their lot but as a part of their heritage. Their mobility contributed to their sense of freedom. If their non-Hmong neighbors mistreated them, or if a government abused them, they could always vote with their feet. Not being tied to the land they could refuse assimilation into the dominant culture of their host country. It was their trump card, and for centuries it had served them well.

This is not to say that the Hmong preferred the migratory lifestyle they had evolved during centuries of oppression. Given the opportunity, the Hmong of Southeast Asia might very well have developed a way of live similar to that enjoyed by their Kweichow brethren during times of peace.

Denied access to the rich soil of the lowlands, these Kweichow Hmong made the best of a bad situation and wherever possible abandoned slash and burn agriculture and transformed the steep slopes of their mountains into terraced fields supported by stone walls and constructed bamboo aqueducts to divert mountain streams to their fields for irrigation. In eastern Kweichow the Hmong engaged in fish farming, raising fish in their rice fields and breeding them in special ponds on the outskirts of their villages. The carp, tench and perch raised in these ponds were used locally and sold to neighboring villages.

There was a thriving timber industry, also in eastern Kweichow, which owed part of its success to the Hmong commitment to conservation. After an area had been clear-cut, new trees were planted to replenish the forest. Consequently, pine, cedar and oak as well as Chu trees used by the Chinese to make paper, were always abundant and in great demand by the Chinese. During the Ming dynasty, it was Hmong timber that was used in the construction of imperial buildings. The best coffins were also made from the Japanese pine marketed by the Kweichow Hmong.

Hmong lumberjacks were famous for their ability to fell trees on the steep slopes and maneuver them down the mountain sides into the rivers below where they were ferried downstream to the Chinese dealers who linked the logs into huge rafts before floating them to the saw mills situated along the rivers across the border in Hunan.

Hmong boatmen sailed up and down these same rivers which were often the only efficient means of transporting goods. Known as the Dragon Boat Hmong, they carried loads of wood oil, hides and timber as far east as the Hunan lake region. Once every year, in May, they staged boat races in slim dugouts, each with a finely carved dragon's head rising above the bow.

Not only were the Dragon Boat Hmong famous for their races, they were also renowned for their ability to navigate their boats through dangerous rapids which increased in number and severity the further one traveled upstream. Descendants of these same Hmong live relatively prosperous lives in eastern Kweichow today.

Then as now, Kweichow was rich in silver, and the Hmong in the province were accomplished silver smiths, a skill they have preserved since, even after migrating to Indochina. It is seldom that a Hmong village of any size in Vietnam, Laos, Thailand or Burma does not possess at least one accomplished silver smith who can be counted on to fashion the silver jewelry worn by Hmong during festivals, and especially by a bride on the day of her wedding.

Unlike these Kweichow Hmong, however, the Hmong of Southeast Asia have seldom enjoyed a stable relationship with the land. Still they did not complain and swidden farming did have its benefits. After the clearing and planting was completed they enjoyed nearly a month of uninterrupted leisure away from the fields. While some of this time had to be devoted to much needed repairs on the family home, and on horse and cattle stables, and pig sties, most of it was set aside for hunting.

Hunting

The Hmong have always been passionate hunters. Superb marksmen with either crossbow or flintlock, the Hmong of Southeast Asia considered nearly everything from mice to elephants fair game, though the most prized quarry were deer, elephant, wild pig and rhinoceros. Because of their passion for hunting and their skill as hunters, all game close to the village quickly disappeared and with it the sounds one normally associates with the forest. Nights in an established village were therefore uncommonly quiet.

In the mid-1930s the German anthropologist Hugo Bernatzik lived several years with the Hmong of Thailand. An avid hunter, he was very much impressed by Hmong daring and skill during the hunt, especially as their only weapons were crossbows and flintlocks, primitive weapons when compared with Bernatzik's high powered European hunting rifle.

Though the Hmong used poison on their arrows, it was not the deadly toxin of old China. Extracted from the sap of certain trees and then boiled into a rubbery mass, the poison was slow acting and took some time to disable or kill a large animal. Like the crossbow the flintlock was a short range weapon, and though a well placed shot might kill a large animal, more often than not it simply wounded. This meant that when hunting big game the Hmong could count on being attacked by their prey. For this reason they seldom ventured forth alone on these hunts. If one Hmong was charged another leaped in to distract the attacker. Often it was necessary for everyone involved to run for cover, a fact that was driven home to Bernatzik after he examined the four inch deep holes punched into a tree trunk by a wounded gaur (a larger and more ferocious cousin of the American bison) trying to get at several Hmong huddled behind the tree for protection.

Yet despite their primitive weapons and the dangers they faced, the Hmong were highly successful hunters, even with the elephants and rhinoceros that roamed the mountain forests. Bernatzik met one Hmong who had in his lifetime killed two rhinoceros and over twenty elephants. In the case of the elephants the shots were fired from only a few yards away, a feat that was due not only to the hunter's stealth but to his cleverness in nullifying the elephant's keen sense of smell by smearing elephant dung over his body.

Between planting and harvest the main occupation was caring for livestock, weeding the crops, and collecting animals caught in traps set around the fenceless fields. These catches not only augmented the Hmong diet, they greatly reduced crop damage caused by wild birds, pigs, rodents, and deer.

Livestock

The Hmong raised pigs and chickens, oxen and horses, though few families could afford to own an ox and even fewer a horse. Oxen served a dual purpose. They were used as draft animals and were sacrificed at funerals. Horses, on the other hand, were used only for hauling and the transport of goods. Though highly valued they were not the same quality of animal as the famed Hmong horses of old.

Centuries earlier Hmong horses were considered by the Chinese to be the best in the empire. They could scale mountains like goats and descend them at a dead run. They were great jumpers as well, and were often jumped over wide ditches for sport and, if we are to believe Chinese accounts, for the selection of officers in the Hmong cavalry. This test consisted of galloping one's mount up the side of a mountain and then dashing down to the bottom where a large ditch filled with blazing logs waited them. It was here the truly superior mounts were separated from the rest, for only they did not break stride before leaping through the flames to the other side. These horses were seldom sold, but when a sale was made it was at an astronomical price, and the buyer was usually a Chinese official who needed an extraordinary gift to ingratiate himself with his superiors.

Though pigs and chickens were the principal source of protein in the Hmong diet, they were not raised primarily with an eye to nutritional needs. Their main purpose was sacrificial. Pigs or chickens, or both, were sacrificed to appease ancestors, to aid shamans in curing illnesses, for the celebration of births and weddings, for funerals and for the New Year festival.

As a matter of simple economics, this was not an efficient use of livestock. At any one time nearly the entire breeding stock of pigs or chickens might be wiped out by special ceremonial or sacrificial needs. While all might eat well on such occasions, there would be little if any meat added to the diet for several months afterward. To an outsider, a westerner, this may seem foolish. But this is to ignore the pivotal role of shamanist beliefs in the Hmong culture.

PART II: THE SPIRIT WORLD

In Hmong cosmography, the creator and ruler of the world is Hua Tai. Unlike the Christian God, Hua Tai has little interest in the affairs of mankind. Indeed they bore him. He lost interest in mankind, in all their bickering and feckless ways, almost as soon as he created them. One of his lieutenants, though, had compassion for man. He is Yer Shau. As the Hmong portray him, Yer Shau is not only God's personal representative to mankind, he is also half man, half God. He is godlike in the sense that he sees and knows all, but he is like a man in that he has material substance and lives in a house. And as a man he is more like the Hmong than any other race of men. He tends a garden and raises pigs. He is an earthy fellow who likes to eat and drink and have long discussions with friends. Also like the Hmong, he is polygamous and has many wives.

It was actually Yer Shau, and not Hua Tai, who saved mankind from the great flood. It was also Yer Shau who saved mankind from Ndu Nyong, the god of sickness and death. Appropriately called "The Savage One", Ndu Nyong is the king of the demons who harass the Hmong and bring them misfortune, sickness and death. He lives in a fortress at the top of a mountain chain where he spends his time devouring living things. His greatest pleasure is to consume thousands of Hmong at a setting, tearing at their flesh and drinking their blood like some wild beast.

Actually, what he devours is one of their souls. The Hmong believe an individual has more than one soul. Some claim the number to be three, others seven or more; disagreement over the exact number does not cause much consternation, for the Hmong are not bothered much by fine points of theology. One of these souls, envisaged in the form of a pig or ox, resides in Ndu Nyong's huge corral where he keeps his livestock, which includes just about anything he can lay his hands on. If Ndu Nyong happens to consume one of these souls, the physical individual also dies. Conversely, when the physical individual dies it is presumed that Ndu Nyong has consumed this corralled soul, which is why an ox is sacrificed at a Hmong funeral ceremony: the soul of the ox will take the place of the consumed soul, and the other souls of the deceased can live on through reincarnation — the implication being that should no new soul take its place all the souls that constitute the perdurable essence of an individual would cease to exist. The imagery is instructive. Ndu Nyong holds every Hmong hostage. He can bring death at any moment.

Ndu Nyong is assisted in his war against mankind by a host of evil spirits, the Dab, who cause pain, sickness and death. Once, long ago, these spirits were not much of a threat to mankind. For at this early date they were not invisible as they are today. And they were also extremely vulnerable. Having no skin, their vital organs were easily pierced by a spear or could even be plucked out by hand. This fatal weakness was exploited by men who killed the spirits for sport until they were reduced to near extinction. It was then that heaven interceded and granted the Dab spirits protection by making them invisible. This was accomplished with a magic dust which camouflaged the spirits so they could not be seen by men. Now that they were invisible and beyond the reach of spears and hands, it was the spirits' turn to harass their former tormentors by causing them misfortune, illness and death.

Fortunately, humans are not completely without protection for Yer Shau has provided them with shamans who have the power to combat Ndu Nyong and his demons in his own domain.

The First Shaman

First practiced by Siberian tribesmen, shamanism spread south to China, southwest to central Asia, and east across the Bering straights to north America. The Hmong probably became shamanist during their sojourn in Siberia and continued to practice the religion when they migrated to China where shamanism was adopted by many other tribal groups and incorporated in the state religion by the early dynasties.

Such facts do not figure in the Hmong account of shamanism. According to Hmong legend, in the distant past mankind prospered and multiplied. This pleased Yer Shau, but when Ndu Nyong surveyed the scene it whetted his appetite and, without Yer Shau's approval or knowledge, he descended to earth and began devouring mankind. When Yer Shau realized what was happening he sent two servants to earth to kill Ndu Nyong. Unfortunately, Ndu Nyong was always able to elude his pursuers because he could fly and they could not. The two returned to Yer Shau to tell him of their failure. He ordered them back to earth while he pondered the matter. In the meantime the two servants had a child. His name was Shee Yee, the first shaman, also known as Ndzo Ying, "the inspired one'. Unhappily for Shee Yee when his parents were called back to heaven they did not take him along. Abandoned and alone, he turned to the Hmong for help. Ironically, the future guardian of Hmong health and welfare was rejected by them when he begged to be taken in. The excuse for this atypical hardheartedness was that the child was as fat as a Chinese mandarin. Rejected by the Hmong, Shee Yee had no other choice than to appeal to the Chinese for aid, which he received from a Chinese Lord who put him to work in his stables.

When Shee Yee reached manhood he spent his leisure walking the countryside around the Chinese Lord's palace. On one such walk he discovered a nest of large, leathery, white eggs. They were not like any eggs he had ever seen before. To his surprise, when he broke

them open he found they were empty. Stranger still, when he returned to the same spot the next day the eggs had miraculously become
whole. Again he broke them open, and again they were empty. But
this time, instead of leaving, Shee Yee remained out of sight and
waited to see what sort of magic was being used to make the eggs
whole. Shortly after dusk his patience was rewarded. An enormous
shadow passed over him in the pale moonlight. When he looked
up he saw a dragon swoop overhead and land near the eggs. After
inspecting the damage, the dragon searched the ground, tearing up
bushes and kicking up stones until it found what it was after. Shee
Yee watched as the dragon uprooted a plant, separated the tubers
from the stalk, crushed them in its talons and placed the pulpy mass
in a bowl of water. The dragon slithered over to the eggs, raised
the bowl to its mouth and blew over it, spraying the water on the
eggs. Immediately the eggs were made whole.

It was then that Shee Yee realized the significance of the event.
Yer Shau had sent the dragon to earth so that he would find and
break its eggs and discover the secret to curing the ill and bringing
the dead back to life.

When the dragon flew away Shee Yee emerged from his hiding
place and hurried to gather as much of the magic herbs as he could
carry before setting out to heal mankind of its illnesses and bring
the dead back to life.

Shee Yee had good reason to make haste for Ndu Nyong was
now devouring so many humans that mankind was on the point
of extinction. Indeed, when "The Savage One" divined what Shee
Yee was up to he flew into a rage and, unable at the moment to
lay his hands on the shaman, attacked and killed the Chinese Lord's
horses, which numbered in the thousands. Perhaps this was also
meant to sidetrack Shee Yee because when the shaman's former
employer begged him to restore the animals to life he did not have
the heart to refuse.

To make up for this delay, and to improve Shee Yee's chances
in his battle with Ndu Nyong, Yer Shau gave him the power of flight
or, more accurately, the next best thing: a winged horse, a Hmong
Pegasus, to serve as his mount and to speed him on his way to raising
the souls of the dead.

Before he left on this mission the Chinese Lord insisted that he
be rewarded for reviving his slain horses. Shee Yee was given two
companies of Chinese soldiers to serve as his helpers in the great
battle that was ahead. The carnage was horrible to behold, for in
an attempt to outstrip Shee Yee's healing efforts Ndu Nyong
slaughtered more humans than ever before. Even so, Shee Yee was
able to match him, soul for soul, and soon it was apparent to Ndu
Nyong that he could never win. It was then that he conceded defeat
and pledged that from that moment on he would remain with Shee
Yee as his servant.

This was not Ndu Nyong's real intention, however. He was biding his time until he could figure out a way to destroy Shee Yee, a task that became all the more pressing with the birth of Shee Yee's first son. If the child reached adulthood there would be no stopping the two. While Shee Yee was away healing the ill, Ndu Nyong murdered the infant, butchered him and used the pieces to prepare a meal which he served to Shee Yee on his return. The first shaman unwittingly consumed his own child. Grief stricken after realizing what he had done, Shee Yee intended to kill Ndu Nyong but was stopped by Yer Shau who ordered him to simply maim "the Savage One" so that he would at last experience some of the pain he had caused so many humans. Shee Yee used his shaman tools to pierce Ndu Nyong's eyes and cast him out of his house to wander among mankind as a beggar.

Though blind, Ndu Nyong was nevertheless able to find his way back to his fortress in the sky. Less powerful than before, but still full of hatred for mankind, he gathered his evil spirits about him and renewed his campaign to cause pain, sickness and death to mankind. There was therefore still much work for Shee Yee to do. Yet, because he had eaten his own son, the strength of his resolve to heal mankind was considerably weakened. And so he departed earth to live in heaven for eternity. But he promised that he would return in a year with his shaman's tools as a gift to mankind so that they could heal themselves. Unfortunately, on the appointed day and hour no one was there to greet him. Furious at this ingratitude, Shee Yee threw the tools to the ground and declared that the sacred healing instruments would never again have the full power to heal, and would work only one out of ten times.

Still, the tools were of some use. One out of ten is better than nothing. Of course, other shamans who followed in Shee Yee's footsteps would have to enter the spirit world to make good use of them. To accomplish this they would have to call on the Neng spirits, another gift from Shee Yee, as guides. These are the same spirits Shee Yee himself had used in his own fight with Ndu Nyong. And it is to the shaman and his Neng helpers that the Hmong turn when seeking protection from Ndu Nyong and his legions of evil spirits.

Though the Hmong believed wandering souls to be the cause of many illnesses, they also acknowledged the existence of organic disease which is best treated with physical rather than spiritual remedies. They were, and remain, pragmatists, and in many cases if someone could demonstrate the physical means to effect a cure for some disease, the Hmong eagerly employed it. On the other hand, it was no easy thing for the Hmong to distinguish between a malady with a spiritual origin and an illness with a clear organic cause. To a westerner, if an arm is broken, a splint rather than a shaman is called for. To a Hmong this would be a careless diagnosis. For even a broken arm might be traced to a spiritual cause. How was the arm broken? Was it really an accident or was a spirit angered and seeking revenge by causing the fall that led to the broken arm? If a spirit was angered, the broken arm may not be the end of things. Other evils may befall the victim and therefore a simple splint will not be enough to really heal the patient. That the Hmong were prone to ask such questions indicates the extent to which they were willing, even when the problem appeared on the surface to be completely organic in nature, to contemplate problems in the spirit world as sources of human difficulties in the physical.

While the head of a Hmong household was familiar with rites and ceremonies useful in dealing with or placating the spirits, only the shaman had the ability to leave his body and enter the spirit world and deal directly with the spirits, demons and genies. This was not an acquired skill but a gift from heaven. To receive the gift was also to accept a calling to heal the sick and prevent evil.

The Shaman's Calling

The manner in which a Hmong received this calling was every bit as dramatic as that experienced by a protestant Christian. There was the recognition that one had been specially selected to serve and there was also a sense of rebirth. The selection was made by the Neng spirits. Sometimes they appeared in a dream and conveyed their selection to the dreamer, but most often they signalled this selection by making an individual seriously ill. Often when an illness did not respond to treatment the affliction was thought to be the result of a visitation by Neng. If a shaman deemed this to be the case he would perform a brief ceremony to invite the Neng to stay with the individual, confirming the calling. If the diagnosis of the illness was correct, the individual usually fell into a deep trance and then completely recovered.

During this trance the individual might experience his soul leaving his body and entering the spirit world. As one shaman described the event, he was dead for seven days during which time his spirit travelled on a long journey to the palace of Shee Yee. During the journey he had to cross a field of fire and jump over a giant caterpillar and finally pass through a door with slashing blades that cut the unworthy but allowed the just to pass unscathed. Shee Yee himself wrote on his chest and back and placed the Book of Knowledge, the book containing the secrets of the shaman's healing art, on his chest. Then one of Shee Yee's helpers gave him the shaman's bell, rattle and drum to use when he would again enter the spirit world.

To receive the shaman's calling not only required dedicating one's life to healing the sick, it meant that one now possessed the unique ability to enter the spirit world and retrieve wandering souls, souls that had not just left a body and remained nearby, perhaps just outside the home or beside a trail, but souls that had actually left the world of man and entered the world of spirits, sometimes travelling as far as Ndu Nyong's fortress. Only the shaman could pursue such a soul and bring it back.

It is also this ability that imparted special significance to the shaman as a representative of the Hmong to heaven. According to Hmong legend, man and God once communicated freely, and now not at all. Only the shaman retains the power, if not to speak directly to God, to at least communicate with Shee Yee and, through him, to Yer Shau who cares about mankind. It is this aspect of Hmong shamanism that has helped to sustain the Messiah myth, the belief that Yer Shau will one day send the Hmong a king who will rule over an independent Hmong nation. If the shaman could not communicate with the spirit world, the Hmong would have no way to appeal to heaven to send them their king, or to know of his impending arrival.

Despite the shaman's unique abilities, there were many things of a spiritual nature the Hmong felt competent to handle without the shaman's aid. Divination was one of them. The object of divination was to predict the future and the tools employed were simple: halved buffalo horns or the parts of sacrificed animals.

Suppose the eldest son of the house planned to travel to a nearby village. The head of the household might throw two halves of a buffalo horn on the floor. Was the flat side of each face up or down, or was one up and one down? If the configuration was wrong, the trip would be delayed and the horns tried again until they came up right. Many adults in a Hmong village would know such divination techniques, as well as many others involving the examination of the tongues, feet or bones of sacrificed animals (usually chickens), and so long as they proved effective to the purpose at hand there would be no need to consult a shaman.

Even if the source of the trouble was a wandering soul, a shaman still might not be needed. Souls could wander for various reasons. They could be enticed out of the body by evil spirits. They could leave the body because they had been frightened or because they were unhappy. Whatever the cause, a wandering soul was considered a serious matter because if it did not return the body would die.

However, if a soul had not wandered far, or if it left the body at a particular place due to a fright, a shaman would not necessarily be required to retrieve it. Often when a child fell suddenly ill, the head of the household would search for an insect on the ground where the youngster had been recently frightened. If one was found, the insect, presumed to be harboring the frightened soul, was carried home where a simple ceremony was held to return the soul to the child's body. Or a chicken might be placed outside the house to scratch the ground in search of the lost soul which, when found, was tucked up under one of its wings. The chicken was then sacrificed and the soul and the child reunited. Sometimes, a bridge was built to help a wandering soul find its way home. The bridge was usually placed where it was thought the soul might have had difficulty finding its way, such as over a stream or at a fork in the road.

On the other hand, a shaman was always consulted when it was believed that a soul had left the physical world and entered the realm of the spirits, which was invariably the presumption when an illness did not respond to conventional home remedies.

Journey Into the Spirit World

A shaman did not accept just any case. The Neng spirits had to be consulted first, not only regarding the cause of the illness and its seriousness, but to find out if the Neng spirits would be able, or willing, to help effect a cure. Often the latter question was decided by an improvement in the patient's condition, a clear sign that the Neng were favorable.

The ceremony to retrieve a soul was not only physically demanding, it was often quite long, sometimes lasting several hours. First the shaman called the helper spirits to assemble for the hunt. When he was confident they had all arrived, the shaman straddled a bench and placed a black veil over his face. Shortly after this his body would begin to tremble and then he would fall into a trance, a sign that he had entered the spirit world. Since the shaman would soon engage in considerable gymnastics, assistants stood close by ready to support him should he loose his balance and begin to fall.

After a few moments the shaman would begin to bounce on the bench as though riding a horse. And so he was. For he had called on the great winged horse of Shee Yee to carry him on his search. The journey was a dangerous one. There was a wide sea that must be crossed, the home of innumerable dragons with the ability to mesmerize passersby with their eyes, transfixing their victims before they leaped up and dragged them down into the depths. If a wandering soul had been captured by a dragon, the shaman was forced to descend into the depths and rescue it, an act that might be signalled by one of the shaman's assistants placing a rock on his lap to help weigh him down and make the descent easier.

Once the sea was crossed the shaman began the search for the lost soul in the forests and fields of the underworld. Like the Hmong's own mountains, the terrain was crisscrossed with thousands of foot-

Shaman's Spirit Tools

Shaman's Alter

paths used by wandering souls seeking the lair of Ndu Nyong. The trails were so numerous that it was easy for a wandering soul to take a wrong turn and lose its way. Some souls became frightened when lost and were eager to return to the world of man but could not find their way back. Other lost souls, steadfast in their resolve to remain in the spirit world but unable to find the way to Ndu Nyong, hid in a hole or under a rock to elude the shaman. While it was believed that few wandering souls ever reached Ndu Nyong, the shaman had to expect the worse. Thus, it was necessary to cover as much ground as possible in the shortest time, overlooking nothing in case a soul had gone to the ground to hide yet never tarrying in one place for long so that he would never catch up with a soul that had happened on the right path to Ndu Nyong's lair. And this is why he had helpers, whom he summoned at the beginning of the ceremony.

Numbered among these were, of course, his Neng. There were also the two companies of soldiers which the Chinese Lord placed under Shee Yee's command and which Shee Yee made available to all shamans. There were also thousands of other helpers, beneficent spirits who joined in whenever the cause was just. Some of the shaman's helpers beat the bushes to flush the lost soul, others scared away evil genies intent on interfering with the hunt. Helper spirits examined every hole, turned over every rock in search of the wandering soul. The pursuit continued, if necessary, to the very door of Ndu Nyong's fortress.

During the search the shaman, still supported by his assistants, might leap to the top of the bench and jump about. Witnesses to the ceremony could only guess at the meaning of these gyrations, and the dangers the shaman faced on his journey into the spirit world. Perhaps he was fighting off dragons or evil spirits, perhaps he was urging his winged horse to attempt giant leaps over mountains. For those with vivid imaginations, the gyrations of the veiled shaman suggested a frightening drama of good against evil, of armies locked in mortal combat, the fate of a soul hanging in the balance.

When the lost soul was found the shaman was always careful not to frighten it. The object, after all, was to bring it back home and keep it there. He therefore gently coaxed it out of its hiding place, assuring it that all would be well, that loved ones longed for its return. Just as gently he led it back home. It was then that the shaman, as well as the lost soul, crossed over into the world of man. And it was only then that the shaman emerged from his trance, often exhausted from his efforts.

On rare occasions a lost soul would find Ndu Nyong and be granted reincarnation. At such times the patient faced certain death unless the shaman acted quickly. While still in a trance, the shaman would urge his mount onward to search every village for the pregnant woman whose fetus had been granted to the lost soul by Ndu Nyong. When the woman was located the shaman would lead the soul away and bring it home, allowing another soul to be reincarnated in its place.

Most often a pig was sacrificed before the healing ceremony began. The bulk of the sacrificed animal was consumed by those in attendance, including the patient (if well enough to eat), the immediate family and close relatives. The shaman received no more than the head as payment. Being a shaman was a vocation not a profession. Even the most successful shaman, his success evidenced by the many jawbones hanging in his house, had to farm like any other Hmong to support his own family.

If the sacrifice of an entire pig was a considerable expense for most Hmong families, a family plagued with illness or a death (which required the sacrifice of an ox) might in a short time find its livestock reduced to a few animals. Even a family enjoying good health was expected to perform ritual sacrifices to ancestors or to appease various important spirits, like the central post spirit, and the door spirit. Such sacrifices were thought essential to safeguard the continued health of the family or to improve it if it was bad.

Considered simply as a health care system and not a religion, Hmong shamanism could be characterized as economically inefficient, as would any health care system that commanded the lion's share of a society's resources. Economically, it meant that those least able to afford this sort of medical care paid the most in proportion to their total wealth. In many cases the consequence was to make wealthier families less wealthy for a time but poor families poverty stricken perhaps forever. For a wealthy family with many pigs and oxen heavy sacrifices depleted their stock but did not reduce it below the level required to build it up again. In contrast, a poor family left with one pig would never have more than that without purchasing or trading for additional pigs.

It is not entirely fair to blame all this on the Hmong religion. As already indicated, the Hmong are very pragmatic and trust results more than ideas. If less expensive medical care had been available it is likely they would have used it. In recent years, Hmong have been quick to use modern medicine when accessible, though they return to the shaman if modern techniques fail to deliver. Nor should one forget that so many sacrifices were made because so much could go wrong. In a world of danger and uncertainty it was foolhardy to trust things to fate. In a safer world the need to sacrifice would be less. For example, I once asked an elderly Hmong emigre to the U.S. why the traditional altar was absent from his apartment. His answer was simple. In America there were no tigers, snakes or enemy soldiers.

Rites of Passage

Birth, marriage, and death are major events in the life of the Hmong, as they are in all societies. For the Hmong they are also rites of passage. A birth signifies the reincarnation of a soul in a new body. In marriage a Hmong assumes the full responsibilities of adulthood. And in death the individual's soul leaves this world to join the world of his or her ancestors to wait until it is time to be reborn.

Birth

In traditional Hmong society it was commonly believed that when a man died he would be reborn as a woman, and if a woman died she would be reborn as a man. It was a belief in cosmic justice, for the lot of the Hmong woman was always a hard one. The independent spirit of most Hmong women was also a factor, for it was not very difficult to imagine they had once been men. Whatever its sex, the birth of a child was a great event. In one sense it was a reunion, a reincarnated soul reentering the world of man. It also meant a family had a new member, and for the Hmong the family was nearly everything. Children in particular were cherished and enjoyed.

Like all peasant farmers, the Hmong recognized the economic benefit of children. An additional child would eventually become an additional worker in the field. This was of special economic importance during the labor intensive opium harvest. A child of seven could contribute much, and one of nine or ten could match the output of a woman carrying an infant. A large number of children also meant there would be someone to take care of you when you were too old to work.

But above all, children were a living testimony to the importance the Hmong have always placed on the family, clan and race. It is these ties, which extend through the generations, both living and dead, that gave life meaning for the Hmong and kept them going in the hardest of times. And the birth ceremonies reflected this.

Three days had to pass after the birth of an infant before it could officially become part of the human community. It was then that a soul was invited to be reincarnated in the infant's body. If an infant died before the third day, no funeral rites were held on the assumption that since the infant had no soul it was not a human being.

If available, a shaman presided over the ceremony during which sacrifices were made to invite a soul to become reincarnated in the infant's body. This was sometimes followed by the throwing of divination horns, or an examination of the tongue of a sacrificed chicken, to determine whether evil spirits were present. If this turned out to be the case, then additional sacrifices might be made to placate them. The family's ancestors would also be asked to unite with the family and bless the event and offer the infant their protection. The infant was then given a silver necklace as a precaution against the newly reincarnated soul wandering from the infant's body. For it was believed that souls like pretty things, and are less likely to leave a body when it is wearing jewelry. This belief also prompted adults, for reasons other than vanity or ceremonial occasion, to wear jewelry.

Hmong children lived constantly in the presence of adults and, contrary to the observation of some ethnologists at the turn of the century, they did not lack supervision or moral education. Quite the opposite, their socialization to Hmong culture began almost immediately. If anything they absorbed the morality of their group much earlier than a child in Europe or America who, in comparison with the Hmong child, remains relatively isolated from the real world of adults until late puberty.

As soon as they were able, Hmong children joined in the work of the house and field. Older children were given the responsibility of watching out after the younger ones. At an early age girls became skilled in cooking and sewing, and boys learned how to hunt and trap. And when there was free time they played. Much of the time this consisted in imitations of adult activity, but they also made toys, modeled in clay, enjoyed games of hide-and-seek or simply frolicked with the family dog.

Marriage

Hmong boys participated in courting as young as fourteen. For girls it began when they reached sixteen. Both boys and girls entered courtship with an adequate knowledge of the fundamentals of sex, for while Hmong parents might tell young children fairy tales when asked about sex they gave straightforward answers to the older children.

The ultimate object of courting was marriage, and the strong incest taboo that operated in Hmong society dictated that courting occur only between members of different clans. If the families in a village all belonged to the same clan a Hmong lad had to travel to another village where there were families from different clans to do his courting. For this reason most Hmong preferred to live in large villages where several clans were represented. Courting had to be discreet. It was bad manners to court a girl in her own home. Her parents would consider it a grave insult. However, a suitor could speak to his beloved on the road or in the field, and, if she agreed, arrange a meeting in the night. Often young men would gather outside a young woman's house and discretely coax her to come out and join one of them for a night of love.

91

Love songs abounded during courting. Some were erotic, as one would expect, but many spoke of unrequited love. And some, like the following love song (sung by a girl) even addressed social issues, such as the inequality between the sexes:

> My beloved, you have nursed at your mother's breast and also shared your father's bed; your face is as radiant as a blossom, as bright as the paper flowers sold by the Chinese.
>
> As for me, I have also sucked at my mother's breast, though I have not shared my father's bed; and my face is tired and creased as the soul of the feet of a Chinese grandfather.
>
> You have been able to lick your mother's spoon and to leave at will to go on long trips; you are the child who cares for the spirit of the center post.
>
> As for me, if I have eaten with my mother and sometimes leave on long trips, I am not able, as you, to protect the house. For that I am unhappy.

Most courting occurred in late December during the New Year festival. It was a time of general merriment and leisure. Even more important for courting it was a time when young people from different clans were brought together in large numbers. Eligible girls and bachelors dressed up in their best clothes. For the girls this might have included fine Hmong jewelry and delicately embroidered blouses and dresses.

Hmong women have long been famous for their fine embroidery which consists of detailed, symmetrical patterns produce by intricate cross-stitching and applique techniques. The traditional patterns of this ancient craft, which the Hmong call Pandau (pronounced "pond dew'), are created by combining five basic shapes: an eight point star, a snail shell, the outline of a ram's head, an elephant's footprint, and a heart. Because of the high quality of Hmong needlework it fetched a handsome price in Chinese markets and was often given as tribute to the Peking Court. Indeed, Hmong embroidery was thought so beautiful that representations of it found their way into Chinese art albums.

To facilitate courtship ball games were held. The boys lined up on one side, the girls on the other. Pairing was by consent. And either the boy or the girl could initiate the invitation. While this posed no difficulties for the boys, a shy girl would sometimes employ a married woman as her intermediary to do the asking. The balls were made of cloth, often of bright colored silk, and were about the size of a softball. The two partners tossed it back and forth. If one of them flubbed a catch, a piece of clothing had to be discarded and handed over to the partner. The boys made few drops, the girls many, though modesty prevented the game from ever going too far. The boy returned the girl's discarded clothes that evening when they met away from her house and out of sight of the villagers. Lovemaking may or may not have occurred during the first evening, but by the third meeting the girl was under considerable pressure

Courting Clothes

to engage in sex, and could lose the attentions of her suitor if she did not. On the other hand, the girl was also free to change partners at will.

The high romance of all this courting was meant to serve one overall purpose, making matches for marriages. Hmong bachelors who sewed their oats without regard to this social end were not only subject to moral reproach they were often forced to pay heavy fines to the girl's family.

When a young man settled on a particular girl he asked his father to begin marriage negotiations. If the choice was not rejected outright by the father, and his voice carried some weight since he paid the bride price, two representatives from his clan were selected to accompany the would-be groom and his best man to open negotiations with the girl's father. When they arrived at the girl's house, one of the negotiators offered the girl's father a gift, usually tobacco, and announced the business at hand. The girl's father then consulted with his relatives and the girl herself. She could reject the match, but unless she was absolutely adamant and threatened suicide she could be overridden. If the girl's family agreed to the marriage, drinks of alcohol were prepared and the bride price discussed. If, on the other hand, the girl's family were against the match, matters ended there.

Negotiations over the bride price sometimes involved more than the price of the bride. Old grievances against the groom's clan could be brought up and reparations demanded before the marriage contract could be finalized. The inclusion of such considerations in the negotiations enabled the institution of the bride price to serve the larger social end of inter-clan solidarity. Of course, this could sometimes have the reverse effect. Reparations could be refused and the negotiations broken off. In such cases, instead of drawing clans closer together demands for reparations might drive them further apart. But if one is to judge by how negotiations proceed today, such untoward results were uncommon. With or without reparations, the bride price was invariably quite high, amounting to as much as several years family savings which, given the high savings rate of the Hmong, was a large financial sacrifice.

It would be a mistake to construe the payment of a bride price as essentially a financial transaction. The bride was not literally bought by the groom's family. Rather, the bride price served to stress the importance of the marriage rather than portray the bride as a commodity to be bought and sold. The high price also helped to insure that marriages would last since a divorce, which was rare, would require a refund.

Brides were sometimes abducted, especially when the couple were deeply in love and the girl's parents dead set against the marriage.

Even here, propriety had to be observed. The parents of an abducted bride had to be notified and a bride price paid.

Bachelors from poor families who could not come up with a bride price could sometimes still marry by paying the bride price on an installment plan, or by agreeing to work for a period of time for the bride's family in lieu of a cash payment.

The actual marriage ceremony began at the groom's house where sacrifices were made to the house spirits and to the ancestors. After the bride price was delivered to the groom's go-betweens, the groom and his party proceeded to the bride's house where more sacrifices were made, the bride price paid and the marriage feast begun. The next day, or several days later if the feast was lavish and there were many guests, the bride accompanied the groom to his house. After sacrificing a pig another wedding party was begun that continued late into the night. One final ceremony remained to be completed. The bride could not become an official member of her husband's family until she was introduced to the house spirits of her new home. Only then was she formally accepted into her husband's clan. This did not mean she was expected to sever all ties with her own clan, nor even change her name. She would still be known by her maiden name, including the surname of her own clan.

Though polygamy has long been condoned in Hmong communities, it has never been widespread save during wartime when it was expected that a widow would be taken in by one of her husband's brothers. The limitation on the practice of polygamy was mostly the high expense entailed by the bride price. And for the Hmong who could afford more than one wife, the decision to become polygamous was colored by the realization that the polygamist was burdened with the obligation to share his affection equally with all his wives. For favoritism, when it occurred, was serious cause for complaint by an ignored wife or wives and could rightfully be aired before relatives or even the general community and, on occasion, even be judged grounds for divorce.

Death

The death of a family member was announced by the firing of three shots in slow succession, each waiting for the echo of the last to fall away before taking its turn. The shots not only served to signal the death and to summon all within listening distance to come and pay their respects, they were also used to frighten away evil spirits who might hinder the journey of the soul of the deceased to the home of its ancestors in the nether world.

The deceased was then washed, and new clothes put on over the old. Stockings and slippers came next. Then the body was placed on a stretcher inside the home and a red veil placed over the mouth of the corpse. For several days while the body remained in state, mourners arrived to pay their respects to the family, tender gifts, and display their grief by moaning and crying, always directed to the mortal remains of the deceased. All who came had to be fed, and if the deceased was a person of some importance, the number of guests could be quite large.

Shortly after the washing of the deceased's body, a rite was held to prepare it for the long journey in the spirit world to the place of its ancestors. A shaman or, if one was not available, someone who knew the rite, offered the deceased a cup of alcohol. Joss sticks or divining horns were then tossed to determine if the offering had been accepted, and repeated until the result was affirmative. Since the soul of the deceased might not know what had happened, it was necessary to tell it that the body it inhabited was now dead. The soul was given assurances that it was not alone and that it would be given directions for undertaking the journey to its ancestors.

Spirit money, bogus slips of bright colored paper, was burned, money that would be available to the soul in the spirit world so it would not enter there penniless. A rooster was killed, roasted without being plucked and placed next to the deceased. The rooster would be a guide and helper on the soul's journey. If the sun became too hot or if it rained during the journey, the soul could find shelter under the rooster's wings. The rooster would also inform the soul when it had reached its destination, for when the two approach a village the rooster would crow. If they had reached the village of the soul's ancestors, roosters in the village would crow back, informing the soul that its journey was at an end.

The soul of the deceased was also provided a verbal map of the route to its ancestors. It was told of dangers such as deceiving genies who would attempt to sidetrack it, or monsters like carnivorous rocks and poisonous caterpillars. It was warned of lakes and oceans so treacherous that they must not be crossed, and of water that was poisoned and must not be drunk. The soul was told of the guards stationed at the portals through which all souls must pass, and the answers that must be given to the guards before it will be allowed to pass through. The soul was informed of all such dangers and instructed how to avoid them. If the soul paid heed to this advice, it would reach its destination and live tranquilly with its ancestors until it was time for it to be reborn and resume its life among mankind.

The body continued to lie in state until work on the coffin was finished, which usually took several days. There might be other reasons for delaying the date of burial, such as the late arrival of relatives who lived far away or the temporary unavailability of an ox which had to be sacrificed before the internment so the beast's soul could serve as a substitute for the one Ndu Nyong had devoured — the supposed real cause of death. When all was in order the body was carried outside the house in the early morning and placed on a litter along with the coffin. The ox was killed, cooked and eaten. In the late afternoon a piper led the burial party to the grave site which was chosen with care, for the placement of the grave would help determine the fortune of the deceased person's soul in his or her afterlife. The arcane rules of geomancy, borrowed from the Chinese, governed the selection. If the site was indeed a good one and the soul of the deceased fared well, it would have no need to make periodic visits to its living relatives to request sacrifices of chickens or pigs to sustain it.

The grave was not dug until the funeral party reached the grave site. The coffin was placed in the grave and then the corpse placed in the coffin, face up. After covering the grave with earth a stone cairn was constructed, the exact size and configuration determined by clan or sub-clan custom. For a few days following the burial, food would be placed beside the grave until it was certain that the soul had at last begun the journey to its ancestors.

Among certain Hmong clans in the Kweichow province of China, care for the dead did not end with the burial ceremony. A year after the burial, relatives and friends were invited to the grave site where sacrifices were made to the deceased. The coffin was then opened and the bones carefully cleaned, wrapped in cloth and replaced in the grave. This ceremony was repeated seven times at one or two year intervals.

The practice stemmed from a belief that a failure to keep the bones of an ancestor clean could make him or her angry enough to cause sickness or death in the family. Appropriately enough, the Chinese called these Hmong the "Wash-bone Aborigines".

Strange as the practice may seem, it is not difficult to imagine how it might have originated. Repeated forced migrations meant leaving the graves of ancestors behind, and Hmong legend indicates that the conquering Chinese often desecrated Hmong graveyards, a matter of critical concern for the Hmong since this would anger the ancestors and possibly bring illness, death or misfortune to the family. For this reason many Hmong began to disguise their grave sites or fashion them in the Chinese way so that invading Chinese would not know they belonged to Hmong. Even today there are Hmong in southeast Asia whose grave sites ape those of the Chinese. Of course, one sure way to avoid desecration was to exhume the remains and transport them during a migration to a new grave site. The practice of exhuming and cleaning bones between migrations might have been a way to symbolically affirm the community's concern with desecration and to put the souls of the departed at ease.

Whatever the exact origin of the practice, it did exist and Vietnamese reports in the 1860s that the Hmong of Quan Ba cleaned, wrapped, and stored the bones of their deceased make it almost certain that there were "Wash-bone" Hmong living in the area at that time.

New Year Festival

Any account of traditional Hmong culture would be incomplete without at least a brief description of the most important communal event in Hmong society.

The New Year Festival officially began on the first day of the waxing moon of the twelfth month of the year. More precisely, it began at the first cock's crowing of that day, which is about three in the morning. Unofficially, it commenced as close to that date as the demands of the harvest permitted.

The New Year Festival was the only Hmong religious ceremony shared by the entire community. As often as not, it included members of neighboring communities. It was the time for courting, a time when eligible bachelors and young Hmong maidens dressed in their finest clothes and when ball games were organized to bring couples together. It was a time for feasting and visiting friends, and in the better-off communities, for bull fights.

The fights were not between man and beast but between bulls. It was a sport the Hmong brought with them from China or, more properly, from Kweichow where buffalo rather than bulls are still used in the ceremonial combats. The fights were not to the death.

Bullfighting

98

Usually the match ended when one bull turned tail and ran. If one bull was in danger of being seriously injured or even killed by the other, referees jumped in with long poles to separate the two beasts. In Kweichow, buffalo were specially raised for the sport and were larger and stronger than those yoked to the plow. There the fights were also a matter of considerable ceremony. Before the contest, the combatants, draped in red cloth and some with silver tips slipped onto their horns, were led around the arena, usually a cleared field, followed by a shaman beating a gong.

In addition to courting and bullfights, ritual sacrifices were performed to placate the spirits of the forest and field, to honor the house spirits, dead ancestors, and the souls of the living members of the family as well as the souls of the family's livestock. Shamans burned the jaws of the pigs that were given in payment for their services during the year so that the souls of the sacrificed animals could be reincarnated. It was a time to honor all beings living and dead, to show gratitude for whatever help they had given the family during the year or, if times had not been so good, to placate them in hopes that the new year would bring better fortune.

The festival lasted three days. And except for the time reserved for ritual sacrifices, during those three days Hmong, young and old, visited friends and relatives, ate and drank, and played games from dawn to dusk. It was a celebration looked forward to and warmly remembered.

CHAPTER

6

THE OPIUM INDUSTRY IN ASIA

The Hmong have grown opium for centuries. However, they did not become famous, or infamous, for their opium farming until after World War II when they were referred to for the first time as "the Opium People". Later they would become the target of considerable criticism for harvesting the lion's share of the opium in northern Laos, Thailand and Burma, a region popularly known as the "Golden Triangle". In the late 1960s Hmong farmers from this region supplied the raw opium for nearly 70% of the world narcotics market in heroin, morphine and smoking opium.

Despite their extensive involvement in opium farming, the Hmong were only tangentially responsible for the post war growth in the international market in illicit opiates. Indeed, they would never have devoted so much of their labor and resources to opium farming if the market for the drug was not already well established and expanding, a market created and carefully nurtured by western governments.

The Hmong have two legends recounting the origin of opium. One is poetic, the other mirrors historical fact. The poetic version has it that opium was discovered by a beautiful Hmong girl who had many suitors. She had remained a virgin longer than was customary and the young men who sought her favors became impatient. One morning while working in her garden she was attacked by one of the suitors and raped. Though she struggled, she was also overwhelmed by the pleasure of the act. The joy she experienced in her humiliation drove her mad. She took one lover after another. At first she was discriminating in her taste, but soon began to seduce any man who happened along, rich or poor, young or old, married or single. Her sexual excesses so destroyed her health that she fell ill and died. But before she died she made a vow. It was that she would be reborn as a flower whose sap would excite passion

100

as had her caresses, and yield pleasures greater than even she had been able to give. And so it happened that an opium poppy grew from her grave. The flower's pod oozed a white sap whose perfume called forth memories in all who inhaled it of the pleasure experienced by all the young woman's lovers. And when they dreamed she appeared to them and revealed the secret of harvesting the sap, and how to prepare it for smoking.

The other legend simply states that opium came to China from a place called England. Indeed no word for opium exists in the Hmong language, and they call it by a Chinese name, "ya-ying," which means tobacco from the west. It is an expression that accurately reflects the origin of opium's use as a recreational drug.

Opium is one of the oldest drugs known to man. Archeological records indicate that some of the pharmacological properties of opium were known as early as 8000 B.C. Tablets from Sumer dating back to 3000 B.C. reveal cuneiform characters for the poppy. Later Assyrian inscriptions list opium as one of the most common drugs, and contain descriptions of the harvesting of the poppy sap that reveal the process has not changed much in five thousand years. Slits were made in the poppy pods and the sap allowed to leak and congeal on the wounds. Iron scoops were then used to scrape off the residue which was rolled into balls and stored in earthen pots.

As early as 1500 B.C., opium was mixed with wine by Egyptian priests as an anesthetic for surgical operations, principally trepanation (cutting or drilling holes in the patient's skull). Centuries later the use of the drug in Egypt had spread from the operating room to the general population where it was widely used as an anti-depressant.

While the exact route remains uncertain, use of the drug eventually spread from Egypt to the eastern Mediterranean. In the *Odyssey*, Homer refers to the curative properties of opium, as does Theophrastus nearly 300 years later. Hippocrates prescribed opium for the treatment of infections; and Dioscorides, in the first century A.D. provided an account of opium that is remarkably close to contemporary descriptions. By this time the drug had spread throughout the middle east. From there it penetrated into the India, Pakistan and China following the path of Islamic conquests.

When Arabs introduced opium to China in the seventh century, they offered it as medical remedy for various diseases and not as a narcotic. The use of opium as a recreational drug came later, and from the west. Indeed, from the ninth to the sixteenth century, Chinese treatises mention opium only in connection with medicine.

When the Portuguese opened trade routes to China in the 1500s they discovered that the Chinese were unwilling to barter for anything but gold and silver. Heavily influenced by mercantilist thinking that gauged a nation's economic vitality by its reserves in gold and silver, the Portuguese sought a substitute for precious metals acceptable to the Chinese. In the late 1500s they brought tobacco from their Brazilian colonies and were greatly pleased to find that it was an immediate success. Having introduced the Chinese to pipe smoking the way was now open for enterprising minds to discover something with an even greater market potential.

BANE OF CHINA

In the early 1600s Dutch merchants observed Indonesians mixing tobacco with opium. Soon the Dutch were smoking the mixture themselves to combat malaria. They also recognized its commercial possibilities and began to sell the opium and tobacco mixture to the Chinese on Taiwan. From Taiwan the practice spread to the mainland where it gained a foothold. The Portuguese quickly added opium to their list of imports to China. By this time the Chinese had discovered the process of preparing raw opium so that it could be smoked alone and the consumption of imported opium increased dramatically.

India would for some time remain the center of world opium production, and when England successfully reduced India to a British colony and opened it up to the British East India company for exploitation, the English were in a position to both dominate and dramatically expand the Chinese opium market. As with the Portuguese before them, the British considered trade which resulted in a net loss of gold and silver a bad bargain. For some time they had been trading Indian cotton for Chinese tea and silk. But the Chinese needed Indian cotton less than British merchants needed Chinese tea and silk, so there was a constant trade imbalance. This resulted in a steady drain of specie from British coffers. The British were quick to realize that opium was the means to effectively close the specie spigot. A member of the Foreign Office stated the British position succinctly in a secret memorandum:

> For the previous 200 years the foreign merchants had been obliged to import silver into China to pay for their purchases of tea and silk, but in opium they had at length found a commodity which the Chinese desired to buy. Down to 1817 a stream of silver was poured into China and remained there... From 1818 to 1830 there was a movement both ways. From 1831 the tide turned, the import was reduced to small amounts, and the trade could be balanced only by increasing shipments of treasure. This drain of silver from China was only checked in later years by the increased production of opium within the Empire.

By 1767 the East India company was shipping 1,000 chests of opium a year from India to China. With the appointment of Warren Hastings to the Governorship of Bengal in 1772 British India's dependence on the opium market became a matter of explicit policy. Opium production was expanded and within a few years exports accounted for one-seventh of all revenues in British India.

Expanding markets naturally invite competition. The Americans quickly moved to monopolize the trade of Turkish opium to China. They were followed by the Portuguese who began to purchase opium from northern India with an eye to increasing their presence in the Chinese market. But neither competitor enjoyed the British advantage which was exploited in a price cutting war that nearly ruined Britain's competitors and greatly expanded the market for the drug. Between 1811 and 1821, British Indian shipments of opium to China averaged 4,532 chests per year—more than a four hundred percent increase in less than thirty years. Remarkably, demand continued to match supply, so that by 1838 exports exceeded 40,000 chests, or approximately 2,400 tons of opium.

The spectacular success of the British opium trade caused serious problems in China. For one thing it resulted in a debilitating trade deficit. But more importantly, it was creating a nation of opium addicts. Early attempts to control addiction were ineffective. In 1729, the Manchu emperor, Shih Tsung, after having already placed a general ban on Christianity as a subversive movement, went on to prohibit opium smoking throughout China. If the ban on Christianity proved needless because of the small number of converts it attracted, the prohibition on opium smoking was unenforceable as long as the importation of opium continued unabated.

It was not until the nineteenth century that the Chinese at last faced the more salient issue. In 1800, in an attempt to stem the flow of imported opium, the Chinese government closed the port of Canton. It was an extreme move for Canton was the principal trading port of China and closing it meant shutting down not only the opium traffic but nearly all import and export trade as well. This, at least, was the intention of the Edict of 1800. Unfortunately, while export trade suffered, opium continued to find its way into China. The opium traffic simply spread out along the southern coast, supported on the sea by Chinese pirates and inland by corrupt officials and criminal syndicates, both of which flourished well into the twentieth century. Recognizing its impotence to enforce the edict, and under the prodding of the British government, the Chinese government reopened Canton for trade.

The negative effects of the opium trade on the Chinese monetary system also became a point of serious concern for Chinese officials. The constant drain of silver inflated its value. This had serious social as well as economic consequences. By tradition, land taxes were paid in silver, or in other coin, usually copper, at the prevailing exchange rate. Unfortunately, the inflation in silver debased the value of other currency. Prior to the nineteenth century the exchange rate held steady at approximately a thousand copper coins per ounce of silver, yet by 1835 the rate had changed to two thousand copper coins for one ounce of the precious metal. This proved a disaster for the peasant class, for the selling price for rice did not rise with the general level of inflation but remained close to the customary level. The higher taxes coupled with unchanging income from rice production resulted in a drastic decline in the real income of Chinese peasants. Moreover, between 1826 and 1850 crop shortages due to natural disasters were endemic, leading to not only declining incomes for millions of peasant farmers but to mass starvation. Not surprisingly, peasant uprisings increased and helped set the stage for the Taiping Revolution.

In 1839 the Chinese government tried once again to control the opium traffic. Lin Tse-hsu was appointed commissioner to Canton. His first act was to prohibit the importation of opium. His second act was to seize over 20,000 chests of British opium. The seized chests were burned and then dumped into Canton harbor, an act of defiance similar to the American colonists's Boston Tea Party.

The British response was to send its warships up and down the Chinese coast, shelling ports and settlements for three years until China was forced to the bargaining table. The result was the 1842 Treaty of Nanking. It was a one-sided affair, the Chinese agreeing to pay $21,000,000 in indemnity, a third of which was for the opium chests destroyed at Canton. The Chinese were also forced to acknowledge the principle of free trade which, from the perspective of the Chinese, translated into the right of the British to exploit Chinese markets and carry out even illicit trade. For the Chinese were still unwilling to legalize either the importation or use of opium. They would soon change their mind.

In southeastern China, in the province of Kwangsi, Hung Hsiuch'uan, a Hakka tribesman who had been educated by Christian missionaries, organized Hakka peasants and then members of other tribal groups, including the Hmong, in a quasi-religious movement. Open insurrection broke out in the summer of 1850 and the revolutionaries gained control over eastern Kwangsi Province, proclaiming a new "Heavenly Kingdom of Peace," or "tai-p'ing t'ien-kuo." The movement gathered force and Hung led his troops out of Kwangsi into Hunan where they were joined by thousands of peasants. From there they marched north through Hupeh and followed the course of the Yangtze to Nanking. In 1853, Hung declared a new dynasty. There followed an abortive attempt to take Peking, and by 1856 the movement began to disintegrate from internal squabbling. The Manchus launched a counter-offensive which limped along for several years until Nanking fell in the summer of 1864.

Not only did the Manchus have to contend with the Taiping rebels during this period, they also had to deal with the British who, under the pretext of the Chinese government's failure to observe the terms of the Nanking treaty, began a new series of naval bombardments in 1857. Fighting two wars on different fronts quickly exhausted government finances. After settling with the British, again on Britain's terms and with the burden of another indemnity, the Chinese reexamined their policy on opium.

Since past policy had proved a complete failure, they were willing to try something new, and quite bold. The government decided on a two-pronged attack on the opium problem. The first was short term and dealt with the pressing need for additional revenue. Opium would be legalized as would its import; this would permit a duty on imported opium, which was first enacted in 1858. The second, and long term, approach to the problem was not only to legalize opium but to actually encourage domestic production and flood the market, forcing down the price to the point where it would no longer be profitable for the British to import it. With the British finally out of the picture it would then be easier to control and, ultimately, eliminate opium from China.

From the 1860s on, Chinese opium production expanded rapidly. In 1880, the peak year for imported opium, 6,500 tons of the drug entered Chinese ports. By 1905 the amount of imported opium had fallen to half that amount while domestic production increased to over 22,000 tons. Indeed, as early as 1885 China was producing twice the amount of opium imported from India and elsewhere. One reason for the increase was that Chinese opium sold at half the price of the imported Indian variety. It could also be re-smoked many more times than Indian opium, making it an especially good bargain for the poor. Unfortunately, once opium became a real bargain opium addiction spread rapidly among the poorer classes. By 1870 there were an estimated 15 million Chinese opium addicts, most of whom were poor.

In 1908, during the last year of her life, the Dowager Empress put the final piece of the grand strategy into place by concluding the Ten Years Agreement with Great Britain. By the terms of the agreement China would phase out domestic production while Britain would concurrently reduce the export of Indian opium to China, which was to end altogether in 1918.

In 1912 the Manchu dynasty ceased to exist and China became a republic. Under the republic China made considerable headway in fulfilling its part of the treaty. Indeed, just prior to the outbreak of the civil war in 1916, the Chinese were well on their way to completely eradicating opium use in their country. The civil war changed all this. It transformed the country into a land of opposing armies, most led by warlords seeking power and profit, some by diehards bent on restoring the Manchu dynasty, and some like Sun Yat-Sen who remained faithful to the republic. In many cases the armies of the warring factions were financed out of profits from opium sales. Wu Lien-Teh, a Chinese physician, travelled extensively throughout China during the civil war period and observed "mile upon mile of land covered with multi-colored poppy plants in Manchuria, Shansi Shensi, Jehol, Jukien, Yunnan and Szechuan, from which the various warlords hoped to derive needed revenue for maintaining their troops."

Chiang Kai-shek, supported by the army of the Kuomintang nationalists, gained nominal control of the country in 1927. In the same year Chiang legalized opium to gain the revenue needed for a campaign to crush all remaining opposition. Public pressure caused a reversal in official policy, though the government continued unofficial sponsorship of the trade until 1934 when Chiang realized that the best way to neutralize his opposition was to dry up their revenue, which meant suppressing opium production. Chiang mounted a vigorous anti-opium campaign. However, Kuomintang officials seldom destroyed confiscated opium. Instead it was hoarded, and a good deal of it entered the illicit market from which Chiang amassed a personal fortune.

The Japanese invasion of China in 1937 drove the nationalists into the interior where officials traded freely in opium with the Japanese who had long recognized the profit potential of drug trafficking. With the return of Chiang Kai-shek to power after the defeat of the Japanese in 1945, China enjoyed the dubious distinction of having become the world leader in opium production.

It required the communist take-over of the country to fulfill, after nearly a hundred years, the grand scheme of effectively ridding China of opium. Nor was it accomplished overnight. Yunnan Province continued a brisk trade in illicit opium, smuggling it to Indochina via remnants of the Kuomintang army operating freely in Burma up until 1955. Furthermore, the Peking government, noted for its excesses in many areas, exercised prudence in dealing with opium producing hill tribes in the most remote areas. There the opium poppy can still be found, some of it farmed by Chinese Hmong.

THE ROLE OF THE HMONG

The Hmong played a part in this history but more as pawns than as major actors. British success in expanding the opium market set the stage for the rapid growth of opium farming in China. And since opium grows best at high altitudes, mountain farmers like the Hmong were best situated to cultivate it profitably: the Hmong especially so because they had cultivated opium for medicinal use long before the British introduced it into Asia as a recreational drug. Not only did the Hmong know how to grow the poppy, they knew which kinds of soils, determined by color and taste, produced the greatest yield of the poppy sap, a knowledge which later earned them the reputation for growing some of the best opium in China.

This specialized knowledge did not guarantee that the Hmong would undertake large scale opium farming, for they lived far from populated areas and lacked the resources to market the drug on their own. Chinese opium merchants resolved this difficulty by paying the Hmong in advance for future harvests and accepting full responsibility for the marketing side of the operation.

Advance payment was crucial in persuading Hmong farmers to neglect their traditional subsistence crops for the labor intensive cultivation of the opium poppy. Even so, the increase in income was a mixed blessing. On the one hand, the switch to cash crop farming made the Hmong more dependent on local markets and itinerant merchants for the provision of many necessities, and the Hmong did not like being dependent on outsiders. On the other hand, the increase in income, coupled with the high rate of Hmong savings, indirectly reinforced Hmong independence. For the accumulation of sizeable nest egg made it economically feasible for a family to afford the expense of migrating to new areas, and even to new countries, when political repression became unbearable.

The role of Chinese middlemen in the expansion of Hmong opium farming was perhaps most fully developed in Yunnan province where the Haw, descendants of the Chinese Muslim converts of Arab traders, induced thousands of Hmong to farm opium as a cash crop. While profit was made on both sides, this close association with the Haw caused the Yunnanese Hmong considerable grief during the last stages of the Muslim separatist movement known as the Panthay rebellion (1818-1873). Though many Hmong allied themselves with the Haw during the fighting, many also held back from the conflict. Unfortunately for these pacifists, Chinese generals charged with putting down the mutiny had little interest in sorting out the guilty from the innocent and killed thousands of Hmong, rebels and noncombatants, indiscriminately. When the uprising was over the Haw had their property confiscated and were barred from engaging in trade. Many Haw migrated out of the province into Indochina, as did many Hmong. In Indochina the Haw invariably settled close to Hmong communities, renewed old ties or established new ones and readied their caravans for the trek back into China where the demand for the drug remained high for the next seventy years.

Despite the high profits enjoyed by middlemen trafficking in the drug, Hmong opium farmers seldom got rich. Most considered themselves fortunate if their annual income from the opium harvest matched those of the average lowland wet rice farmer. Still, it was a definite step up from grinding poverty. And growing opium made good economic sense. Ordinarily the Hmong lost out in competition with lowland farmers who enjoyed higher per acre yields and lived closer to final markets. The larger crops and lower transportation costs meant lowlanders could charge less for their produce and still make a profit. Opium was one of the few crops that did better in the highlands than in the lowland valleys, and this gave the Hmong a competitive advantage. Also, the yearly harvest for a single farmer seldom yielded more than a few pounds of raw opium. A small caravan could therefore easily transport the entire output of a village or even several villages which, given the high street value of the drug, reduced the transportation cost per pound to such a level that the Hmong never lacked for Chinese merchants eager to market their crops.

While the Hmong considered the economic benefits from growing opium to far outweigh the evils of drug addiction for their own people, they nevertheless acknowledged it to be a serious problem. For even if they did not view addiction as a sin they nevertheless considered it a debilitating vice and a sign of a weak will, especially in a young person. If recent surveys can be considered representative of long term trends, Hmong addiction rates have been lower than the average in China and southeast Asia and atypically concentrated among the elderly, principally victims of chronic pain who became addicted after prolonged use of the drug to combat the suffering associated with rheumatism, tuberculosis, or cancer. While this was tolerated as perhaps a necessary evil, young healthy adults who became addicted were often treated as social pariahs. Invariably they were poor family providers and, if they were bachelors, they had great difficulty in finding a bride.

Despite their condemnation of opium addiction within their own communities, it is unlikely that Hmong opium farmers ever suffered pangs of conscience for supplying the raw material to support the habits of millions of Chinese addicts. Especially since, by the mid-1880s, the opium market was either legalized or directly managed by Asian governments. Indeed, in the late 1800s, local Chinese authorities in Kweichow province forced the Hmong to pay taxes in raw opium. Sanctioned by law and sustained by strong markets, Hmong opium farmers had no more difficulty justifying their crops than Kentucky farmers today who, with the sanction (and subsidies) of government, grow the tobacco that sustains the nicotine addiction of millions of Americans.

OPIUM IN INDOCHINA

For a time, the opium market in southeast Asia lagged behind the ever expanding market for the drug in China. A series of events not only reversed this trend but eventually made southeast Asia the locus of world opium production.

A change in China's demographics was one of these events. By the early nineteenth century China had become a country of more than 400 million. The nation's agriculture had not kept pace with its population. In many provinces famine seemed always just around the corner. The coastal provinces of Kwangtung and Fukien were hit particularly hard, and during the rest of the century peasants from these areas left the country in large numbers. Some emigrated to America and Mexico where labor for huge railroad construction projects was in short supply. Most, however, emigrated to southeast Asia where the British and French were expanding their empires.

Large numbers of these immigrants were opium addicts who formed the nucleus of a new, and vigorous, opium market evidenced by a precipitous rise in opium imports to the region. The development was not unopposed. In Thailand, three kings in succession fought the growth of drug trafficking. The undertaking was doomed from the start. Harsh penalties, including execution, were enacted, but they affected only the native population and resident Chinese. The British who brought the opium into the country were beyond the reach of the law. Conceding defeat and eager to increase sagging government revenues, king Mongkut legalized the trade and granted the Thai opium franchise to wealthy Chinese in the late 1850s. Eventually the Thai government stepped in and assumed full responsibility for retail sales while the British continued to manage imports.

The French moved nearly as fast as the English to spread opium addiction in southeast Asia. As soon as the French gained control of an area they integrated their official opium monopoly into the colonial administration, which meant that trafficking was not just tolerated, it was organized and backed by the prestige and power of the French government.

From its inception the rapid expansion of opium trafficking alarmed Vietnamese emperors. They objected to it on both moral and economic grounds, although the economic side of the question soon loomed as the most pressing because the constant drain of silver into the vaults of the French opium monopoly was rapidly inflating the value of silver. However, efforts to restrict illicit opium trafficking were abandoned in the late 1850s after the French launched a successful military invasion, first against Hue and then against Saigon. In order acquire the necessary revenue to pay for the large indemnity demanded by the French as punishment for Vietnamese resistance, the Vietnamese emperor reluctantly endorsed an opium franchise in the Tonkin region.

The French colonial administration not only managed the import of Indian and, later, Chinese opium, it established official retail outlets for the drug as well as government run opium dens which, by 1918, numbered in the thousands. Managers of the state run opium refinery, erected in Saigon near the turn of the century, spent years perfecting a fast burning smoking opium with an eye to increasing demand, an aim that was also served by the importation of large amounts of Yunnanese opium. Far less expensive than the Indian variety, Yunnanese opium made addiction possible for even the impoverished lower classes of Indochina.

Colonial revenues from the southeast Asian opium trade were enormous, at one point amounting to 40% of all revenues. Even in bad times opium revenues seldom dropped below 20%. Indeed, it was opium that placed the French experiment in imperialism in Indochina on a profitable footing right from the start and provided justification for more intensive colonization of southeast Asia. From their foothold around Saigon the French moved north and west, eventually conquering all of Vietnam, Cambodia and Laos. While a good deal of the necessary infrastructure was financed out of opium revenues, the pace was so rapid and so poorly managed that deficits began to mount. One response to the deficits was to expand the opium trade.

In 1878 public opinion forced the British parliament to pass the Opium Act which severely limited England's participation in the opium trade and restricted British sales of opium to registered Chinese and Indian addicts. In British Burma where addiction had spread beyond the Chinese minority to the native population, trafficking among the Burmese was also strictly prohibited. Britain's 1908 agreement with China to phase out the importation of Indian opium was followed by a second agreement in 1911 which aimed at speeding up the process. By 1915 most Chinese provinces were barred to all foreign opium and England's complicity in international drug trafficking was at last drawing to a close.

Unfortunately, Britain's retirement did not appreciably alter the size or intensity of the international narcotics market since other nations quickly moved in to take up the slack. This included not only France but many former British colonies such as Burma, Pakistan, Iran, Afghanistan, and Thailand. Within a few decades, however, France achieved the dubious distinction of having successfully replaced England as the world's foremost trafficker in opiates.

Just prior to the outbreak of the Second World War France was importing nearly sixty tons of opium annually from Turkey and Iran to supply the more than 100,000 addicts who were the nucleus of the Indochinese opium market. The war severed this supply line. With the Japanese occupation of Indochina, all shipping to the region was interdicted by the British navy. The French were therefore forced to turn to domestic opium production to replace lost imports.

While the Hmong of Laos and north Vietnam had been selling their raw opium to the French for decades, they did not produce enough to meet the needs of the opium monopoly. To increase Hmong production, the French raised the official purchasing price for raw opium and placed Hmong notables on the Opium Board to guarantee delivery of all the available opium harvested by Hmong farmers.

Hmong opium production skyrocketed, and continued to increase even after 1946 when, in response to international public opinion, the French dismantled their opium monopoly. The monopoly was gone, but not the French sponsored opium traffic which went underground. Until the mid-1950s the French continued to encourage Hmong opium production to raise revenue to support their war against the Vietnamese communists. Even after the French departed Indochina, the traffic in opium continued to grow with much of the raw opium that supported it coming from the Hmong. French narcotic syndicates allied with Vietnamese gangsters and corrupt South Vietnamese officials used Hmong opium to supply not only the southeast Asian narcotics market but the growing market in Europe and the U.S.

When the Vietnamese communists gained control of north Vietnam in the mid-1950s they effectively brought an end to opium farming in the north, the heartland of Vietnam's opium industry. In Laos, however, the Hmong continued to grow opium and actually increased production until the late 1960s when massive U.S. bombing devastated most of the prime opium growing areas in that country. But by then the Laotian Hmong were so preoccupied with mere survival that the loss of their opium fields seemed of little consequence.

CHAPTER
7

THE HMONG AND THE FRENCH: UNEASY ALLIES

In 1885, Ton That Thuyet, the advisor to the Vietnamese Emperor Ham Nghi, persuaded the young sovereign to rebel against the French. The rebellion failed, but Ton That Thuyet and Ham Nghi escaped and sought refuge in the highlands of Laos where they organized a government in exile. Though the French had installed their own hand picked puppet, many Vietnamese remained loyal to Ham Nghi. It consequently became a matter of high priority for the French to locate the deposed emperor and eliminate him once and for all from the Vietnamese political scene. But forays into the Laotian mountains turned up absolutely nothing. It was like looking for a needle in a haystack. Only after the Hmong consented to be their guides did the French capture Ham Nghi and defuse a potentially explosive situation.

Cooperation in the capture of Ham Nghi not only earned the Laotian Hmong praise it alerted the French to their strategic importance for future operations in the Laotian highlands. A change in policy immediately followed. French officials began to bypass Laotian middlemen and deal directly with Hmong communities and their leaders. It marked the beginning of a special relationship between the French and the Laotian Hmong that would continue until France was forced to withdraw from Indochina. It was not all smooth sailing, however. French insensitivity to Hmong interests, and especially their failure to appreciate the devastating effect of tax increases on the already low Hmong standard of living, periodically incited large numbers of Laotian Hmong to armed rebellion.

TAX PROBLEMS

In 1896, the French raised taxes in Laos. The new taxes struck the Hmong as particularly unfair because they were applied almost exclusively to them. In Laos, opium cultivation was predominately a Hmong occupation. The French were fully aware of this. They were also eager to obtain a cheap source of raw opium for their opium monopoly, which is why they required the Hmong to pay a portion of the tax in opium, and at an assessed value far below the market price.

The Hmong appealed to their kiatongs for help. It did not take much to urge them to action. They were already incensed over the fact that the French had failed to consult them about a tax which so adversely affected the Hmong community. Nor were tensions eased by the decision of the French Commissioner for Xieng Khouang to try to intimidate the Hmong by ordering a mixed contingent of Laotian and Vietnamese militiamen to conduct patrols in the Hmong highlands.

The governor of the province, Prince Kham Huang, also had an axe to grind with the French. Descended from a long line of Xieng Khouang princes who ruled the province as an independent kingdom, Kham Huang chafed under French rule. His lack of cooperation earned him a demotion from Prince to provincial governor. Seeing that the Hmong were in a rebellious mood, he advised their nominal leader, the Lo kiatong, to organize an armed resistance.

The first attack was against the military post at Ban Khang Phanieng on the eastern edge of the Plain of Jars. Though the Hmong failed to take the post they did give a good account of themselves. The second assault was more ambitious. It was directed against the provincial headquarters at Xieng Khouang city. There the Hmong found themselves outnumbered and outgunned. They were cut down by modern French rifles before they could get close enough to fire their flintlocks, which are only effective at short range. After suffering many casualties the Hmong were forced to withdraw into the mountains.

The defeat so damaged the prestige of the Lo kiatong that the leadership of the Laotian Hmong passed to the kiatong of the Moua clan, Moua Tong Ger, who represented the Hmong in negotiations with the French at Ban Ban, a small town north of the provincial headquarters. It was the French who initiated the negotiations. Though they had defeated the Hmong, they had stirred up a hornet's nest that still buzzed and might yet sting. At Ban Ban, Moua Tong Ger proved to be an able diplomat. Not only did the French Commissioner agree to lower Hmong taxes, he pledged to consult Hmong leaders in the future before implementing policies that might adversely affect Hmong interests.

Laos and its Provinces

While a climate of close cooperation between Hmong political leaders and French officials became the norm in Xieng Khouang province, elsewhere in Indochina Hmong communities complained bitterly about increasing exploitation. It was not the French who were doing the exploiting, but Tai, Laotian, and Vietnamese officials. This would not have necessarily affected French and Hmong relations except that the exploiters often attempted to intimidate the Hmong and deter them from contemplating retaliation by claiming to be acting with the full knowledge and backing of the colonial administration.

The Vietnamese Hmong living in the prime opium growing areas surrounding the high plateau of Dien Bien Phu perhaps had the most cause for complaint. Opium taxes exacted by the Tai lords in the lowlands were so high they bordered on expropriation. Entire communities that had once enjoyed a modest prosperity were impoverished within a few years. The region was ripe for rebellion, though it would take nearly two decades of simmering before the pot finally boiled over. And, when it did, not only the Tai but the French became the target of the rebellion.

BLACK FLAGS

This is not to say that it was all dark clouds. As late as 1914, many Hmong communities throughout Indochina welcomed French military protection against groups of marauding bandits known as the Black flags.

In 1884, France and China signed the treaty of T'ien-Tsin in which China acknowledged French sovereignty over all of Vietnam. Prior to the signing, China had maintained military garrisons along its common border with Vietnam, some inside Vietnamese territory. The French naturally expected the Chinese troops to be recalled. But instead of returning home they pillaged and then occupied various sectors of the frontier. Their generals became warlords, each with his own army, each exercising absolute sovereignty over the native population under his control. Since these renegades chose a black flag as their standard, the French fell into the habit of calling them, as well as all Chinese bandits in Indochina, the Black Flags.

These warlords and bandits were not without their supporters, however. Vietnamese emperors as well as Tai tribesmen opposed to French colonial rule had, at various times, allied themselves with the bandits and set them loose on the French. While the Black flags seldom bested the French in combat, they did inflict many casualties.

One encounter in particular transformed the name"Black Flag"into a rallying cry for French infantry. In 1874 Captain Henri Riviere led 600 French troops against Black Flags who had gained control of Hanoi and the surrounding countryside. After driving the bandits out of Hanoi, Riviere pressed on northeast to the coal mining town of Hongay which he meant to place under French control. A Black Flag ambush not only frustrated this aim but cost Riviere his life. After slaughtering the French troops, the Black Flags carried Riviere's head from village to village to celebrate their victory and to graphically thumb their noses at the French.

The Black Flags not only caused the French headaches, they were a constant threat to the Hmong who were favorite targets of the bandits because of their opium which could be traded across the border in China for supplies and munitions. The Hmong therefore shared a common interest with the French in destroying these brigands.

In November 1914, Black Flags crossed the Vietnamese border and entered Sam Neua province in Laos and attacked the French garrison near Sam Neua city. After suffering heavy losses, the French colonial troops abandoned the garrison and fled for their lives. Reinforcements were sent to retake the garrison, but they were ambushed and driven off. It was only after more reinforcements were sent from Vietnam that the French were able to liberate Sam Neua city. The Black Flags retreated into Vietnam where they launched successful attacks on the French garrisons at Dien Bien Phu and Son La. These victories bolstered their confidence and they once again entered Laos, but this time further north in Phong Saly province.

The Hmong in Phong Saly did not wait for the French to arrive and drive out the bandits. They mounted an expedition of their own. After establishing a position overlooking a Black Flag encampment inside a pass near the Vietnam border, they cut down trees for barricades which they mounted on logs for wheels and descended the trail to engage the enemy. Alerted, the Black Flags raised their banners and attacked the Hmong. Barrages of rifle fire chipped away at the barricades which moved relentlessly downward, closing the distance between the Hmong and the bandits. When the Hmong were nearly on top of the Chinese they abandoned their protection and closed on the enemy.

Though the Black Flags suffered heavy casualties that day, the Hmong had not scored a decisive victory. They had only defeated one contingent of the bandits. The main body, encamped near the battlefield, was soon in hot pursuit of the much smaller force of poorly equipped montagnards. The Hmong had no choice but to retreat. They mounted several ambushes against Black Flag outposts after that, but on their own they could not hope to drive the bandits out of their province. Fortunately, the French dispatched two full regiments to Phong Saly from Hanoi in December of 1915. With nearly two thousand pack mules and several pieces of mountain artillery, the French clearly anticipated a long campaign. After rooting the Black Flags from their entrenched positions, French troops harried the bandits for over three months until they were driven out of Laos into China.

The success of the Laotian campaign encouraged the French to step up their lagging offensive against Black Flag strongholds in northern Vietnam. One Hmong, Yang Yilong, had already begun a campaign of his own against a group of Black Flags who had for years tyrannized the montagnards around Ha Giang, robbing them of food, livestock and opium, and carrying off the most beautiful women of each village to serve as concubines for Black Flag notables.

Yang Yilong organized his Hmong volunteers into small guerrilla bands of two or three men. Their weapons were crude: knives, swords and axes. They attacked isolated units of Black Flags and only when it was certain that all could be killed. The slain bandits were buried or thrown into deep grottos. Yang Yilong did not want reprisals. Missing soldiers tell no tales.

The sudden and mysterious disappearance of a number of his soldiers puzzled the Black Flag warlord until he learned from an informant that it was all the work of the Hmong. Yang Yilong was captured and imprisoned. But on the day of the scheduled execution he succeeded in generating an argument between the guards over which of them would get his clothes. A fight broke out and, in the confusion, Yang Yilong sneaked out of the prison compound to freedom.

Yang Yilong collected a number of his guerrillas and led them to the French garrison at Bao Lac, a small mountain village fifty miles east of Ha Giang. After listening to Yang Yilong's description of his guerrilla operations against the Black Flags, the post commander immediately donated sixty rifles to the cause. While Yang Yilong could have used twice that number, sixty rifles were sufficient to support more daring operations against the bandits.

Three months of incessant harassment finally forced the Black Flags of Ha Giang to abandon their strongholds and return to China. Not all of them made it across the border. Yang Yilong's guerrillas always kept several days ahead of the fleeing Chinese, preparing rock slides to greet them when they passed by.

After Yang Yilong's victory over the Ha Giang Black Flags the French began to recruit other Tonkin Hmong for the final push against the remaining Black Flags. Sometimes the Hmong served only as guides. At other times they fought alongside the French. And, on other occasions, they coordinated their own independent operations with those of their French allies.

One joint operation proved particularly costly for a group of Black Flags who had been driven from their mountain stronghold by the French. Deprived of the sanctuary they headed south toward the Red River delta. On their way they attacked a Hmong village situated north of Nghia Lo where the French maintained a well armed garrison. Hmong scouts had spotted the Black Flags earlier so the village was empty when they arrived. The bandits scoured the village in search of the opium the villagers had wisely carried away with them on their retreat into the forest. The Black Flags immediately set out after them.

Once in the dense forest, however, the Chinese were easy prey for Hmong ambushes. Poisoned arrows from Hmong crossbows thinned out their ranks. It was now the Black Flags' turn to retreat. The Hmong kept close on their heels until the Chinese made the mistake of entering a deep grotto. They were outflanked by the Hmong and boxed in. More Black flags felt the bite of Hmong arrows. When the bandits finally broke out they left behind so many dead that the grotto was later renamed the"Valley of the Dead Chinese".

The enraged survivors of this carnage pillaged and burned every Hmong village they came across. Another mistake. Hmong chiefs in the area swore a blood oath to destroy the brigands. Contact was made with the French garrison at Nghia Lo where plans for a joint operation were worked out. The Hmong would engage the Black Flags and drive them south where the French would be in place to cut off their retreat.

The Hmong assembled their forces on the outskirts of a village the pirates had occupied, and remained at the forest's edge waiting for the signal to attack. A large cannon, made of wood and banded with iron, was already in position at the top of a rise overlooking the rice paddies that ringed the village. The cannon was the handiwork of a Hmong blacksmith named Nao Ku Hlau. He had already loaded the cannon with powder and stuffed its wide mouth with old knives, axes, chains and whatever else he had been able to retrieve from the scrap pile at his shop.

Nao Ku Hlau walked down the rise to a clearing where he began waving a white flag and taunting the Black Flags in the village. A detachment of bandits was sent to capture the impertinent Hmong. By the time they reached the last paddy, Nao Ku Hlau was already standing beside his cannon. He lit the fuse and ran for cover. The cannon roared and belched its junkyard at the advancing Chinese. While Nao Ku Hlau waited for the smoke to clear so that he could assess the effectiveness of his invention, his compatriots streamed out of the forest onto the paddies, stumbling over dead and dying bandits in their headlong rush for the village.

The Black Flags stood their ground until they were overrun. From then on they had to fight in retreat. The Hmong drove them south into the waiting arms of the French. Trapped, the Black Flags had no choice but to attempt to fight their way out. The few who succeeded were dogged by the French and Hmong all the way to the Chinese border.

THE DECEIT OF LO BLIAYAO

While the experience of fighting a common enemy helped to improve relations between the French and Hmong, the momentum of other events soon strained them to the breaking point.

The French raised taxes in Laos in 1916. However, the taxes were not applied equally to all Laotians. Tribal minorities such as the Hmong were forced to shoulder a heavier burden than the ethnic Lao in the lowland valleys. In particular, the Hmong were now forced to pay several kinds of taxes. There were two annual per capita taxes, as well as a semi-annual tax. And for the first time widows and adolescents were taxed. Also, adult males were obliged to provide two weeks of free labor on government work projects.

The new taxes were burdensome and the grumbling from those forced to pay them quite audible. To insure that taxes were paid, elements of the colonial militia made the rounds with the tax collectors. Hmong who could not pay were jailed until their relatives could make good on the delinquent taxes. Accustomed to mountain living and habituated to a migratory lifestyle, the Hmong have always found imprisonment intolerable, and it was this aspect of the new tax policy as much as the higher taxes themselves that led to a growing rebelliousness among the Hmong.

Then there were the new roads. Looking to the future, the French decided to develop an all weather road system in Laos that would link it to Vietnam. The network of new roads was to serve a dual purpose. First, it would make it easier to transport troops from Vietnam to Laos in case Thailand attempted to exercise its former hegemony over Laos. Second, a communication link between Laos and Vietnam would prepare the way for linkages between the two economies. The hope was that, at some point, the investment in the Vietnamese economy would, through a process of economic osmosis, pay off for Laos as well.

Since the French were still unwilling to spend much on Laos, the local population would have to both pay the taxes to raise the necessary revenue for the project and supply the labor for the construction of the new roads. The Hmong of Xieng Khouang and Phong Saly provinces supplied most of the manpower for the work crews. Major roads were to be constructed through both provinces to the Vietnamese border. Since the roads would have to be constructed through mountains the work was particularly arduous, and because it was mountainous terrain the available pool of local labor was small. It meant that the Hmong not only had to work hard, they had to work for weeks at a time. This resulted in neglected crops, poor harvests and, consequently, less income to pay taxes. In parts of Phong Saly province the burden on some Hmong communities was so great that entire villages simply pulled up stakes and moved away. Many did not return until work on the roads

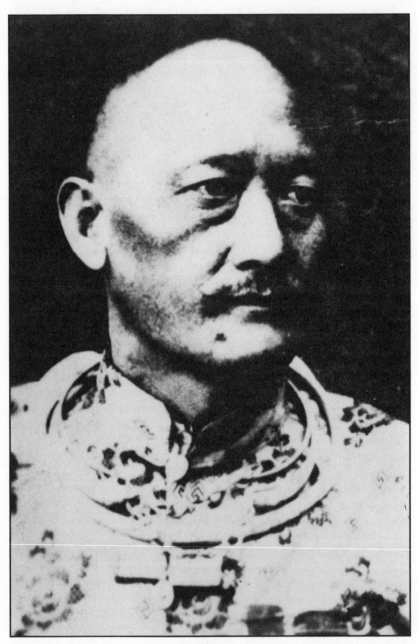

Lo Bliayao

was completed in 1924. While few Xieng Khouang Hmong opted for this solution, they nevertheless complained bitterly about their plight.

The French justified the forced labor by pointing out that, after all, the workers were paid. However, the wages were low and, equally important, workers received wages only after the first fourteen days of work, which had to be donated free. The French had another, more cogent, reason for ignoring the complaints of Hmong recruited for work on the road crews. Hmong leaders had been consulted before the plan was put into effect and they had endorsed it; as far as the French were concerned, they were keeping to their earlier promise to undertake nothing affecting Hmong interests without prior consultation with Hmong notables.

Sometime in late 1917 or early 1918, the village chiefs of Xieng Khouang province appealed to the Lo kiatong, Lo Bliayao, for relief. Selected as the kiatong of the Lo clan in 1910 and appointed that same year as the aging Moua kiatong's assistant, Lo Bliayao took over as the leader of the Xieng Khouang Hmong when Moua Tong Ger retired from all official duties in early 1917. One reason the Xieng Khouang Hmong had tolerated the corvee system as long as they did was that the French had relied on Lo Bliayao to organize the work crews and pay them their wages, which up to that time amounted to two Laotian kip per day. Even so, it had become painfully clear that the wages were too low. Since the average yearly tax load per Hmong family had risen to around 13 kip, three weeks of work on the road crews (two unpaid, one paid) left a worker with just enough wages to cover his tax liability. It also cost him nearly a month's work on his own fields.

Though Lo Bliayao eventually demanded, and received, higher wages for the road crews, very little of it reach the workers. In place of two kip per day, workers were to be paid three. But instead of passing on this extra pay to the Hmong, Lo Bliayao set it aside for himself. There were two exceptions, however: his nephew, Lo Song Zeu and his son-in-law, Ly Foung. They were his top aids for the corvee project and received the full three kip per day for organizing the labor gangs and distributing the short wages.

Whether it was because they weren't allowed to share in the graft or because they couldn't stomach such calloused behavior toward fellow Hmong, the two assistants became increasingly disenchanted with their boss as they watched him become the richest Hmong in Laos. While the experience radicalized Lo Song Zeu and set him on the path of rebellion, Ly Foung's plan for revenge was more long range: to patiently work to advance the political careers of his sons and eventually take over the leadership of the Xieng Khouang Hmong. Lo Bliayao's deceit did not remain undetected. Whether, as one Hmong recounts, he arrogantly (and foolishly) told the

Hmong to ask the French why they were not receiving higher wages, or whether his aids quietly let it be known that Hmong on the road crews were being short changed, the truth of the matter became common knowledge and resulted in a general strike.

When Hmong selected for work crews did not show up, Lo Bliayao enlisted French aid to use colonial militiamen to intimidate the strikers and force them back to work. This did not put out the fire, it fanned the flames. The time was ripe for a general Hmong uprising in north eastern Laos. Indeed, in Vietnam one had already begun. The leader of the rebellion was Pa Chay.

PA CHAY

Pa Chay was born in a small village in southern China just a few miles from the Burmese border. Orphaned at a young age, he left China in his teens and migrated to north Vietnam where he was taken in by Song Tou, a member of the Vue clan who lived in a village near Dien Bien Phu. According to legend, Pa Chay was able to speak and write not only Chinese, but Vietnamese and Laotian, all without ever having attended school, the sort of thing one would expect from a Hmong messiah, although Pa Chay never claimed to be anything more than a messenger of the long awaited Hmong savior, a Hmong"John the Baptist"whose mission was to prepare the way for the master.

Pa Chay received this revelation sometime in 1917. A part of this revelation was that he must assume leadership of the Dien Bien Phu Hmong and lead them in a holy war against their Tai oppressors who, by their abusive treatment and excessive taxes, had reduced the Dien Bien Phu Hmong to near slavery and abject poverty. Vue Song Tou presumed Pa Chay had gone mad and tried to dissuade him from taking up arms. Fearful that the argument might turn violent, Vue Song Tou's wife tried to intercede and calm things down. It was too late, Pa Chay had already picked up a spear. Meant for her husband it caught her in the chest. When Pa Chay came to his senses he fled to the safety of the mountains.

Vue Song Tou ran to the authorities to report the incident and to beg for protection from Pa Chay. The treatment he received was hardly sympathetic. He was accused of being in league with his adopted son and imprisoned at Lai Chau (north of Dien Bien Phu) along with his four sons. During his incarceration, Vue Song Tou committed suicide by taking an overdose of opium.

Meanwhile, Pa Chay was busy organizing a rebellion. It was reported by some of his early followers that he used magic to gather a following and to authenticate his claim that he was sent by the Messiah to liberate the Hmong from their Tai oppressors. On one occasion, it is said, he fell into a deep trance before a number of

Hmong seated around him in a villager's home. To their astonishment he suddenly leaped from the floor right up through the roof of the house. When he descended through the roof a few moments later Pa Chay held several eggs which he placed in a rice grinder. After working the handle of the grinder, he retrieved the eggs. Not one of them was broken. In a related story, during a village celebration Pa Chay was supposed to have wadded up a piece of cotton and thrown it into the air where it miraculously exploded.

Pa Chay's first act of rebellion was to convince many of the Hmong around Dien Bien Phu to refuse to pay their taxes. The French responded by sending troops to the area, though they were unable to capture Pa Chay and were repeatedly ambushed by his guerrillas.

Again, Pa Chay supposedly employed magic to best the French. According to one Laotian Hmong, Vue Shue Long, every effort to capture Pa Chay failed. First, the French sent four soldiers to capture him. Pa Chay's men killed two and spared two, whom they released so the French would learn of Pa Chay's power. Unimpressed, the French sent twelve more soldiers. Ten were killed and two released. More soldiers were sent and more killed. Pa Chay sent no more than a few Hmong on these ambushes. And he was careful, for reasons only he understood, that the number sent was never odd. Pa Chay's followers were amazed by his ability to know when soldiers had been sent by the French and just the route they would take, which made ambushes easy.

The legend also tells how Pa Chay continued to use magic to insure the success of his rebellion. He performed the egg ceremony before sending his men out on a mission. Now, however, the eggs were distributed to the soldiers. Each wrote his name on his egg and placed it in the rice grinder with the others. Those whose eggs broke were exempted from the mission on the understanding that this was a message from heaven foretelling their injury or death. Those with unbroken eggs were guaranteed complete safety. Pa Chay also distributed sacred water to his men which was supposed to make them invulnerable to injury once they drank it.

As the rebellion progressed, Pa Chay introduced other ceremonies. He made a flag which he claimed was magical. It was placed in a special area. Before engaging the enemy he ordered his soldiers to throw spears at the flag. If any spear pierced the flag, Pa Chay took this as a bad omen, a sign that the time was not yet ripe for an attack. Pa Chay entrusted another magical flag, this one white, to a Hmong virgin, the seventeen year old Ngao Nzoua. Pa Chay told her that by waving the flag she could deflect bullets aimed at his soldiers. Ngao Nzoua led Pa Chay's soldiers into several battles against the French, each time protecting the Hmong with her white flag and, if we are to believe the French officers who witnessed the events, was never once struck by a French bullet.

In December of 1917, Pa Chay stepped up his campaign and ordered attacks on several Tai military posts around Dien Bien Phu. Pa Chay himself led eighty Hmong against one of them. After a brief struggle the Tai surrendered. According to legend, he spared their lives on condition they treat the Hmong fairly in the future.

Alarmed by Pa Chay's successes, the French sent the best of their troops stationed at Son La against him. The detachment was ambushed and badly mauled. More troops were sent, with similar results. For nearly a year Pa Chay bested the French in one engagement after another. Then the tide turned. By early 1919 Pa Chay had suffered numerous defeats and was forced to retreat across the Vietnamese border into Laos where he eventually sought refuge in Xieng Khouang province. There he encouraged the Xieng Khouang Hmong to join his rebellion, drive out the French and establish an independent Hmong kingdom with Dien Bien Phu as its capital.

Many Hmong responded to his call, among them the Lo kiatong's nephew, Lo Song Zeu, who assumed leadership of one contingent of the Xieng Khouang rebels. With the support of Pa Chay's guerrillas, the new rebels gained control of the province's highlands. From there they conducted successful attacks against major Tai, Lao and French installations in the region. During one of these attacks, Lo Song Zeu led the Hmong under his command on a detour to Lo Bliayao's house with the intention of settling an old score. After his men surrounded the house Lo Song Zeu called Lo Bliayao out. The kiatong emerged from his home and stood defiantly before his nephew. Lo Song Zeu ordered his men to open fire, but none wished to take responsibility for killing a kiatong and Lo Bliayao escaped.

The local French garrisons, manned mostly by Vietnamese and Laotians under the command of French officers, were no match for the Hmong. Each time they ventured into the mountains to crush the rebels the Hmong employed rock slides and home made artillery to drive the colonial troops back to the safety of their garrisons.

It was Hmong artillery more than the rock slides that demoralized the colonial militiamen. Each piece was constructed from a hollowed out tree trunk, about six inches in diameter and ten feet long. Once loaded with gun powder and topped with shot, the butt of the mini-cannon was braced against the ground while the barrel was placed in the V of a forked stick. Elevation was controlled by the placement of the forked stick along the length of the barrel. The cannon was fired by lighting a wick that ran from the powder to the cannon's mouth.

The utility of these cannons did not only lie with their killing power. They also had a marked psychological effect on the enemy.

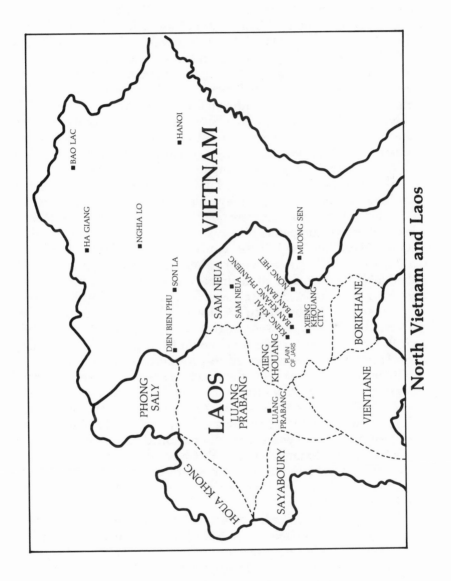

North Vietnam and Laos

The spray of shot nearly always struck one of the militiamen. This led to the belief that the rebels were incredible marksmen. Each time they fired their guns a militiaman fell. The Vietnamese and Laotians began to talk of the Hmong possessing magical powers. The resulting loss in morale brought the campaign against the Hmong rebels to a standstill. The tide would eventually turn, however.

One Laotian Hmong, eighty year old Vue Tong Leng, recalls that the event which precipitated this change was Lo Bliayao's eagerness to help the French suppress the rebellion. The kiatong explained to the French that, while the Hmong are indeed excellent marksmen, they are not as good as the superstitious Vietnamese and Laotian militiamen supposed. He informed them of the existence of the Hmong cannons and explained how they could be nullified. Since the wicks of the cannons could not be lit in the rain, Lo Bliayao urged the French to remain in their garrisons until the rainy season and then launch an all out campaign against the rebels.

It is unlikely, however, that Lo Bliayao's information was the primary reason for the rebels' eventual defeat. After finally realizing that the local garrisons were no match for the Hmong, the French brought in two companies of regular infantry from Vietnam to beef up the operation. With these reinforcements the French launched a vigorous pacification program aimed at depriving the rebels of their local support. Similar in aim, and more successful in outcome, to the United States'"Strategic Hamlet"program in South Vietnam in the early 1960s, the French pacification effort continued for nearly a year. Entire villages were singled out for relocation. First their crops were burned so that they would be of no use to the rebels, then the villagers were moved to protected areas.

By the beginning of 1921, the effects of the pacification program began to tell on Pa Chay's forces. Food and ammunition were everywhere in short supply. Casualties began to mount, and many rebels were captured, including Lo Song Zeu who offered his uncle bribes for his freedom and was eventually poisoned by one of his jailers. Morale was understandably low. Pa Chay saw many of his original converts leave the movement and return home to Vietnam. Soon the Xieng Khouang rebels were also returning to their homes. The revolt was all but over.

Pa Chay finally conceded defeat and vowed that he would never fight again. Accompanied by a few of his most loyal followers he left Xieng Khouang province and settled in northern Laos where he lived in a small hut in the heart of the forest. On November 17th, 1922, he was tracked down and assassinated.

To Pa Chay's followers the collapse of the great rebellion, later known as the"Mad Man's War"was due not to superior French forces or even to the treachery of Lo Bliayao. Pa Chay simply lost his magic. According to one legend, when Pa Chay suffered his first defeat against the French he tried to raise the spirits of his followers by announcing that heaven would soon send him something that would guarantee their victory. On the same day a large wooden box magically appeared in the village. There was a note attached that warned the box was not to be opened for three years. Several months later a curious Hmong opened the box and found it was full of grasshoppers. As Pa Chay was supposed to have explained later, if the box had remained closed for three years the insects would have been magically transformed into men and formed the nucleus of his future army. Now that they were gone he admitted the Hmong had no hope of winning the war against the French.

Another story tells how Ngao Nzoua, the Hmong virgin entrusted with the magic flag, was violated by some of Pa Chay's soldiers and as a result lost her power to protect the rebel troops. A related account indicates that it was not Ngao Nzoua who was violated, but a French woman. Pa Chay had ordered his men to take a town in which there were French civilians. Before they left for the mission he expressly warned them against committing any wicked act against French civilians, for to do so would lose them the support of heaven. Not heeding his warning his men raped and murdered a French woman. Pa Chay knew of the event the minute it occurred. And when the soldiers returned he informed them that their crime would cost them the war. A sign confirming this prediction supposedly occurred a short time later when Pa Chay performed the egg ceremony before leading his troops into battle. For the first time all of the eggs broke.

Like the explanation of his defeat, the account of Pa Chay's death blends fact with legend. Part of this legend is that Pa Chay predicted his own death. The night before he was assassinated he heard a tiger roar and a deer pawing the ground. He told his few remaining followers that this meant he would die the next day. He asked them to bury him in the forest on the spot where the deer had turned the earth to guarantee he would return in fifty years to once again lead the Hmong in their struggle for independence.

The identity of Pa Chay's assassins remains uncertain. By one account they were Kha tribesmen, bounty hunters eager to collect the price the French had placed on Pa Chay's head, which they delivered to the French as proof of his death. In another account, the assassins were Hmong — former rebels who had served under Pa Chay and to whom the French had promised 150 silver piasters if they could deliver Pa Chay to the French authorities at Luang Prabang. If they could not take him alive, then they were to bring his head. They were also to deliver his rifle, a one of a kind Hmong flintlock with a copper stalk. The French knew that a Hmong and his rifle are inseparable; he will part with it only in death. Since no Frenchman knew for sure what Pa Chay looked like, his rifle would constitute good evidence that the rebel leader had indeed been killed.

The two Hmong knew just where to find Pa Chay. And when they found him he did not put up a fight. He simply sat quietly in front of his hut, consigned to the fate which he himself had prophesied. After they shot him, they cut off his head, fetched his rifle and immediately set off for Luang Prabang and their reward.

As the story goes, the trip back was uneventful until they approached the Nam Ou River. That was when it began to rain. They had crossed the Nam Ou in a makeshift raft just a few days earlier. Since it was the beginning of the dry season the river was shallow and the crossing easy. They had pulled the raft up on the shore and marked the location so they could find it when they returned. Now, because of the unexpected downpour, when they found the raft the river was up by several feet, the current rapid, and the water churning. The two Hmong debated whether they should risk the crossing or wait out the storm. The lure of the reward waiting for them in Luang Prabang overpowered their good judgment; they decided to chance a crossing. They were no more than a few yards from the shore when they realized their mistake. They could not control the raft. The swift current whipped them around and then pulled them out to the middle of the river where the little craft bobbed and pitched uncontrollably for a few minutes before capsizing. The two Hmong struggled to right the raft, but it was no use. All they could do was hold on for dear life and trust that the raft would eventually come to shore downstream. By the time it did the river had claimed Pa Chay's head. Then, as suddenly as it had started, the rain stopped.

The two assassins spent a day and a half walking the river bank looking for Pa Chay's head. They found it lodged in the branches of a half submerged tree. But it wasn't Pa Chay's head. It was the head of one of the two assassins, Yang Koua, or at least a double since Yang Koua's head was still firmly attached to his shoulders.

The two were more than a little puzzled, they were frightened. Even so, there was the 150 silver piasters to consider. Despite their misgivings they continued on to Luang Prabang with the strange head and delivered it, along with Pa Chay's rifle, to the French.

The French officer was as mystified as the two Hmong when they presented him the head. Mystified or not, he knew one thing: unless the rebel leader was Yang Koua's twin brother the head did not belong to Pa Chay. On the other hand, there was the rifle. It seemed authentic enough. The officer lowered the reward to 100 piasters. The two Hmong complained. After some hard bargaining they received the full 150 piasters.

They left the head with the officer and set off for the local marketplace to buy a few things before returning home. On the way,

Yang Koua stumbled and fell. When his companion bent down to help him up he saw that Yang Koua had no head. It had been cut off, and the blood that covered his neck and shoulders was dark and dry as though he had been decapitated days earlier.

In this apocryphal account of Pa Chay's assassination, shortly after his death a new species of flower mysteriously appeared in the mountains of Laos. The flower is real, even if its origin is questionable. Its delicate blue blossoms dot the mountain slopes in the late fall. To the Laotian Hmong it is a living memorial to Pa Chay, and to this day they call it Pa Chay's Wheat.

Touby Lyfoung
(approximately 40 years old)

CHAPTER
8

TOUBY

When Pa Chay was assassinated in 1922 the Hmong rebellion he inspired officially ended. Ironically, in an earlier and equally bloody suppression of a Hmong rebellion in China, events had already been set in motion that would culminate in the rise of another Hmong leader, Touby Lyfoung, whose renown would eventually rival even Pa Chay's. Like Pa Chay, Touby was committed to Hmong independence. But unlike Pa Chay, he sought to achieve this through political reform rather than rebellion. A consummate politician, Touby assumed the leadership of the Laotian Hmong in the 1940s and was instrumental in shaping the history of the Hmong in that country for the next two decades.

In the early 1860s, Ly Nghia Vue led the remnants of his clan from southern Szechwan to Laos and to a new life. His father remained behind to hold the pass, as it were, against Chinese troops engaged in one of the many campaigns to crush the Great Panthay Rebellion led by the Haw.

The Hmong in both Yunnan and Szechwan provinces had long maintained amicable relations with the Haw who regularly traded with them. When the Hmong took up opium cultivation, their relationship with the Haw was strengthened, for the Haw served as their middlemen, purchasing Hmong opium and then delivering it to sometimes distant markets. And so it was natural, once the Haw were drawn into armed conflict with representatives of the empire, that the Hmong often fought at their side.

Not all Hmong, however. Some tried to remain neutral, though without much success since their protests of neutrality were seldom thought genuine by Chinese generals charged with pacifying the region. Consequently, many neutralist Hmong were drawn into the conflict simply out of self-preservation. Some, no doubt, harbored ill feelings toward their Hmong brothers who had openly allied themselves with the Haw and by doing so made life miserable for the rest of the Hmong who wanted nothing more than to be left alone. There is reason to suppose that the Szechwan Ly who migrated to Laos belonged to this group and that they continued to nurture ill-feelings toward Yunnanese and Szechwan Hmong who had, by their active participation in the conflict, forced them to abandon their homes and fields for a strange land.

In 1865 another member of the Ly clan arrived in Laos. He settled near Nong Het where the earlier contingent of Ly had located. Even though he belonged to the same clan, the newcomer was not welcome. It was not only that he was from Yunnan while they were from Szechwan. His traveling companion to Laos had been a Haw. This was construed as evidence that he had not been a neutralist during the rebellion and was one of the troublemakers who had forced the Szechwan Ly to abandon China for Laos.

Obliged to live apart from his fellow clansmen, the ostracized Ly joined a small Hmong village near Nong Het, where he married and raised three sons. One of them, Ly Foung, was unusually bright, having mastered at an early age not only Chinese, but Vietnamese and French. He seems also to have quite early set his mind to removing the taint on his family name by marrying into one of the most prominent of the Laotian Hmong families, that of the Lo kiatong, Lo Bliayao.

Ly Foung's marriage to Lo Bliayao's daughter, Lo May, took place in 1918. The marriage was reportedly by abduction, though it is inconceivable that Ly Foung would have attempted anything so bold without first having made certain that a marriage by force would meet with the Lo kiatong's approval. Ly Foung found immediate employment as the kiatong's personal secretary and the fortunes of the once outcast Yunnanese Ly family improved both economically and socially. Ly Foung's new employment pulled the family out of poverty, and his close association with the Lo kiatong meant the Ly Foungs were at last accepted by the Szechwan Ly as clansman in good standing.

RIFT BETWEEN THE LO AND LY

Ly Foung and Lo May had two children, a son and a daughter — Touby and Mousong. While Lo May must have taken considerable pride in the fact that little Touby was every bit as precocious as his father, her marriage turned sour when Ly Foung took a second wife whom he favored over her. While such favoritism was contrary to the spirit of Hmong polygamy, there was little Lo May could do but complain, and for which she reportedly received numerous beatings, something that was also contrary to the spirit of Hmong marriage, polygamous or not. No doubt relatives on both sides tried to bring Ly Foung to his senses, but before anything was resolved Lo May committed suicide by taking an overdose of opium.

Not only did Lo May's suicide cause a serious rift between Ly Foung and Lo Bliayao it strained relations between the Lo and Ly clans. In 1922, Ly Foung was dismissed from his position as Lo Bliayao's personal secretary. Sensing that tensions between the two clans might lead to armed conflict, Hmong elders approached the French and recommended that authority over the district of Nong Het be divided between Lo and Ly. With the memory of the Pa Chay rebellion still quite green, the French were eager to do anything to smooth rough waters. The Ly were given authority over the Nong Het subdistrict of Keng Khoai and the Lo were allowed to administer the subdistrict of Phac Boun. For over a decade, until Lo Bliayao's death in 1935, an uneasy peace was maintained by means of this compromise.

It was during this period that the first Laotian Hmong attended school. Moua Nao Tou, the head of the Moua clan in Xieng Khouang province, was the first to send his children to school; in addition to his two sons, Yang and Chu Chao, he financed the education of three of his nephews, Ya Tong, Chue No and Nao Pao. In due course, two more Hmong began their lessons at the French elementary school (Groupe Scholare) in Xieng Khouang city. They were Ly Foung's sons, Touby and Tou Zeu. Of the handful of Hmong children who entered school at this time, only the two Ly boys went on to the Lycee and received baccalaureate degrees. Touby also attended college at the School of Law and Administration at Vientiane. And Tou Zeu was one of the first Hmong to graduate from college.

The value of a French education for future Hmong politicians was not lost on Lo Bliayao who packed up three of his younger sons, Faydang, Nghia Vue and Fong, and enrolled them in the French school. The kiatong's eldest son, Song Tou, was too old to attend school and was appointed tasseng (administrative head) of the Keng Khoai subdistrict of Nong Het. The aging kiatong pinned his hopes on Song Tou to take over after his death and outwit and outmaneuver the Ly clan in what had become a struggle for political leadership of all the Hmong of Xieng Khouang providence. Lo Bliayao was certain that before his body was cold Ly Foung would begin to jockey for power and, if successful, pass it on to his talented son, Touby. The kiatong must have expected the worst for on his deathbed he left instructions that should the Ly begin to gain the upper hand his family must immediately sacrifice several oxen as a sign to his spirit to return to Nong Het and help Song Tou in his struggle against the Ly.

Song Tou was certainly in need of any help he could get. Lo Bliayao died in 1935, and in the years that followed Song Tou's political incompetence became a matter of record. Instead of discharging his duties as tasseng he spent his days hunting and gambling. This got him into trouble with the French. While the colonial administration might look the other way when native administrators abused citizens, they considered tax collection a sacred trust. Not only did Song Tou fail to regularly collect taxes, by one account he sometimes used tax revenues to pay off gambling debts.

When Ly Foung offered to make up for the lost tax revenue out of his own pocket the French displayed their gratitude by dismissing Song Tou and giving Ly Foung his post. Ly Foung immediately appointed Touby tasseng over Phac Boun, expanding the Ly power base which now encompassed nearly all of Nong Het district.

Song Tou and the Lo clan were disgraced. Song Tou appears to have been less affected by his fall from power than his younger brother Faydang who travelled all the way to the Royal Palace at Luang Prabang to lodge a complaint. Prince Phetsarath granted him an audience as well as a concession. While the decision of the French could not be reversed, Phetsarath promised that on Ly Foung's death, authority over Keng Khoai would revert to the Lo clan and Faydang himself would be made tasseng of the subdistrict. It was an attractive compromise since Ly Foung was already quite old and not in the best of health. In fact, he died just nine months later, in September of 1939.

The French, however, chose not to honor Phetsarath's promise to Faydang. The tasseng position was given to Touby instead. One reason for the bad faith was the perception that Faydang had obstinately defied French authority by going over the heads of local colonial administrators and directly appealing to the royal court at Luang Prabang for a redress of grievances. Put simply, the man was not to be trusted. Of equal importance, however, was Touby himself who not only spoke fluent French and was something of a Francophile but whose training in French law and administration, as well as his talents as a bureaucrat, made him an ideal choice. In fact, the French were as eager as Touby to see his political star rise.

LOOKING TO THE FUTURE

Touby's ambitions were larger than even the French imagined. It was to build a Hmong power base that enjoyed French confidence and support and then to use it as a lever to gain concessions for schools and government positions for the Hmong and eventually to demand the integration of the Hmong into Laotian national politics.

At the time, most Laotian Hmong would have viewed Touby's aspirations as hopelessly utopian. They had always been treated as second class citizens by the ethnic Lao and exploited by Laotian officials. It was particularly humiliating to the proud Hmong to have to literally grovel before Laotian bureaucrats, crawling on hands and knees, head down, up the steps of the official's office to his desk where they had to kneel patiently until the Laotian recognized their presence. Trade with the Laotians was a constant reminder to the Hmong of their inferior status. They were charged several times more for goods than Laotians, and when they sought employment in lowland towns their wages were invariably half of what a native Lao received for the same work. Few Hmong expected this to change. The general perception was that the most that could be hoped for was an increase in village autonomy so that the Hmong might get by with as little contact with Laotian officials as possible.

The principal strategy behind Touby's plan to raise both the social status and political clout of the Hmong was at once simple and persuasive. It was to make the French dependent on the Hmong. Should such a dependency come to pass, the Hmong could pressure the French to exert their considerable influence over Laotian political elites to concede political power to the Hmong.

Whether Touby had, at this early date, worked out in his mind the details of what this concession should include, a reading of his later actions suggests that quite early on he considered it imperative for the Hmong to find representation in the councils of the national government and to be granted political autonomy at the local level.

These were actually two sides of the same coin. Local political autonomy would bring an end to the exploitation of the Hmong by local authorities who would now be Hmong rather than ethnic Lao. And with more Hmong occupying positions of power in provincial bureaucracies the level of political maturity of the Hmong would naturally rise and with it their chances of becoming a permanent political force in the country.

This was not just wishful thinking. Laotian demographics dictated it as the natural course of Laotian politics. While ethnic minorities make up a large proportion of the populations of every nation in southeast Asia, only Laos can justifiably be called a nation of minorities. Fewer than 50% of Laotians are ethnic Lao, the rest are Kha (Khmu), Tai, Akha, Lolo, Lisu, Lahu, Yao, Vietnamese, and Hmong. The ethnic Lao monopolized power only because the other ethnic minorities remained politically backward. Touby meant to turn things around, at least as far as the Hmong were concerned. With French patronage, the Hmong would have representation in the national government and establish a political base at the provincial level of sufficient size and strength to give their representatives bargaining power with the Lao elite. In time, this would translate into new schools for Hmong children who would, at last, be able to compete on an equal footing with the Lao. There would also be new hospitals. And new roads would be constructed to integrate Hmong communities into regional markets, permitting the diversification of the Hmong economy and economic growth.

However, before all this could come about the Hmong would have to become indispensable to the French. Hmong opium was an obvious candidate to satisfy this requirement for the French opium monopoly was one of the most profitable enterprises of the colonial administration. But opium was not the only possible candidate. The Japanese occupation of Indochina between 1940 and 1945 provided Touby the opportunity to demonstrate the military value of the Laotian Hmong to the French.

SUPPORTING THE MAQUIS

When France fell to Germany in 1940, it was relatively easy for the Japanese to obtain the concession from the colonial administration for the free movement of Japanese troops in French Indochina. Isolated from the home government in France, the French colonial administration headed by Admiral Decoux adopted a policy of business as usual. No military action was mounted against Japanese troops, and every effort was made to avoid confrontations that might antagonize the Japanese and lead to reprisals. For their part, the Japanese were perfectly content to permit the French to administer Indochina so long as it did not hamper the Japanese occupation or hinder efforts to monopolize exports of rice and certain minerals such as tin, tungsten, and manganese needed by Japanese arms and munitions factories to meet the growing demands of the Japanese war machine in the pacific.

With the liberation of Paris in August 1944 all this soon changed. De Gaulle quickly set about planning a resistance movement in Indochina. French commandos (maquis) were parachuted onto the Plain of Jars in November with orders to establish guerrilla bases. When Japanese intelligence learned of the event it was misinterpreted as a preparation for an allied invasion of Indochina, a view that was reinforced several months later by U.S. air raids on Japanese ships in Vietnamese harbors and rail yards in the Red River Delta region of north Vietnam. In March 1945 the Japanese moved quickly to disarm and imprison thirteen thousand French soldiers. Some French garrisons, like the those in Hue and Tonkin, put up a fierce resistance, inflicting heavy casualties on the Japanese before surrendering.

In Laos, new life was breathed into the French resistance when more French commandos were parachuted in from India. The commandos received much needed logistical support from a handful of colonial army officers and noncoms who, with the help of Touby and his Hmong partisans, had managed to elude the Japanese dragnet. When the Japanese caught wind of Hmong involvement in the operation they arrested and imprisoned Touby. He might very well have been executed had it not been for the intercession of Monsignor Mazoyer, the Catholic bishop of Vientiane, who advised the Japanese that mistreatment of one of the leaders of the Hmong could easily invite a Hmong uprising. Touby was released, wiser but hardly repentant. In short order he presented himself to Captain Bichelot, who commanded the French maquis at Phoun San on the eastern edge of the Plain of Jars, and pledged Hmong support to the beleaguered commandos. Since the Hmong did not have modern weapons and were no match for Japanese units equipped with machine guns they played chiefly a support role for the maquis, serving as guides and interpreters and hiding French officers from the Japanese in Hmong villages.

Hmong support was not without its costs. In an attempt to intimidate the Hmong and to coerce them into abandoning the maquis the Japanese repeatedly attacked Hmong villages, nearly all defenseless, suspected of helping the French. It was testimony to Touby's rising popularity that despite the attacks the Hmong rallied solidly behind him. The French were appreciative, too, promising Touby that, at the close of the war, the Hmong would be guaranteed positions in the colonial administration and especially in the ministry of education to insure that there would be schools for their children.

Not all the Hmong supported the French. Faydang, still seething over the French refusal to honor Prince Phetsarath's promise to grant him the tasseng position at Keng Khoai, actively collaborated with the Japanese in hunting down French commandos. His guiding principle, which he would publicly avow a year later, was simple: "Whatever Touby and his men do, I and my men will do the opposite."

REOCCUPATION

When the war was over the French lost no time attempting to regain control of Indochina. They reoccupied the southern delta region with relative ease, though to France's discredit this was accomplished with gratuitous savagery. The reoccupation of the north was another matter.

There were nearly two hundred thousand Chinese troops in north Vietnam when the Japanese surrendered. The French paid a high price to get them to leave. In February 1946, France signed the Chungking agreement in which China promised to pull all troops out of north Vietnam for France's promise to relinquish its concessions in Shanghai, Tientsin, Hankow, and Canton.

The next item on the agenda was the Vietminh. Supported by the U.S., Ho Chi Minh had organized the Vietnamese military resistance against the Japanese. The Vietminh army, led by Vo

Nguyen Giap, had grown to dangerous proportions, which became all the more ominous when the Japanese, preferring to surrender to Asians rather than westerners, handed over their weapons to the Vietminh. On the political side, the Vietminh had spearheaded an independence movement, conducted elections, and installed Ho as the president of an independent Vietnam. While the French refused to formally acknowledge the legitimacy of the new government, they nevertheless invited Ho to Paris in the hope that he might be persuaded to accept the status quo ante with only minor modifications. To strengthen their position, the French installed a puppet regime in the south which claimed to represent the entire nation. Once in Paris, Ho realized the hopelessness of his position and was forced to accept a loose agreement that included a national referendum on the independence issue that was to be followed with a resumption of negotiations sometime in 1947 on full Vietnamese independence.

An uneasy peace between the Vietminh and the French forces who had reoccupied the Red River delta region was shattered in late November of 1946 when a dispute between Vietminh and French custom officers over tax authority in Haiphong harbor led to an exchange of gunfire. The French then shelled the city of Haiphong, killing some six thousand Vietnamese citizens. Within a month the Vietminh responded with coordinated attacks against French military and civilians in Hanoi and guerrilla raids on French installations throughout Vietnam before retreating into the north Vietnamese highlands and settling in for a long war.

Compared to the troubles the French encountered in north Vietnam, the reoccupation of Laos was relatively uncomplicated. True, troops had to be held back from northwestern Laos until China's 93rd Infantry Division pulled out. The 93rd had remained in Laos after the agreed upon withdrawal date so they could confiscate all the Hmong opium they could carry home. For the French the delay was an inconvenience, nothing more.

Of greater concern was the Laotian independence movement led by Prince Phetsarath. The movement had earlier received an unexpected shot in the arm when, in March 1945, the Japanese occupation force imprisoned all French colonial administrators and demanded that king Sisavang Vong proclaim Laos an independent state and formally sever all political ties with France. Phetsarath quickly persuaded the Japanese to fill the Laotian civil service with pro-independence Laotians. By October of that same year he succeeded in organizing a new government (the Lao Isalla or Free Laos) in Vientiane. A constitution was drawn up and members of a provisional people's assembly selected.

In response, elements of the French commandos who had been parachuted onto the Plain of Jars in northeastern Laos several months earlier occupied the royal palace at Luang Prabang and forced the aging king to renounce independence and strip Phetsarath of all power. Though Phetsarath felt obliged to obey the edict of his king, other members of the Lao Isalla turned to the Vietminh for support, granting Vietminh military units complete freedom of operation in Laos. Vietminh agents were hurriedly dispatched to Laotian towns with large Vietnamese populations where they encourage their Vietnamese brothers to whip up support among the ethnic Lao for the Vietnamese communists.

The Vietminh flag waved in many of these communities. However, in Xieng Khouang province the Vietnamese community at Khang Khay did more than just wave flags, they armed themselves with weapons stolen from the Japanese and declared Xieng Khouang a prefecture of Vietnam. With the arrival of Vietminh troops from Hanoi, joined later by units of the Lao Isalla dispatched from Vientiane, the Vietnamese dug in and prepared to defend the newly claimed territory from being reoccupied by the French.

SETTLING OLD SCORES

By this time Touby's forces had received modern weapons and he was eager for every opportunity to prove the worth his Hmong guerrillas to the French. In November 1945, in a joint action with French commandos, Touby and his Hmong routed the Vietminh forces and drove them out of Xieng Khouang province. By January, when French reinforcements arrived in the province, the Lao Isalla partisans had already departed, retreating across the Plain of Jars to safety. Fearing French and perhaps even Hmong reprisals, thousands of Vietnamese living in Xieng Khouang packed up and left the province for Vietnam. With French approval Hmong settled in the abandoned villages, many of which contained the best farm land in the region.

Now that the province was firmly under French control, Touby turned his attention to the matter of settling old scores. Lo Faydang was in the area, still carrying on his war against the French, his most recent triumph being an ambush against sixty troops commanded by two French officers. Armed only with traditional crossbows his Hmong killed eight of the soldiers and sent the rest packing for the safety of their garrison.

Touby itched to get his hands on the rebel. When he learned from two of his partisans that Faydang's brother, Lo Nghia Vue, was in Nong Het visiting his father-in-law, Moua Nao Tou, he sent thirty of his soldiers to capture him.

Nghia Vue had an ulterior motive for visiting his father-in-law. Moua Nao Tou was a direct descendant of the Moua kiatongs, the leader of his clan, and was much respected by the leaders of the other clans. When Touby's work for the French maquis took him to Nong Het he often stayed at the Moua home. Nghia Vue believed that if anyone could help mend the rift between the Lo and Ly clans it was Moua Nao Tou. When he broached the issue the old man immediately agreed to act as an intermediary and suggested that if Faydang was sincere about returning to the fold a simple monetary penalty might be sufficient to settle matters. He even offered to help raise the needed funds if that proved necessary.

Nghia Vue went to sleep that night with high hopes that an end to the clan feud was near at hand. They were shattered when he was dragged out of bed by Touby's partisans in the middle of the night. Moua Nao Tou was furious that Touby had so little respect for their friendship and his own standing in the Hmong community that he would sanction the raid. He ordered the soldiers out of his house. Not only did they refuse to obey, they proceeded to beat Nghia Vue, breaking his ribs and knocking him unconscious.

By this time other villagers had gathered around the home, most of them Moua clansmen. One of them, Moua Chia Xa, confronted the soldiers. He pointed to Moua Nao Tou and asked why they did not show him the respect he deserved. When one of Touby's partisans suggested that perhaps Moua Chia Xa would like a little of what they had given Nghia Vue, Moua Chia Xa went to the front door of the house and called his fellow clansmen to arms. In short order a small army of Moua riflemen were gathered in front of the house. "If it is a fight you want," Moua Chia Xa announced, "we will oblige you." To prevent bloodshed, Moua Nao Tou ordered the partisans to take their prisoner and leave the village. Though Moua Nao Tou did not like turning Nghia Vue over to them, it meant the partisans could leave and still save face. He also knew they did not relish the thought of returning to Touby with the news that in the process of attempting to capture Nghia Vue they had started a feud with the Moua clan. Touby's partisans hastily carted Nghia Vue out of the house and left for the village of Phou Do where Touby was headquartered at the time.

When Nghia Vue recovered from his beating Touby had him taken to Xieng Khouang city, perhaps with the intention of handing him over to the French. On the way Nghia Vue escaped into the forest and made his way back to his brother's village near Nong Het. When Touby learned of the escape, he decided to attack Faydang before he had a chance to retaliate for his brother's mistreatment. But when Touby arrived at the village with sixty of his men he found it deserted. Faydang had been warned of the attack and moved his forces across the Vietnamese border to the village of Mouong Sen.

Touby opened a brief, but inconclusive, round of negotiations with Faydang by mail. Bargaining from a position of strength, Touby expected Faydang to be conciliatory. He was not. Though

Faydang desired peace between the two clans, he was unwilling to admit guilt when he believed it was all on the other side. It was Touby and the French who had wronged him and not the other way around. Touby rounded up his men and headed across the border for Mouong Sen. Only a few Lo clansmen were killed during the assault. Faydang and the rest of his men (about two hundred in all) escaped and fled deeper into Vietnam.

Shortly after this incident, Faydang made contact with the Vietminh who promised to support him in his struggle against Touby. Two months later he was guiding a Vietminh column into Laos. The die was cast. After that the French considered him a communist, a conviction that was reinforced in the summer of 1950 by Faydang's participation (as a minister without portfolio) in the Pathet Lao's First Resistance Congress. Branded a communist and outlaw by the French, it was impossible for Faydang to ever again live freely among the Laotian Hmong unless the French were driven out of Laos. And when the Americans replaced the French, it meant he would never be free unless the Vietnamese backed Pathet Lao (Laotian Communists) succeeded in their efforts transform Laos into a communist state.

TOUBY AND OPIUM

As Touby had hoped, Hmong support for the French maquis during the Japanese occupation fortified the ties between the French and Hmong. There would be many other occasions when the Hmong would demonstrate their military value, not only to the French but to the Americans who, through the mechanism of SEATO (Southeast Asia Treaty Organization), became increasingly involved in Laotian politics and military affairs following the 1954 Geneva Conference in which Laos was at last granted status as an independent state. But Touby had not relied on Hmong military prowess alone to ingratiate his people to the French. He very early realized that Hmong opium might prove an even more effective means to this end.

When shipping to Indochina was interrupted during the Second World War the French were no longer able to rely on imported opium to supply the needs of the colonial opium monopoly. They therefore turned to domestic sources in hopes of filling the gap. Touby immediately realized the implications for the Hmong. As the principal producers of raw opium in Laos the Hmong were in a good bargaining position to gain French support for greater Hmong political and economic equality in Laos.

But before this could come to pass the Hmong would have to dramatically increase the size of their opium harvests. Touby used his influence with the French to land a position on the Opium Purchasing Board, the first Hmong to ever do so. Touby sat on the board for eight years, long enough for the transformation of much of the traditional Hmong economy in Laos from subsistence to cash crop farming, and to increase the yield of the annual opium harvest from around fifteen to forty tons. The key to this transformation was new taxes. With Touby's blessing, the existing per capita tax was doubled. Given the meager incomes of Hmong farmers, the tax asked the impossible. Many Hmong did not earn that much in a year. Touby knew this, but then the object of the tax was not to directly increase tax revenues but to indirectly increase opium production. And to serve this end the new tax had a loophole. It was simply this. The Tax could be paid in kind rather than specie. The specific amount was two kilograms of raw opium, nearly twice what the average Hmong farmer harvested prior to the new tax scheme which went into effect in 1943.

Few Hmong welcomed the new tax. Even fewer understood Touby's reasons for backing it. Certainly he did not make the rounds of Hmong villages advertising the tax as a way to expand opium production and increase French dependency on the Hmong. It is doubtful many would have found the scheme plausible anyway. And even if this were not so, the coercive nature of the new plan was sufficient to make it unacceptable.

Realizing that the incentives for evading the new tax would be high, Touby made Hmong authorities responsible for collecting the tax and offered them incentives for performing their jobs well. The minimum aggregate tax was determined by a census. Village chiefs informed sub-district heads of the number of adult males in their village. This information was passed on to the Hmong tasseng who counted up the total and delivered the figure to the French. On the assumption that the lion's share of the tax would be paid in opium, the census provided the opium board with a ball park figure of the amount of Hmong opium that would be available to the French opium monopoly. However, the estimate was only reliable so long as the Hmong paid the tax in opium rather than piasters. And this would only occur if they did not sell their opium on the black market and pay the tax out of the proceeds.

Since the in-kind provision of the tax fixed the price of a kilogram of raw opium at a little over two piasters, Hmong farmers had every reason to sell their harvest to private agents if they offered them a better price, which was highly probable since the cessation of imports had caused the black market price of opium to skyrocket. The simple solution was to prohibit private agents, mostly Chinese Haw, from purchasing Hmong opium in the prime opium growing provinces of Xieng Khouang and Sam Neua provinces. While a French edict to this effect substantially achieved this goal, it did little to prevent enterprising Hmong from taking the place of the interdicted

Haw. Indeed, the likelihood that this would occur was extremely high. With the Haw removed from the scene, Hmong agents would enjoy a near monopoly status and be able to amass a fortune by making the rounds of Hmong villages and selling the opium they collected to traders in Vietnam. This might have the salutary effect of increasing opium production but at the expense of the opium monopoly which would face stiff competition from a healthy black market.

To counter this, Touby persuaded the French to offer a cash bonus to Hmong officials charged with collecting taxes. Village chiefs, sub-district officials and tassengs who delivered opium in excess of census estimates received kickbacks proportionate to the surplus. Judging by the fortunes made by some officials, amounting in certain cases to hundreds of bars of silver, the program was a remarkable success. The only drawback was that successful efforts by local officials to police the black market reduced the potential income of Hmong farmers and created hard feelings between them and their leaders. Even so, Touby's prestige remained high. Not only did the French increase Hmong autonomy at the local level, they became less tolerant of Lao abuses of the Hmong. For the first time a marked, albeit grudging, deference was being shown by native Lao in Xieng Khouang province toward their Hmong neighbors. For Touby, this was just one of many changes he was certain would inevitably follow increasing French dependence on Hmong opium.

However, by 1946, events forced Touby to ponder whether it was feasible in the long run to rely on Hmong opium to gain political leverage with the French, for in that year France at last gave in to international public opinion, officially dismantled the opium monopoly, and launched a five year program to cure opium addiction in Indochina.

If the colonial administration had been sincere the program might very well have succeeded for by the early 1950s the post-war surge in imported opium declined precipitously and then came to an abrupt halt. This was the result of two events: the 1949 communist takeover of China and the 1953 United Nations protocol on international opium trade.

Under Mao, China finally eradicated opium production on Chinese soil. The move was not entirely humanitarian. Yunnan was the principal opium producing province in the country, and much of the opium smuggled out of the province into Burma was controlled by the remnants of Chiang Kai-shek's Nationalist Army. Revenue from these operations kept both the army and Chiang's dreams of a counter-revolution alive. Every poppy field eliminated in the province reduced that revenue which, by the mid- 1950s, declined to almost zero. Not only did this affect the fortunes of Chiang Kai-shek, it cut Indochina off from this once lucrative source of raw opium and increased its dependency on imports from the Middle East, and in particular from Iran which had become the major exporter of raw opium in the area.

Iran, however, was unable to make up the difference. Indeed, it could not even maintain its customarily high level of exports, for as one of the signatories to the 1953 U.N. protocol, Iran was obliged to reduce its opium production. By 1955 this obligation was nearly met for the opium harvest yielded only 4.1 tons of raw opium, approximately 16% of what Iran had produced five years earlier.

If this dramatic reduction in imports had been coupled with a zealous program of opium crop reduction in Indochina, the French could have significantly diminished the size of the narcotics market in southeast Asia. This did not occur. Instead, southeast Asian opium production was dramatically increased, and continued to increase for another fifteen years until, by 1970, southeast Asia not only produced enough opium to supply its own markets but had become the major supplier of raw opium to the illicit international narcotics market.

A principal cause of the failure of the French to reduce opium production in Indochina was that, whatever the official declaration, they did everything to expand it. The opium monopoly did not actually disappear, it simply went underground. And for good reason. The financially strapped colonial administration was in desperate need of funds for the war against the Vietminh. Correspondingly, Hmong opium increased in importance. But this was not only because it was a crucial source of revenue; it was also because the Hmong were playing an ever more active role in the war itself and purchasing their opium was perceived as an important way to retain their loyalty.

At least this was the situation in the early 1950s. However, in 1946, when the French officially dismantled the opium monopoly and the war with the Vietminh was just heating up, the incentive to increase opium production had not been so high. It is possible that Touby sensed that the Hmong were at a crossroad. For the short term, the French would continue to purchase Hmong opium. Indeed, a 1948 edict issued by the High Commissioner for Indochina granted the Hmong a virtual monopoly in opium farming in Laos. On the other hand, Touby knew full well at that time that one of the reasons the French were purchasing nearly every kilo of opium harvested by the Hmong was to keep it out of the hands of the Vietminh who could exchange opium for arms on the Chinese border and outfit a full division with the harvest from one province. If the Vietminh were to lay their hands on the majority of Hmong opium in Laos and north Vietnam they could easily outfit an entire army, for in 1947 alone the estimated value of the opium harvest was 400 million piasters, nearly equal to the revenues for rice exports for all of Indochina for that same year. But purchasing Hmong opium just to keep it out of the hands of the Vietminh was not the sort of relationship Touby wanted between the Hmong and French. It made the Hmong and their opium a nuisance which circumstances forced the French to tolerate—hardly the kind of situation that increased French dependency on the Hmong.

Fortunately, the French High Command was already considering an expansion of a montagnard supported maquis, modeled after the joint operations that had functioned so well during the Japanese occupation, into a major guerrilla force that would employ the same hit and run tactics against the Vietminh that the communists used with devastating consequences against the French Expeditionary Corps. And, because of their previous support, the Hmong occupied a pivotal place in these ruminations.

In 1948 Touby was flown to Saigon to discuss the possibility of launching a much expanded Hmong maquis. While it would take nearly two more years for the French to fully commit to the plan, Touby realized that whatever the ultimate fate of Hmong opium the chances were good that the French would continue to depend heavily on his people, this time not as opium farmers but as guerrillas.

Thus, by 1950, Touby was pleased to acknowledge that all of his earlier fears about the declining utility of the Hmong for the French had been entirely unfounded. Now not only did the French need the Hmong for their war, it was clear that they meant to finance many of their operations from opium revenues.

Beginning in 1951, and continuing until 1954 with the full knowledge and support from the High Command of the French Expeditionary Corps, a secret operation dubbed "Operation X" supplied much needed revenue for clandestine military operations in Indochina. Its purpose was to airlift Hmong opium from northeastern Laos to Saigon where it was sold to representatives of international narcotics syndicates and the revenues set aside for the provisioning and training of French sponsored guerrillas. The first major shipment was actually stored in a military warehouse and accidently discovered by a French customs inspector, causing a considerable scandal. More circumspect methods were employed after this incident.

Touby's role in "Operation X" was to collect the shipments from Hmong farmers. Whenever he had gathered close to a ton of raw opium he was flown to Saigon where Le Van Vien, former head of a South Vietnamese criminal syndicate and then Chief of the Saigon police, received the illicit goods and tendered payment. Out of this sum Touby set aside five thousand silver piasters that were earmarked for training and equipping his Hmong maquis. The rest was distributed as payment to the farmers who had supplied the opium for the transaction. During this brief period nearly $4 million was collected for the support of Hmong guerrillas under French command.

With the French dependent on Hmong guerrillas, and the revenue from Hmong opium set aside to support them, Touby had every reason to be optimistic about future relations between the French and his people. Indeed, that relationship had already begun to pay large dividends to the Hmong. In 1946 the French granted autonomous status to Laos as a free state in the French Union and helped organize elections for a national assembly. In Xieng Khouang province a Hmong stood for one of the seats. He was Toulia Ly-foung, Touby's older brother. Not only did Toulia win the election, he pressed hard in the national assembly for greater recognition of the rights of ethnic minorities at both the national and provincial levels of government. Though the other deputies to the assembly refused to deal with the issue, it was settled for them by a new constitution which, due partially to pressures from the French, contained provisions that guaranteed equal citizenship rights to all Laotians regardless of ethnic origin, and provided for proportional representation of ethnic minorities on the provincial councils. This resulted in the creation of two new Hmong subdistricts (cantons) in Xieng Khouang province and Touby's appointment as a deputy to the provincial governor (and former schoolmate), Chao Say Kham. At the time the position offered Touby greater power than a seat in the national assembly, for it gave him the opportunity to consolidate Hmong political power in the province and work for an expansion of the number of Hmong cantons, which eventually numbered twenty-four (a seven canton increase since the end of the Second World War).

Even greater political victories were to come, but what Touby could not foresee at the time was that the French were near the end of their rule in Indochina, and if the Hmong were to have sponsors for their cause they would eventually be forced to look elsewhere.

When the Americans took over from the French they became the likely candidate, but by that time Touby's very success with the French damaged his cause with the Americans who considered the French bunglers for having lost Indochina. However, another Laotian Hmong, a professional soldier by training and temperament, would rise to take Touby's place as the representative of his people before a foreign power. The Americans would lavish far more on the Hmong than the French could have ever afforded, had they even had the will to attempt it. But, in the end, the Americans would also demonstrate that they were no more adept at governing Indochina than the French, and certainly no more faithful to the Hmong who supported them.

CHAPTER

9

THE FALL OF TONKIN

While Touby was busy collecting opium and organizing Hmong guerrilla units to combat incursions of Vietminh in northern Laos, the French had their hands full with the Vietminh in northern Vietnam. In January 1950, fifteen Vietminh battalions overwhelmed a small French outpost in the Black River valley, due east of Dien Bien Phu. This offensive was followed by another, and larger, operation further north close to the Chinese border. Several towns were taken and French forces badly mauled.

A few months later, in May, four Vietminh battalions, newly trained and supplied by the Communist Chinese, engaged and routed three companies of French infantry defending the border town of Dong Khe located on the edge of Colonial Road 4, a single lane dirt road that ran from Cao Bang in the north all the way to the Gulf of Tonkin. Since the road was the only link the French had with the north they quickly organized an airborne strike force to retake Dong Khe and regain a foothold on Colonial 4. The town was recaptured but only after French forces suffered heavy casualties.

An urgent request was made to France for reinforcements to keep the road open. Not only was the request denied, a force reduction of nine thousand men was ordered. It could not have come at a worse time for Dong Khe was attacked again in September, leaving Cao Bang isolated in the north. Since the mandated troop reduction ruled out a major offensive to regain control of the north, the French decided to withdraw existing troops to the security of the Red River delta. The commander of the garrison at Cao Bang was ordered to immediately evacuate all of the garrison's troops, as well as all Cao Bang civilians, after blowing up the garrison's heavy equipment, including trucks and jeeps. He was then to lead the evacuees south to Dong Khe. A task force of nearly four thousand

147

was already on Colonial Road 4 rushing to Dong Khe. Its mission was to retake the captured town a second time and hold it long enough to keep the road open for the Cao Bang refugees.

The majority of the refugees never made the link-up. The commander at Cao Bang did not blow up the equipment as ordered and was forced to stay on the main road with his trucks and heavy artillery. Only after repeated ambushes did he finally realize the wisdom of the original order and, at last, destroy the trucks and artillery. By then precious time had been lost. There were more ambushes on the 85 mile march, mostly over mountain trails, to Dong Khe. After four days the few survivors of the march joined what was left of their badly outnumbered rescuers who had retreated to the hills just outside of Dong Khe to make their last stand. It was there that the two groups finally linked up and held out against repeated assaults just long enough for three battalions of paratroopers to join them and share their deaths.

By the end of the year the French had lost almost all of the northern border region of Tonkin to the Vietminh. Communist Chinese support for the Vietminh had turned the tide. By providing sanctuary, arms, and training camps the Chinese communists gave the Vietminh what they sorely needed to mount a major offensive against the French.

Communist Chinese support was also a primary reason why the Vietminh concentrated their operations in northern Tonkin, and especially against French garrisons near the Chinese border. The object was to maximize the effectiveness of Chinese aid. For despite China's willingness to provide supplies to the Vietminh they could only be delivered to military units by coolies travelling at a snail's pace over mountain passes and through dense jungle. This was not only time consuming it was labor intensive. Forty thousand coolies were required to maintain a supply line to an infantry division in the field.

It was therefore imperative for the long term prospects of the Vietminh to drive the French from their border enclaves, and begin construction on supply roads into China and replace the coolies with trucks.

For the French the Vietminh offensive was a military disaster. They suffered heavy casualties. Six thousand French troops were killed in action, equal to fifteen percent of all French losses in the war since 1946. Even more alarming was the fact that supply routes from China were now wide open. And once coolies were replaced by motor vehicles the war would be as good as lost. This was not just Vietminh wishful thinking, even members of the French high command accepted this assessment.

The one unforeseen bright spot for the French was that the Vietminh offensive had coincided with the outbreak of the Korean war.

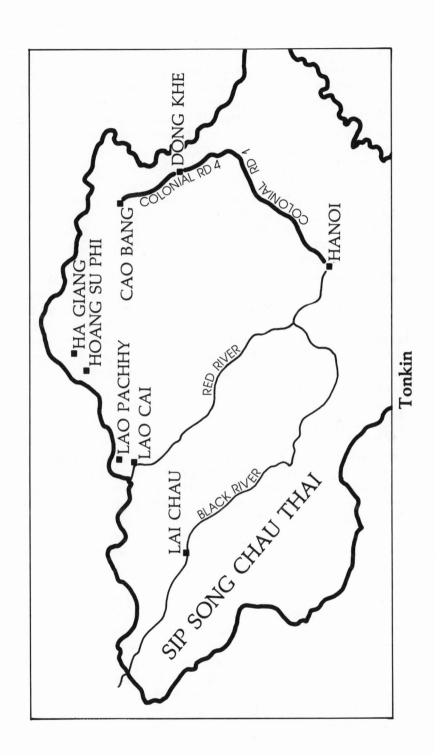

Rhetoric about a communist takeover of southeast Asia now had a ring of reality. President Truman was at last persuaded by the hawks in his cabinet to increase military aid to the French. In the next four years the French would receive $3 billion from America to continue the war. Yet, even with the prospect of increased American aid, the French high command was forced to admit that the Vietminh could not be defeated by continuing to adhere to traditional tactics alone. If the war was to be won at all, it was imperative to harass and wear down the Vietminh in their own sanctuaries, to cut their supply lines and, if possible, to regain control of border territory. But for this guerrillas were needed.

The original idea was to style them after the American and British jungle fighters, Merril's Marauders and Wingate's Chindits, who had performed so well during the last war. But part of the success of the Marauders and Chindits was due to their ability to return to safe bases behind their own lines after each mission to rest, regroup and be resupplied. French guerrillas could not count on this luxury. They would have to work more or less permanently behind enemy lines and live off the land. Few in the French high command imagined that even their best commandos could survive for long under these conditions. On the other hand, montagnards like the Hmong, able to live off the land and to count on support and supplies from their own people, might be expected to carry off this kind of operation.

THE G.C.M.A

In early 1950, Colonel Grall was placed in charge of the newly formed G.C.M.A. (Groupement de Commandos Mixtes Aeroportes — Mixed Airborne Commando Group) and given twenty French officers to recruit, train, and equip the new guerrillas. It was a clandestine operation. Indeed, although nominally under the authority of the French Expeditionary Corps, the G.C.M.A. was actually run by the S.D.E.C. (Service de Documentation Exterieure et du Contre-Espionage), the French equivalent of the American CIA.

There was good reason for all the secrecy. The scope of G.C.M.A. operations was large. Not only did it involve the organization of a montagnard maquis, it included close cooperation with Saigon criminal syndicates in monitoring and sometimes interdicting the activities of communists and pro-communist Vietnamese in the Mekong delta. Then there was the collection and sale of opium to finance G.C.M.A. projects, an activity that contradicted official French policy and would be a cause of embarrassment if it became public knowledge.

The first recruits for the new maquis to arrive at the training school at Cap St. Jacques (present day Vung Tau), a seaside resort just forty miles southeast of Saigon, were not Hmong but montagnards from the High Plateau in south Vietnam. The High Plateau region was just one of the four areas where guerrillas were to be organized. The other three were Laos, north Vietnam, and south Vietnam. Laos (especially Phong Saly, Sam Neua and Xieng Khouang provinces) and north Vietnam had top priority, however.

Grall brought in Colonel Roger Trinquier to take charge of the organization of the maquis in the two most important areas. By the beginning of 1951, Trinquier had recruited Touby into the new guerrilla force. After receiving training at Cap St. Jacques, Touby and a handful of his Laotian Hmong returned to Laos to organize a network of Hmong maquis in Phong Saly, Xieng Khouang and Sam Neua provinces.

THE TERRESTRIAL DRAGON

While guerrilla operations in northeastern Laos were important, especially in denying the Vietminh sanctuary after conducting operations west of the Black River in the troublesome ethnic Thai region of Sip Song Chau Thai (The Land of the Dozen Thai Fiefs) near the Laos-Vietnam border, what Trinquier really needed was an effective guerrilla force in northern Tonkin where, up to now, the Vietminh had been able to operate with complete impunity. He even had someone in mind for heading up the operation—Chao Quang Lo, a Hmong chieftain from Lao Cai, a town near where the Red river flows across the Chinese-Vietnam border.

Chao Quang Lo was born near Lao Cai in the small village of Lao Pa Chay, so named, it would seem, in honor of the famous Hmong rebel Pa Chay. Given the course of events which unfolded after the evacuation of the French from the region, the location of Chao Quang Lo's birthplace seems, in hindsight, almost prophetic.

Chao Quang Lo was an imposing figure of a man. He was extremely tall for an Asian, and slightly stoop shouldered. His appetite matched his strength which was twice the ordinary man's. Despite his size, he was blessed with the remarkable endurance that is so common to his race. More than once when pursued by superior forces he led his guerrillas on forced marches covering as much as two hundred kilometers over difficult mountain trails, stopping only occasionally to permit his soldiers to eat.

Chao Quang Lo was blind in one eye, the result of an ancient Hmong flintlock that exploded in his face when he was a boy. The accident did not effect his marksmanship, though. Indeed, his reputation as a marksman spread from Vietnam across the border into China. And from time to time a Chinese wanting to test his mettle against this renowned Hmong rifleman travelled to Lao Cai for a contest. The stakes were high, a fine rifle or even a horse. Shots were fired nearly seven hundred feet to the target, a small bronze coin imbedded in a tree trunk. Chao Quang Lo seldom missed, a fact evidenced by his ever growing collection of horses and rifles.

Chao Quang Lo's personality was as imposing as his person. He had an aversion for lying that bordered on the obsessive. Any officer under his command who lied to him was summarily shot. Nor did he have much sympathy for cowardice. Few who served under him contemplated retreat or desertion. It was as good as a death sentence. And though Chao Quang Lo appreciated the economic necessity of growing opium as an export commodity, he detested opium smoking and would not tolerate it among his troops. Nor would he trust a civilian who smoked the drug, not even his rich uncle whose social prestige perhaps merited confidence but whose habit made the old man untrustworthy in his nephew's eyes. Convinced his uncle would sell him out for a pipe of the drug, Chao Quang Lo told him nothing at all about his activities, which was wise because the Vietminh would later periodically interrogate the old man who was always able with complete honesty to plead total ignorance of his nephew's whereabouts.

Chao Quang Lo possessed two other traits. He was a natural leader and, as the Vietminh and Chinese soon discovered, a superb guerrilla commander. Equally important, he had supported the French in the past and was an avowed enemy of the Vietminh who had more than once tried to confiscate the opium crops of the Hmong in the area around Lo Cai. Just the sort of man Trinquier needed to command a montagnard maquis in northern Tonkin. Unfortunately, Trinquier's attempts to recruit the Hmong chieftain were aborted when he was informed by intelligence that Chao Quang Lo was presumed dead.

When Lao Cai was evacuated along with Cao Bang after the Vietminh captured Dong Khe, Chao Quang Lo had refused to abandon the area and remained behind hidden in the forest with a portable radio post to keep the French informed of Vietminh troop movements. Within a month, however, his messages ceased. The logical conclusion was that he had been killed or captured by the enemy. To Trinquier's surprise and delight he later learned from two Hmong refugees in Hanoi that Chao Quang Lo was still alive.

The cause of the communication break was a Chinese battalion that had crossed the border into Vietnam to sweep the area around Lao Cai for French partisans, and in particular for the one-eyed maquisard, whom the Chinese would later nickname the "Terrestrial Dragon". The Chinese were called in because the Vietminh had mistakenly presumed that with the French gone the Hmong would offer no resistance. To their surprise, when they sent their com-

152

missars to Lao Pa Chay to confiscate weapons Chao Quang Lo politely, but firmly, refused to hand them over. The commissars paid another visit to the village later on, but this time in the company of Vietminh troops. Chao Quang Lo again refused to relinquish the arms, and in language that turned the commissar's face red with rage. "You want our weapons but we very much regret that it is not in our power to grant this wish. On the other hand, if you need bullets, we are able to supply them. More, I trust, than you want." Chao Quang Lo escorted the commissars to the edge of the village and bid them adieu.

The Vietminh attacked that same night, were repulsed and repeatedly ambushed as they vainly tried to retreat to safety. More skirmishes followed until, toward the end of 1951, Chao Quang Lo completely routed the 148th Vietminh regiment stationed at Lo Cai. It was after this humiliating defeat that the Vietminh appealed to the Chinese communists for help.

The Chinese launched a surprise attack against Chao Quang Lo's village. The guerrilla chief put up a fierce resistance, but after a day and a half of constant artillery bombardment he was forced to retreat into the forest and regroup. The morale of his partisans was low. They were not eager to engage the Chinese a second time. But that is just what Chao Quang Lo ordered. Indeed, the attack was to take place that very night for Chao Quang Lo was certain the Chinese would be celebrating their victory and never expect the defeated Hmong to launch a counterattack. He placed his own father in charge of one contingent, an uncle in charge of another. They were to attempt to retake Lao Pa Chay from the east and west while he would assail it from the south. Most of his partisans no doubt imagined that they were being sent on a suicide mission. What they did not know was that Chao Quang Lo had held back a store of machine guns and mortars for just such an occasion, which accounts for his confident remark to one of his men that "tomorrow we shall have lunch together in my home village. There will still be Chinese there, but they will all be dead." The assault transpired just as Chao Quang Lo had planned. Not only were the Chinese taken by surprise, they predictably responded to the assaults on their two flanks by withdrawing into the center of the town where they were easy prey for the Terrestrial Dragon's mortars and machine guns. By first light the battle was over. The only Chinese who survived were those who had fled during the night. Chao Quang Lo had lunch in the village that afternoon and observed that there were indeed still Chinese there but, as he predicted, they were all dead.

The French knew next to nothing about these exploits at the time and were eager to contact the Hmong chief and organize a maquis, later code named "Chocolate'. In February 1952, two Hmong refugees boarded a plane in Hanoi and took off for Phalong, just

153

north of Lao Cai, where they parachuted down with a message to Chao Quang Lo from his cousin in Hanoi, Lo Wen Teu. The essence of the message was simple: prevent the Vietminh from taking over the area at all costs. Of course, the task was already well underway when Chao Quang Lo received the communique. What he needed, however, was not inspiration but arms and munitions to equip his rapidly expanding partisan following.

ARMS AND MUNITIONS

Once the French were apprised of the situation arms and ammunition were immediately airlifted from Hanoi to Chao Quang Lo's forces. At first only 100 rifles were parachuted in, then 400 more dropped from the sky a week later. By April 1952, Chao Quang Lo had received 2,500 rifles from the G.C.M.A., and was well on his way to establishing complete control over the 60 mile stretch of mountainous terrain between Lao Cai and Hoang Su Phi.

Trinquier was so pleased he awarded Chao Quang Lo the Croix de Chevalier and integrated him into the regular army, advancing him to the rank of lieutenant. Though Chao Quang Lo would never serve with the French Expeditionary Corps, the gesture was properly interpreted as a great honor. Trinquier very much wanted to personally award the medal to the Hmong chieftain, but Chao Quang Lo still operated in complete isolation from the French behind enemy lines and the rough terrain made it impossible to clear even a landing field large enough for a Cricket, the nickname for the Morrane-500, the Expeditionary Corps's all purpose reconnaissance plane. And while a helicopter could certainly have negotiated a landing, the G.C.M.A. did not have any at that time. Under such conditions the best Trinquier could do was fly over the Hmong lieutenant's field headquarters and drop the medal to him.

Chao Quang Lo assembled 500 of his partisans at the old French post at Phalong for the occasion, all standing at attention as Trinquier flew by in a Dakota. As the colonel passed over the makeshift parade ground he gave a quick salute and dropped the medal which floated down to the assembly dangling from a small parachute. While it was not much of a ceremony, it was better than nothing at all and it provided Chao Quang Lo with a cherished memory. Trinquier would remember it also, for as his Dakota veered away and began to climb Vietminh anti-aircraft guns opened up. Fortunately, he had worn a flack jacket for the occasion. It stopped several large pieces of shrapnel from ripping open his chest and making the brief fly-over not only his shortest but his last official ceremony as a French officer.

CHINESE REINFORCEMENTS

By April of 1952, the remaining survivors of the Chinese battalion charged with defeating Chao Quang Lo fled across the border into China, which was cause for celebration for the Terrestrial Dragon's Chocolate maquis. But Chao Quang Lo knew they would be replaced. The Vietminh simply could not allow the region to slip from their control. It would hamper their supply lines and leave them constantly open to debilitating ambushes. Moreover, as documents captured from the 412th Vietminh reconnaissance battalion revealed, the Vietminh were not in a position to siphon the necessary manpower from other units to assemble the division sized force necessary to defeat what Vietminh intelligence estimated to be a rebel force of 2,000 men. Chao Quang Lo therefore presumed more Chinese troops would be sent against him. In preparation he radioed Hanoi for a thousand land mines which he had placed along a mountain corridor that encompassed an area of nearly sixty square miles. The placement of the mines was a massive undertaking. To avoid having to divert all his troops to the task, Chao Quang Lo recruited Hmong from all the surrounding villages for the task. Every male over fifteen was encouraged to participate and, given Chao Quang Lo's prestige, the turnout was high. Special instructors from Hanoi were parachuted in and dispatched to the local marketplaces where village chiefs gathered the volunteers for their training. After receiving their instruction each man carried four land mines home to his village charged with the task of strategically placing the mines on mountain paths where the Chinese might be expected to come when they attempted to infiltrate the region. Later, men were sent to each village to learn of the exact placement of each mine so that when the invasion occurred Chao Quang Lo could either draw enemy fire and lead the unsuspecting Chinese over the mine fields or, if the Chinese were routed, herd them toward the mines.

On June 18th, 1952, three regiments of the 302nd Chinese infantry division crossed the border into Vietnam. Within eight hours after they were first spotted Chao Quang Lo had mobilized all his forces. They engaged the leading regiment high in the mountains, assaulting it in waves. The battle lasted for days until the Chinese finally retreated, goaded on by the Hmong who, like sheepdogs herding a flock to the slaughter, maneuvered the Chinese regiment onto heavily mined trails. Land mines exploded every few minutes. The Chinese soldiers panicked and ran only to discharge more mines. White handkerchiefs began to appear everywhere. Hundreds surrendered and were marched down the mountain to Hmong villages below. Within a few days another six hundred laid down their arms and were taken prisoner.

After gathering together all the captured weapons, Chao Quang Lo had the prisoners divided into groups of ten and each group taken to a separate village with orders that they were to be accorded good treatment. The intent of this was to convince the prisoners that the Hmong really had no quarrel with the Chinese. A number of their officers were persuaded to write letters to that effect and to emphasize that there were no French among Chao Quang Lo's guerrillas, that it was a popular uprising and no threat to the Chinese. Mention was also made of the devastating defeat they suffered at the hands of Chao Quang Lo's Hmong. These letters were then delivered to the commander of the Chinese People's Army headquartered in southern Yunnan.

Whether or not the letters were well received is unknown. In any case, there were still two other regiments of the 302nd division to contend with. Their approach was announced by exploding land mines. The mines began exploding late in the evening and continued into the next morning. Everywhere the advancing division went, each trail, every path, had mines. Members of the Chocolate maquis worked their way up the mountains until they were above the advancing enemy. Dead and dying Chinese were everywhere. And yet they continued to advance under the prodding of their commander who used his men as human mine sweepers. Though hundreds had been killed, there were hundreds still left and soon the mines would all be exploded. Chao Quang Lo called a war council. His few hundred guerrillas were no match for a division of Chinese regulars equipped with machine guns and artillery. Their only chance was to split up into small groups. Chao Quang Lo ordered the majority of his maquis to retreat north across the border into China and wait for his instructions. He led the rest south along the Clear River to Song Chay.

Shortly after his departure two more Chinese divisions (104th artillery and 103rd infantry) advanced on the area. One village after another was attacked. Though Chinese machine guns riddled Hmong huts there were few casualties since most of the Hmong had already left their homes and moved higher up into the mountains. If they had remained there they would have been safe. But when the Chinese opened up with heavy artillery, many villagers panicked and rushed down the mountain slopes to the valleys below where they were easy prey for the Chinese troops.

Chao Quang Lo was having a hard time also. It was not so much the constant harassment of the Chinese, who seemed to be everywhere at all times, as it was the lowland climate of Song Chay that led to so many casualties. He lost more men to illness there than he had to enemy bullets during all his previous campaigns. Chao Quang Lo had no choice but to return to his mountains. This time, however, it was not to fight but to flee through enemy lines into China.

When the French again made contact with the Chocolate maquis in late 1952 it consisted of only a few dispirited partisans. Hundreds of rifles were dropped from Dakotas in hopes of reviving the Hmong guerrilla organization. The gesture raised the spirits of many who had given up hope and abandoned the fight. Soon hundreds of former maquisards were back in harness, collecting new recruits and planning missions.

THE DEATH OF CHAO QUANG LO

When Chao Quang Lo got wind of the revival he immediately marched south with three hundred men to join his former comrades. Requests were made to Hanoi for machine guns and mortars. Within a few days thousands of Hmong had joined the refurbished Chocolate maquis. One after another, captured villages were liberated from the Vietminh and Chinese. The enemy was everywhere in retreat. But not for long. In August 1953, the 103rd artillery and 104th infantry divisions, revitalized with fresh troops, began a new offensive against the Terrestrial Dragon. They attacked from the east. They were joined by the Vietminh 118th division from Lao Cai which attacked from the west. The Chinese set up anti-aircraft guns to prevent the French from dropping more arms and ammunition.

It was an effective ploy. Fighting nearly day and night on two separate fronts not only resulted in high casualties for Chao Quang Lo's men, they were running out of ammunition. By late August, many of Chao Quang Lo's maquisards were near starvation, and he was forced to lead what was left of his guerrilla force up into the mountains where they hid in a deep grotto. Completely encircled by two Chinese divisions, their only hope was that the enemy would not find them and give up the hunt. And it might have happened that way if the Chinese had not earlier captured Chao Quang Lo's adopted son and tortured the truth out of him.

The Chinese struck in the night. They wanted Chao Quang Lo alive and expected him to surrender once he realized he was surrounded and escape futile. It was not to be. With a revolver in one hand and a machine gun in the other and a carbine slung over his shoulder he rushed the enemy. Before he emptied the machine gun he had cut down the first line of Chinese. When he breached the second line his carbine was empty. Armed only with his revolver he continued the charge until he was brought down by a barrage of AK-47s.

His body was carried from one village to another and put on display so the Hmong would know that they no longer had a leader. It was then transported to China to bolster the spirits of Chinese infantrymen and as material proof that the Terrestrial Dragon was not invincible. His valiant death did not go unacknowledged by the French, however, and Colonel Trinquier awarded him, posthumously, the Legion of Honor.

THE INVASION OF LAOS

With northern Tonkin under control the Vietminh concentrated its efforts in the southwest and sent three divisions against French posts located in the Thai tribal territory near the Laotian border. The ethnic Thai in the region around Dien Bien Phu had long been strong supporters of the French who assigned them the task of blocking Vietminh incursions into northeastern Laos. With northern Tonkin now firmly under Vietminh control, the French did not want to see northeastern Laos suffer the same fate. Should that occur the Vietminh could use it, as they had used northern Tonkin, for supply depots and a sanctuary to which they could retreat from the forces of Expeditionary Corps. In addition, there was the growing realization, confirmed by later events, that a successful invasion of Laos by the Vietminh would so shock French public opinion at home that it would make the continuation of the war impossible.

Unfortunately, the Thai proved to be no match for Vietminh regulars and fears mounted that, emboldened by their recent successes, the enemy might mount a major offensive into Laos the following spring. In anticipation of this event a training camp for Laotian Hmong guerrillas was established on the Plain of Jars, and five hundred special Hmong recruits were flown to Saigon for training at Cap St. Jacques. An air field was quickly constructed on the Plain of Jars so that regular troops and armor could be flown in to beef up the operation. And none too soon for in early April 1953 a combined Vietminh Pathet-Lao offensive was launched in Sam Neua province.

Giap, the Commander in Chief of the Vietminh armed forces, had not only concluded that a successful invasion of Laos would turn public opinion in France against continued support for the war, he saw a chance to draw the French across the border and stretch their supply lines thin. Should they foolishly decide to fight under these conditions the results might prove catastrophic, as the fall of Dien Bien Phu would later attest.

The combined Vietminh/Pathet-Lao offensive was conducted as a two-pronged attack. Fifteen battalions drawn from the 308th, 312th and 316th Vietminh divisions marched south through Sam Neua and attempted to occupy the Plain of Jars. Five more battalions drove due west toward Luang Prabang.

Faydang and his men took part in the first prong of this offensive and when the communist forces veered southward into Xieng Khouang province he no doubt contemplated the possibility that he might at last be in a position to settle old debts. Because of the excellent information supplied by Touby's Hmong the French were ready for the Vietminh when they reached the Plain of Jars. The French had transformed their main position on the plain into a fortified camp bristling with barbed wire and protected by heavy artillery and tanks. The invaders were quickly beaten back. In anticipation of new assaults, forty to fifty small forts were constructed at strategic locations on the Plain. Four colonels from the G.C.M.A. were dispatched to Laos to meet with Touby and his second in command, a remarkable young Hmong officer by the name of Vang Pao. The agreement was that Touby and Vang Pao would station their Hmong on the crests of the mountains to report on enemy movements and, when feasible, to conduct guerrilla raids and ambushes while the Expeditionary Corps concentrated on protecting the Plain of Jars.

Smarting from the earlier encounter and defeat, the communist forces did not attempt another assault on the Plain of Jars. Instead they pushed on to link up with the other five battalions heading for Luang Prabang, the royal capital of Laos where the forty-nine year old Laotian king, Sisavang Vong, was in residence. By April 28, the combined communist forces were on the edge of the city. The population of Luang Prabang was thrown into a panic. Many urged the king to flee. He refused, partly out of a stubborn defiance of the invaders, and partly because of the prophecy of a blind monk who claimed that the Vietminh would not set foot in the royal capital. As it turned out the blind soothsayer was correct. Fearing the prospect of his twenty battalions getting bogged down and cut off from their supply lines, Giap ordered his troops to withdraw to the safety of Vietnam. Like Ho Chi Minh, Giap was a patient man. There would be other invasions and one day Vietnamese troops would remain for good and fulfill Vietnam's destiny to rule all of Indochina, a grand design that had been only temporarily thwarted by the imposition of French colonialism on Indochina nearly a hundred years earlier.

Such is the weakness of objectivity in even the keenest minds that Giap perceived no inconsistency between his hatred of French colonialism and his own vision of the future, shared by his comrades in Hanoi, of a "free" Indochina united, by force of arms if necessary, under the iron-fisted rule of the Vietnamese communist party.

Vang Pao
Drawing by K.P. Lui—*Asiaweek*

CHAPTER
10

VANG PAO

With the fall of Dien Bien Phu in May of 1954 France's days in Indochina were numbered. Later in the year a Geneva agreement reduced France's presence in Indochina by mandating the withdrawal of French forces from both Laos and north Vietnam. The Vietminh were also supposed to remove their troops from Laos but many remained to support the buildup of the Pathet Lao, the military arm of the Laotian communist party, the NLHS (Neo Lao Hak Sat), which at that time was locked in a struggle with the Laotian royalists for control of the country. The contest remained a stalemate until 1957 when, over the protests of the United States, Laotian communists gained representation in a new coalition government. The new government lasted only eight months. Its collapse was precipitated by the Vietminh occupation of border provinces near the Ho Chi Minh trail. Pro U.S. rightists captured power and imprisoned NLHS representatives, a move that prompted the Vietminh to step up their military support for the Pathet Lao. In mid 1959 fighting broke out between units of the Royal Laotian Army and Pathet Lao forces, plunging Laos into a civil war. The scale of the fighting was magnified by the involvement of foreign powers. The U.S. supplied the royalists with arms and military advisors and the Vietminh supported the Pathet Lao with both arms and personnel.

In late 1960, Kong Le, a captain in the Royal Laotian Army, led units under his command into Vientiane and took over the government. Declaring himself a neutralist, he sought to end the civil war by banning all foreign troops from Laotian soil. Within a few months he was ousted by CIA backed rightists, forcing the neutralists into an uneasy alliance with the Pathet Lao. Though the rightists controlled the city of Vientiane, they suffered repeated defeats on the

**Laos:
The War Years**

battlefield and, in July 1962, agreed to form a new coalition government that included both communists and neutralists. This coalition, too, was doomed to failure. Frustrated by U.S. efforts to diminish the influence of the leftists in the National Assembly, the communists pulled out of the coalition and took to the battlefield, precipitating a resumption of the civil war.

The war seesawed back and forth until 1968 when the U.S. employed massive air power on the Plain of Jars to break the deadlock. Between 1968 and 1972, the number of bombs dropped on the plain was greater in total tons than all the bombs dropped by the U.S. in both the European and Pacific theaters during World War Two.

In late 1972 the U.S. informed Laotian Prime Minister Souvanna Phouma of its intention to settle the war in Vietnam and urged him to come to terms with the Pathet Lao before the U.S. pulled out of the region. With the prospect of a cut-off of all U.S. aid, Souvanna Phouma hastily concluded negotiations with the Pathet Lao, conceding nearly everything to bring the fighting to an end. On February 21, 1973, a new government was formed and the next day a general cease fire was officially declared. Unofficially, the communists hedged their bets by continuing their military buildup and engaging in sporadic fighting to expand the territory directly under their control.

In the following year the Pathet Lao maneuvered to take control of the government while continuing to consolidate their forces in the field. Fighting broke out in earnest again in 1974 and an undeclared civil war continued through 1975 until, on March 27th of that year, Pathet Lao forces accompanied by Vietminh regulars launched a massive offensive against what was left of the Royal Laotian Army on the southern edge of the Plain of Jars. By the end of August the Pathet Lao had captured Vientiane and organized a "revolutionary committee" to serve as an interim government until something more permanent could be arranged.

The last piece fell into place with the establishment of the Lao People's Democratic Republic (LPDR) on December 1976, less than a week after the forced abdication of the king. Souvanna Phouma was permanently retired from Laotian politics and his half-brother Prince Souphanouvong, who had helped found and organize the Laotian communist party, was made President of the new communist state. Three divisions of North Vietnamese regulars remained on Laotian soil to insure it would not be an independent communist state.

Actually, Laos would have fallen to the communists much earlier if it had not been for the Laotian Hmong who did most of the fighting for a free Laos and, one must add, most of the dying. Nearly one third of the Laotian Hmong perished during the conflict, which included close to half of all males over the age of fifteen. All through the struggle the Laotian Hmong placed their fate in the hands of one man, General Vang Pao — the first and only Hmong to rise through the ranks of the Royal Laotian Army and achieve the rank of General.

FROM COURIER TO GENDARME

Vang Pao was fourteen years old when the Japanese invaded Laos. Too young to serve in the maquis as a guerrilla he nevertheless itched to be a part of the war effort. With Touby's help he landed a job as a messenger and interpreter for the French. Though he had only a few years of schooling, starting late and ending early (to paraphrase his own description), Vang Pao was a quick student and, like many Hmong, mastered foreign languages with relative ease. Much of Vang Pao's time during this period was spent as a courier carrying messages between different units of Touby's maquis. On occasion, he led French officers parachuted in from India to the safety of Hmong villages or to hideaways deep in the mountain grottos. By the time the Japanese capitulated he was accompanying French officers on military missions, including the retaking of Xieng Khouang city.

Vang Pao performed his duties with distinction and Touby was eager to reward him with a position in the Xieng Khouang provincial bureaucracy. Restless and always on the move, Vang Pao balked at the idea. He simply did not have it in him to become a career bureaucrat. What he wanted instead was to be assigned to the newly formed provincial police force under Lieutenant Ticot who had recently arrived from Pakistan to take command of the paramilitary unit.

Beginning as a raw recruit in late 1947, Vang Pao was promoted to corporal in March 1948 and sent a month later to the non-commissioned officer school for corporals of the gendarmerie at Luang Prabang. No doubt the fact that the Xieng Khouang gendarmerie did more than merely keep the peace helped his cause, for Vang Pao's unit often engaged Laotian rebels and the Vietminh units supporting them in the field, providing many occasions for him to reveal his natural aptitude for command.

Vang Pao graduated first in his class. In January 1949, he was promoted to chief-corporal and sent to the National Gendarmerie school where he again graduated first in his class and was promoted to Sergeant-Major. He received two more promotions, achieving the rank of adjutant in October 1950. If Vang Pao was to advance further in rank he would have to become a commissioned officer.

It was during 1950 that Vang Pao's company of gendarmes participated in a joint operation with a battalion of Laotian riflemen against two enemy battalions, one Vietminh and the other Pathet Lao, operating southeast of Xieng Khouang city. The Pathet Lao battalion held a position near the Mo river while the Vietminh occupied the village of Ban Hang. Vang Pao's mixed group of gendarmes and riflemen assaulted the Vietminh at Ban Hang while another group of Laotian riflemen attacked the Pathet Lao near the Mo river.

The assault on Ban Hang lasted through the night and into the early morning when the Vietminh retreated toward the border, leaving many dead behind. However, the pursuit of the fleeing enemy was frustrated by repeated ambushes accompanied by heavy casualties. The French officers in charge were divided over what to do next. In particular, Lieutenant Casteri who commanded the forward position stubbornly refused to lead his men into any more ambushes. Vang Pao offered to command a contingent of his gendarmes and attempt to gain control of the pass through which the Vietminh would have to travel to launch new ambushes, and hold it until the rest of the battalion advanced and linked up. It was a dangerous mission. Fortunately, Vang Pao and his comrades were well dug into defensive positions before the first Vietminh appeared on the trail. There were six of them. Three were killed, and three escaped, two of them with wounds.

The next day the rest of the battalion caught up and hounded the Vietminh across the border to the Vietnamese village of Muong Sen, a Vietminh stronghold, which they overwhelmed. Their forces broken and scattered, the Vietminh were obliged to adopt guerrilla tactics, operating in small units and using hit and run tactics. Accustomed to conventional warfare, the Laotian riflemen performed poorly against these assaults.

The French turned to Vang Pao who was eager to help so long as he was given a free hand in the matter. He had formed some ideas on how to deal effectively against guerrilla units, none of which included slavish conformity to conventional tactics. Moreover, he intended to rely heavily on Hmong soldiers who, accustomed to guerrilla fighting, did not warm to strict army discipline in any case.

Vang Pao correctly assumed that the key to gaining the upper hand over the Vietminh lay with winning the trust of the civilian population in Vietminh occupied areas. They were the best source of military intelligence, for they knew better than any one else the exact deployment and strength of Vietminh units in their locale.

This meant it would be necessary to infiltrate enemy territory without being detected by either civilians or enemy units. The Laotian riflemen had consistently failed to comply with this dictum. Invariably when they conducted maneuvers in enemy territory they were quickly spotted by civilians who informed the Vietminh of their presence. Just as invariably, ambushes followed. This might have been avoided if the Laotians had travelled off the beaten path, but this required trudging up steep inclines through rough terrain. The Hmong were used to this sort of thing, but the Laotians were not.

Vang Pao's Hmong unit performed up to expectation. Not only did it operate undetected, the civilian population proved to be very cooperative. Unlike the Vietminh who often impressed civilians into corvee labor and robbed them of their food and livestock, Vang Pao's Hmong never accepted food or shelter from villagers unless it was freely offered. And civilians were never mistreated. Moreover, Vang Pao carefully avoided situations where attacks on the Vietminh might involve civilian casualties.

In fact, Vang Pao's most successful military operation during this period might have been aborted if the villagers in the Vietminh occupied town of Hin Hong had not been away in the fields harvesting their poppies. With the villagers absent, however, the Vietminh were fair game. The attack came early in the morning when the Vietminh, sleeping contentedly in the village chief's home, were just beginning to stir. Vang Pao's Hmong surrounded the house and on his signal opened fire. Only one Vietnamese escaped. But he was wounded, and Vang Pao followed the blood trail to a mountain grotto. He asked the Vietnamese to surrender, but he refused. Two grenades lobbed into the grotto changed his mind, however, and he was taken prisoner.

The man carried important documents which were turned over to Captain Fret, the French officer overseeing Vang Pao's operations. One of the documents revealed the location of the meeting place where couriers from the Hin Hong Vietminh (whom Vang Pao had just liquidated) exchanged weekly information with their comrades at Muong Phanh near the Vietnamese border. Captain Fret suggested that Vang Pao and a few of his Hmong take the place of the departed Viets and surprise their Muong Phanh confederates. There were two of them. Vang Pao shot them both, killing one and wounding the other who scurried up a hill and took a position at the base of a large tree. Vang Pao rushed him and was nearly struck by a grenade that exploded a few yards behind him. He tossed his own grenade which found its mark. The courier carried papers detailing the organization and operations of the Vietminh units in the region.

OFFICER MATERIAL

Captain Fret was not only pleased with the find, he was thoroughly impressed with Vang Pao's military prowess and insisted that the Hmong adjutant apply for candidacy to officer training school. The written exam was parachuted in to the military camp at Muong Ngan and Vang Pao took the exam in the military barracks with Captain Fret looking over his shoulder. When Fret realized that Vang Pao could write almost no French at all he remarked, "it is a pity you will damage your career because you do not have a command of grammar or tenses," and then proceeded to dictate the correct answers to the exam questions. After passing the oral exam at Vientiane Vang Pao traveled by dugout canoe down the Mekong River to the Officer Training school at Dong Hene near Savannakhet.

Vang Pao's studies at the school lasted fourteen months, from the beginning of 1951 until March 1952. He graduated seventh in his class. Despite the traditional training he received at the school, he persevered in his conviction, confirmed by his encounters with the Vietminh in 1950, that only non-traditional tactics would prove effective against the Vietnamese communists. This explains his lack of interest in all the gadgetry of the French High Command at Hanoi during a mandatory two week post-graduation tour. Organization charts, complicated chains of command, and set piece battles had not defeated the Vietminh in the past and it would certainly not defeat them in Laos in the future.

THE 14TH INFANTRY

Three months after his graduation second lieutenant Vang Pao was assigned to the 14th Infantry company stationed at Muong Hiem on the eastern border of Luang Prabang province close to communist strongholds in neighboring Sam Neua province. The gendarmerie had been absorbed into the regular military and Vang Pao was now an officer in the Royal Laotian Army. As the only Hmong in the company, his job was to establish contacts with the Hmong in the area who had not been forthcoming with information about communist forces in the province. Their reluctance was understandable. Laotian authorities had abused them for years and it would take some persuading to get them to cooperate with their former oppressors. Not only was Vang Pao successful in gaining Hmong cooperation in gathering intelligence, he was able to recruit seventy-one of them into the 14th. Shortly afterward he was promoted to First Lieutenant.

In late March of 1953, when the Vietminh invaded Laos with seven thousand regulars, the post at Muong Hiem was ordered to fortify its position and hold it at all costs in order to receive the French and Laotians retreating from their overrun positions in Sam Neua province. Nearly three hundred French and Laotians actually made it to Muong Hiem, leaving many dead and wounded behind. But when it was learned that fifteen battalions of Vietminh were preparing for a major assault on Muong Hiem orders were sent from Vientiane to evacuate the town. The order came nearly too late, for the Vietminh were already swarming in the hills around the town. The plan was to sneak out at night before the enemy had a chance to launch an attack. To mask the retreat, torches were placed all around the post and buglers ordered to sound the call for the evening meal. With the enemy convinced that the camp was settling in for the night, the entire camp population was evacuated shortly after dusk. After a five hour march to the top of one of the mountains overlooking the post, the evacuees paused to watch the fireworks below. All the post's artillery and all the ammunition that could not be carried out had been stockpiled in one place and explosives set for detonation when the 14th and its Sam Neua refugees were well away from the area.

Unfortunately, the explosion alerted the Vietminh to the escape and they set off in hot pursuit. Since Vang Pao was familiar with the countryside, the French commander placed him in charge of the retreat. Along the way, information provided by Hmong villagers repeatedly saved the column from being ambushed by the Vietminh. And food provided by villagers saved them from starvation. But the French and Laotians were nearly dead from exhaustion trying to keep up the pace Vang Pao was setting. Not only were they covering much ground, he was keeping them off the main roads and trails, following the mountain crests where the enemy was not likely to go.

Several days into the march Vang Pao was wakened early in the morning by a wild goat. He took it as an omen sent to him by his ancestors that it was unsafe to remain camped in the area and he roused the column to push on, against the protests of the French who considered talk of omens and messengers from ancestors pure nonsense but who also had no knowledge of the terrain and were therefore at Vang Pao's mercy.

By early morning they had descended the mountain and reached a river valley. All seemed innocent enough, but Vang Pao suspected a trap because it was precisely the sort of terrain he would himself choose for an ambush: an open field surrounded by thickly wooded hills with the way out of the valley partially blocked by a large butte.

The French commander, Captain Cocostequy, sent out patrols to scout the area with the remainder of the 14th following behind. If the enemy was deployed as Vang Pao suspected, they would all be drawn into a murderous cross fire. Now it was Vang Pao's turn to protest. But Cocostequy was not about to leave the valley and return to the mountains. He had his fill of tramping over mountain crests and intended to do the rest of his retreating over flat valley trails. When the French commander refused to listen to reason Vang Pao simply left the group and began to climb up the mountain the way they had come. Other soldiers began to follow, among them some French officers. At that moment the Vietminh, stationed just where Vang Pao had suspected, opened up on them with machine guns and mortars. The Lao soldiers panicked and threw away their rifles so they could grasp the bushes and with both hands as they desperately clawed their way up the mountain. Only the Hmong soldiers held on to their rifles, a habit drilled into them from childhood.

Again Vang Pao led the column to the crests where it remained until Captain Cocostequy collapsed from exhaustion. Cocostequy transferred command of the Hmong soldiers to Vang Pao and the Laotians were turned over to one of their own officers. Convinced he was going to die he ordered both groups to leave him behind and continue on as best they could. The Laotians set off for Luang Prabang while Vang Pao led the remainder of the column, including several French officers, southwest toward Sop Khao, a town on the edge of the Khan river. Before departing, however, he placed Cocostequy in the charge of one of his Hmong with orders to deliver him to a Hmong village and hide him until someone could be sent back to retrieve them both.

When Vang Pao reached Sop Khao he learned from some Hmong there that the unarmed Laotians had been easily captured by the Vietminh and marched back to Muong Hiem, which had become the new communist headquarters in the region. He also learned that the Vietminh had been spreading rumors in Hmong villages that he had also been captured in hopes that the Hmong would lose heart and cease providing the French intelligence and sanctuary.

During the second week of May Vang Pao reached the fortified French camp on the Plain of Jars. By this time the Vietminh assault had bogged down. One cause of the stalled offensive was Touby's maquis who had harassed the communists' supply lines and provided excellent intelligence to the French regarding Vietminh movements and force levels.

FIRST COMMAND

The 14th artillery was no more. However, Vang Pao was at last given his own command: a special commando unit of over seventy men. A few months later he was brought into the G.C.M.A., sharing responsibility with Touby for the Hmong maquis whose guerrilla network encompassed Xieng Khouang and Sam Neua provinces. Until May of 1954 Vang Pao conducted guerrilla operations around Nong Het on the eastern border of Xieng Khouang province. The imminent fall of Dien Bien Phu changed his itinerary.

By April of 1954 it was clear to the French that Dien Bien Phu would fall to the communists unless the Americans could be convinced to employ massive air power against Vietminh artillery on the mountain slopes overlooking the French garrison below. When the Americans finally backed out of the air assault, code named "Vulture", the French high command planned a rescue operation, "Condor", involving four infantry and four airborne battalions whose mission would be to approach Dien Bien Phu from the south by way of Laos and break through the Vietminh forces blocking the besieged fortress's southern escape route and attempt to evacuate the survivors. As it turned out, the French could not lay their hands on enough transport planes to supply the mission with air drops in the field and only the four infantry battalions were brought into play. They advanced no further than the bend of the Nam Ou River at the Vietnam/Laos border where they met stiff enemy resistance.

With Condor bogged down and Dien Bien Phu ready to fall, it was decided at the last moment to substitute another plan. In keeping with the bird motif it was named "Albatross'. It had the more modest goal of using guerrilla units to infiltrate the area around Dien Bien Phu and help escapees, if any, find their way back to safety.

Touby's guerrillas were to play a pivotal role in the operation, that is if Touby could be persuaded to go along with the plan. And there must have been some trepidation in this regard for General Navarre, Commander-and-Chief of the French forces in Indochina, authorized Colonel Trinquier of the G.C.M.A. to offer each of Touby's soldiers a silver bar for undertaking the mission. As it turned out, doubts about Touby's loyalty to the French were utterly groundless. He refused any payment for the mission and reminded Trinquier of his past loyalty which he had supposed by now was beyond question.

French commandos and Hmong guerrilla units in Phong Saly province were closest to Dien Bien Phu and took major responsibility for infiltrating the border region near the doomed garrison. Another group of Hmong guerrillas was to be dispatched from Xieng Khouang province as a rear guard for the operation. Touby assigned this mission to Vang Pao who was ordered to lead over three hundred Hmong north through Sam Neua province toward Dien Bien Phu. On the way Vang Pao paused long enough for his troops to be inspected by Colonel Trinquier who had not seen him for some years. Trinquier was struck by the change in the Hmong soldier. As the French officer later recalled: "He now had an extraordinary radiance, he was a leader of the highest order."

CAPTAIN VANG PAO

Vang Pao had just entered Sam Neua province when he learned of the fall of Dien Bien Phu. He was too far from the fallen garrison to be of any help to escapees who, as it turned out, numbered only 78. Most were saved by Hmong villagers who hid them from the enemy until they were well enough to travel to the nearest French post.

In December 1954, Vang Pao was promoted to Captain and, in 1955, assumed command of the 21st Volunteer battalion. In February of the next year he took charge of a battalion at Vientiane and, in June 1958, he was appointed director of the non-commissioned officers school at Khang Khay. Vang Pao itched to get back in the field and in 1959 was given command of the 10th infantry battalion encamped on the Plain of Jars close to the headquarters of the Pathet Lao 2nd battalion.

At that time the 2nd battalion was targeted for full integration into the Royal Laotian army in conformity with the provisions of the 1957 coalition agreement, but it was suspected that the Pathet Lao battalion was instead preparing for an assault against the 10th infantry. Vang Pao was ordered by Colonel Xang, the commander of the 2nd Military region, to visit the Pathet Lao camp and assess the situation. Vang Pao found it armed to the teeth and battle ready. When he reported this to his superiors his battalion was immediately ordered into position on a hill overlooking the Pathet Lao camp while another battalion took up a position on the main road near-by. That same night the enemy camp went up in flames. The Pathet Lao had put the torch to their own headquarters and fled.

When Vang Pao learned from his scouts what had happened he naturally expected the other battalion guarding the road to launch an ambush against the retreating communists, and was astonished to learn that it had never materialized. The Laotian commander guarding the road had simply refused to fire on his own countrymen. The incident reaffirmed Vang Pao's growing conviction that the war against the communists would never be won if the Laotian government relied exclusively on the ethnic Lao to do the fighting.

Not wanting to let the Pathet Lao 2nd battalion off scot-free, Vang Pao mobilized his unit and headed for a narrow mountain pass near the Vietnamese border which he was certain the fleeing Pathet Lao would use to reach the Vietminh post at Muong Sen just inside Vietnam. Unfortunately, when Vang Pao reached his destination he discovered that a unit of Vietminh had linked up with the fleeing 2nd battalion and that it was these veterans rather than the cut-and-run Pathet Lao who had taken charge of guarding the pass. The Laotians under his command wanted nothing to do with the Vietminh who were nicely positioned to pick them off at their leisure should they try to rush them. Vang Pao and another Hmong, a non-com from the Ly clan and a superb marksman, undertook the mission alone.

The two worked their way up the mountain side, dashing and ducking behind boulders for protection until the Vietminh were within range of their rifles. The sentries were not all grouped together, but strung out in pairs. The first two were cut down in quick succession, then the next two and so on until they had picked off an even dozen. The remaining guard, no doubt feeling a bit like the last bird in a turkey shoot, ran for his life but was finally cut down.

By this time another company of Royal Laotian Army soldiers had caught up with Vang Pao's group and the two units pushed on through the pass, routing the Vietminh who followed their Pathet Lao brothers into Vietnam leaving a large cache of food and weapons behind.

Another promotion seemed in order for the resourceful Hmong officer but none was forthcoming until the end of 1960 when the faltering rightists turned to him to help save the nation from a communist takeover.

KONG LE

On August 9, 1960, Kong Le, a neutralist, wrested power from the rightists in a successful coup. While Vang Pao had a grudging admiration for the young Laotian colonel, he was convinced the neutralists were playing into the hands of the communists. A month prior to the coup Pathet Lao and Vietminh troops had attacked Royal Army posts in Sam Neua province and launched another campaign to the south along the Ho Chi Minh trail in the Laotian panhandle. It was no small operation. The Vietminh threw three regiments and a battalion into the Sam Neua campaign and sent four more regiments and another battalion to support the Ho Chi Minh trail maneuvers. By the time Kong Le declared a new government they were well on their way to taking over all of Sam Neua province. Meanwhile, Prince Souvanna Phouma, the neutralist prime minister, did nothing but talk of conciliation.

The rightists, led by Phoumi Nosavan, shared Vang Pao's perspective and sought him out as an ally. Though Vang Pao was reluctant to become involved in the intrigues of Vientiane politicians, they did have the king's backing. There were two other considerations. One was that the Vietminh gave every evidence of preparing for a push to occupy the Plain of Jars and use it as a staging area for the conquest of the rest of Laos. Thousands of Hmong lived in the area and, because of their past support for the French, Vang Pao believed they would become prime targets for communist "reeducation". The other consideration was nationalistic. Vang Pao was convinced that only a revival of the old Hmong guerrilla network — but this time on a much larger scale — could halt the communist takeover.

With the blessings of the rightists Vang Pao began organizing a Hmong army at Lat Houang on the southeast edge of the Plain of

Jars. It was the first step in a much larger undertaking, that of building a network of nearly seventy thousand Hmong from two hundred villages throughout the highlands surrounding the Plain of Jars. When the communists moved to occupy the plain Vang Pao would give the signal and thousands of Hmong would relocate at seven preselected mountain tops overlooking the plain in strategic positions to cut enemy supply lines.

Although Vang Pao believed this task was manageable from a military standpoint, the politics bothered him. He felt he lacked sufficient prestige to deal effectively with the politicians backing the plan. This was Touby's element. Unfortunately, Touby was in Vientiane where he had been serving as deputy to the national assembly since his election in 1958. Vang Pao had no way to contact him from the field. Furthermore, Touby had allied himself with the neutralists and, in particular, with Prince Souvanna Phouma who had become his political mentor.

Vang Pao asked Ya Shao for assistance. Considered the most powerful of shaman in Xieng Khouang province, Ya Shao was famous for his ability to contact the spirits and learn where people had left lost articles or, if they were stolen, identify the culprit. Some Hmong claimed they witnessed him remove imbedded shrapnel from the legs and arms of Hmong soldiers using nothing more than a leaf which he placed on the wound of the victim and crumpled into a wad to which the metal fragments were miraculously transported. Ya Shao was also one of the few shamans who could successfully combat the effects of Ku magic. Originally practiced by the Chinese, Ku was the ability to magically reduce the hide of a cow to the size of a mustard seed and flick it toward the victim whose body it entered. An agonizing death resulted when the hide slowly grew back to its original size. Ku magic struck terror in the hearts of most Hmong, and anyone able to combat it was thought to possess enormous powers.

Ya Shao sacrificed two steers to Vang Pao's ancestors for their help in alerting Touby and making him favor the project. Three days after the animals were sacrificed Touby arrived by plane. After being apprised of the situation he came over to Vang Pao's side and allied himself with the rightists. Perhaps Ya Shao's influence with the spirits facilitated things, but the fact that Souvanna Phouma got wind of the operation also helped. The prime minister dispatched Touby to the scene to see what he could do to dissuade Vang Pao from staying the course. That Touby went over to Vang Pao's camp might also be explained as simple political expediency. Vang Pao enjoyed the support of many village chiefs, and, ultimately, they were Touby's real power base.

In short order, Vang Pao had over three hundred Hmong volunteers marching with him to the Royal Army camp on the Plain of Jars. By the time he arrived the rightists had already taken over the government at Vientiane. Vang Pao distributed weapons to all his men and took command of the camp with time left over to greet the neutralist commander of the 2nd military region who arrived by plane to take charge of what he presumed were his own troops. He was placed under house arrest and flown to Vientiane.

Meanwhile, the rightist commander, General Phoumi, was making a botch of things. After retaking Vientiane, he let Kong Le's forces escape to Vang Vieng. Not only had Kong Le left most of his heavy armor behind but the choice of Vang Vieng was a poor one. The town could not be easily defended. In Vang Pao's opinion, if Phoumi had given pursuit and launched a major attack the neutralists would have been out of the picture for good. Instead, Phoumi took three days off from the war to celebrate his Vientiane victory. This was time enough for Kong Le to be resupplied by Soviet cargo plans and joined by Vietminh advisors. By the time Phoumi was ready to again take up arms, Kong Le was already engaged in a diversionary action toward Luang Prabang. Phoumi panicked and sent six battalions against him only to see the neutralist quickly change course and make a dash for the Plain of Jars, supported all along the way by Soviet airdrops and Vietnamese paratroopers.

All that stood in Kong Le's way was Vang Pao, newly promoted to Lieutenant Colonel. But he was without his company of Hmong whom he had dispatched to his home town of Nong Het to beat back a Vietminh attack. And he was having difficulty getting the panicked Laotians under his command to mount a defense of any kind. One lieutenant who had been trained in artillery in France feigned total ignorance of artillery. Furious, Vang Pao loaded six cases of dynamite onto the side litters of a medevac helicopter and had the pilot fly him to the bridge at Nam Yen just six miles from the base. With the bridge out, Kong Le would have difficulty getting his armor close enough to level the already supine post.

The pilot landed the helicopter about a thousand yards from the bridge and waited while Vang Pao dragged the six boxes of explosives to the bridge, placed the charges, and lit the fuses. The charges went off just as the first armored vehicle loomed into view.

When Vang Pao returned to the base he found it nearly empty. He was able to find only five soldiers to help him harness the only heavy artillery available, two 105 millimeter Howitzers, to the back of a Dodge truck and drive it, along with another loaded with ammunition, to the main road where they set up the cannons and waited for the enemy's column to appear. The six of them held Kong Le off for over four hours until they ran out of ammunition.

When Vang Pao landed in Xieng Khouang he found the city in a panic and preparing for a mass evacuation south toward Savannakhet, the site of Phoumi Nosavan's former military headquarters. Vang Pao reluctantly joined the evacuees but soon left them to again attempt to organize a resistance.

He established a small air base south of the Plain of Jars and made radio contact with Vientiane to inform them that he was prepared to make a stand and needed supplies and munitions. General Phoumi flew in, accompanied by a U.S. officer who asked Vang Pao what he needed, wrote everything down and, without making any promises, unceremoniously departed. Meanwhile, after decimating one of Phoumi's airborne battalions, Kong Le advanced on Vang Pao's position. The first artillery rounds were exploding when Vang Pao led his soldiers and the civilian population in the area to Padong, a plateau surrounded by Hmong villages.

Every day supplies and arms were parachuted in to equip new Hmong recruits. Vang Pao set women and children to work constructing a makeshift airfield. Each new day brought volunteers in from the countryside, mostly Hmong but also Kha and even a few Laotians. Capitalizing on the rising enthusiasm, Vang Pao resumed the organization of his Hmong resistance network begun earlier at Lat Houang. He rapidly organized ten resistance zones. Each zone encompassed twenty or thirty villages, and the ten zones formed a ring encircling the Plain of Jars. In short order he had eighty-four companies of Hmong infantry under his command.

A HMONG WAR

By mid 1961, the U.S. government had seen enough of Phoumi's military bungling to conclude that the Royal Laotian Army was incapable of ever holding back, let alone defeating, the communists. It was decided to divert nearly all ongoing military support to Vang Pao and his Hmong. Moreover, past experience with corrupt Laotian officials, both in and out of the army, who were not beneath selling U.S. arms on the black market, convinced them to bypass the normal supply channels and deliver arms and supplies directly to Vang Pao's troops. The defence of Laos was rapidly becoming an all Hmong operation, and deliberately so. On recommendation from advisors in the field who witnessed the contempt Laotian officers had for Vang Pao simply because he was a Hmong, it was decided that all efforts to mount joint operations between the Royal Army and Vang Pao's forces were bound to end in disaster. The Laotian officers could never be trusted to provide full support.

Hmong civilians living on the mountains surrounding the Plain of Jars were made to suffer for Vang Pao's rising importance in the war effort. Pathet Lao and Vietminh units regularly raided their villages, beat and executed their village chiefs and burned their homes, turning thousands of Hmong into refugees. In time, nearly all the Hmong in the region would become refugees and the logistics of relocating them to protected areas and supplying their material needs would turn out to be as difficult to manage as the war effort itself. Nor would it have likely succeeded at all without Touby's help. In 1962, under the new coalition government, Touby was appointed to the upper house of the Laotian legislature, the King's Council, which not only passed on legislation but formed the nucleus of the prime minister's cabinet. As Minister of Health, Touby administered U.S. funds for refugee relief and insured that they went to the refugees instead of lining the pockets of Vientiane politicians and army officers.

A retired Indiana farmer was also instrumental in the success of the refugee program. Edgar "Pop" Buell arrived in Laos in 1960 as a volunteer with the International Voluntary Services (IVS). By mid-1961 he was working hand-in-hand with Touby to organize a massive relief program that would eventually serve nearly two hundred thousand displaced civilians, most of them Hmong. Buell was also responsible for the creation of an unofficial Hmong school system that brought one room school houses to hundreds of mountain villages, and was later expanded to include nine junior high schools, two senior high schools, and a teacher training school. By 1969 three hundred Hmong were attending the most prestigious high school in Vientiane, and twenty-four Hmong went on to attend universities in Australia, France and the United States.

Toward the middle of 1961 another attempt was made to reestablish a coalition government. To facilitate negotiations, a cease fire was officially declared on May 3, 1961. The Pathet Lao and Kong Le's neutralists celebrated the occasion with an all out assault on Vang Pao's headquarters at Padong. During the night Vang Pao, assisted by several American Green Berets attached to his headquarters, evacuated everyone, civilians and military personnel. The civilians were led to Yat Mu where nearly 9,000 Hmong refugees displaced by earlier communist maneuvers were already camped. Vang Pao relocated his military headquarters at Pha Khao on another mountain south of Padong.

While the loss of Padong was a setback, it did little to dampen Vang Pao's eagerness to engage the enemy. However, the makeup of the communist forces he faced was rapidly changing. At first Vang Pao's volunteers faced only Pathet Lao and Neutralist units, but over the months north Vietnamese soldiers began to appear among their ranks. It was not long before the Hmong were facing fully equipped Vietminh regulars at battalion and even division level strength. Shortly after the evacuation of Padong, a combined force of nine hundred Vietminh regulars and five hundred Pathet Lao laid siege to Vang Pao's mixed company of Hmong and Kha at Muong Ngat near the Vietnamese border. The defenders were finally forced to abandon the post, but not before killing nearly a third of the enemy.

Enemy casualties at Muong Ngat were so high because the Viets sent waves of a hundred men at a time against machine guns and over land mines. Not only was the aggressiveness of Vietminh troops disconcerting, the willingness to suffer such losses exposed the Achilles Heel of Vang Pao's army in a protracted war. Ho Chi Minh once pointed out to a French official that France was doomed to lose a long war with his communists. It was simple arithmetic. He was willing to sacrifice ten of his Vietminh for every French soldier killed. It was a high cost, but one which the Vietnamese could pay and the French could not. The commander of Ho's army, General Giap, not only shared this view he had long ago adopted a philosophical attitude toward death which he used to justify the heavy sacrifices he repeatedly asked of his troops. "Every minute, hundreds of thousands of people die on this earth." What then is "the life or death of a hundred, a thousand, tens of thousands of human beings, even our compatriots." The Vietminh had the will, and the numbers, to suffer casualties in the tens of thousands in engagements against the Hmong, and they could do so and endure. Such losses would decimate the Hmong.

In early 1962 Vang Pao again relocated his headquarters. The new site was thirty-five miles southwest of Xieng Khouang city at Long Cheng, an immense high plateau ringed by limestone mountains. The location had two features to recommend it. The vastness of the plateau made it an ideal location for a large airstrip. And the protective barrier of the limestone mountains made it a difficult place for the communists to attack. The C.I.A. immediately set to work laying a four thousand foot landing strip that could accommodate large cargo planes. Power plants, paved roads, living quarters and recreational facilities soon followed. By 1966 Long Cheng had become one of the C.I.A.'s largest field head-quarters, second only to the agency's installation at Saigon. Work on a less grand scale was also underway at Sam Thong, a village nine miles north of Long Cheng, where a logistics center for the refugee relief program was established.

The furious pace of the C.I.A. construction crews at Long Cheng was matched by the Hmong work teams in Vang Pao's ten resistance zones. They built hundreds of mountain top airstrips that enabled Hmong pilots, trained by the U.S. in Thailand, to routinely leap-frog from one village to another in small reconnaissance planes and helicopters, bringing in supplies and gathering information about enemy movements.

The airfields also served another purpose. For the first time opium merchants (mostly French until 1965) were able to fly in and collect raw opium from thousands of Hmong farmers living around the Plain of Jars. Later, when Vang Pao's guerrilla's gained control of Sam Neua province, additional airfields were built and the network rapidly expanded to cover most of the prime opium growing areas in northeastern Laos. While this breathed new life into opium farming, it was really the last gasp of a dying industry. Within a few years the best opium growing areas would come under communist control, and this, coupled with U.S. saturation bombing of enemy held territory, forced thousands of Hmong to leave their fields for crowded refugees camps around Long Cheng.

Vang Pao was a grateful but wary recipient of C.I.A. largess, for he could not help but wonder whether it might stop as quickly as it had started. It was inevitable that the enemy would seek an end to all support for the Hmong army in any negotiations on a new coalition government. To hedge his bets, before the outcome of the 1962 Geneva Conference became a matter of history, Vang Pao ordered his guerrillas to begin stockpiling arms and ammunition. And well he did, for the final agreement resulted in a cutoff of all military aid to his army.

Because of the cut-off, Vang Pao had to scale down his operations with the predictable result that the communists stepped up theirs. Vietminh convoys traveling down highway 7 from Sam Neua province brought new troops and munitions to the Plain of Jars. For the moment, the most Vang Pao could do was send out commandos to blow up passes and bridges to reduce the momentum of the buildup. There was one bright spot. The alliance between the Pathet Lao and neutralists was finally coming completely unravelled and most of the fighting on the Plain of Jars was between their forces. This diversion permitted Vang Pao's self-defense units to mount repeated ambushes and employ hit and run tactics against communist positions in Xieng Khouang province without fear of a major retaliation. By spring 1963 Vang Pao had gained control of nearly 75% of the province.

The relentless Pathet Lao assault on Neutralist positions finally convinced Souvanna Phouma that not only was the so-called coalition government doomed but that the communists meant to capture power by force of arms. He turned to the U.S. for support. C.I.A. cargo planes once again landed at Long Cheng and Vang Pao received enough arms and ammunition to mount a new offensive. This time he pushed into Sam Neua province and advanced to within a few miles of the Pathet Lao general headquarters at Sam Neua city.

Pha Thi was one of the trophies of the offensive. Situated northwest of Sam Neua city and within a stone's throw of the north Vietnam border, the small Hmong village of Pha Thi sat like a bird's nest atop the 5,680 foot limestone mountain that shared the village's name. More aptly described as a giant, wedged shaped promontory than a mountain, Pha Thi was an unlikely site even for a Hmong village. To reach the flattened top of what the locals aptly called "the Rock" one had to trudge through thick underbrush up narrow, nearly vertical trails. Only a Hmong, or a goat, could have considered Pha Thi inhabitable. However, the "Rock's" close proximity to north Vietnam coupled with the obvious difficulty of mounting an offensive against troops stationed on its crest was of some strategic significance to the U.S. military. The Joint Chiefs of Staff were already developing contingency plans for the bombing of north Vietnam by mid-1964. The village of Pha Thi was an ideal spot for radar to guide American bombers to targets in north Vietnam. Toward the end of 1964 construction on a radar installation was underway. With the commencement of U.S. air raids on north Vietnam in early 1965, Pha Thi assumed a strategic importance for the Vietminh. And, as subsequent events revealed, they were willing to invest enormous amounts of time, supplies, and lives to destroy it.

This was all in the future, however. For the moment Vang Pao basked in the glory of his army's achievement. His Hmong now controlled most of northeastern Laos. But capturing so much territory so quickly was a double edged sword. His guerrillas were mobile assault units highly skilled at hit and run. Now that they had actually forced the communists out of their strongholds Vang Pao's troops would be obliged to switch roles and become defenders. Vang Pao attempted to adjust by consolidating his commandos into battalion sized units. But if they were restricted to defending fixed positions even these battalions would be no match for a division of Vietminh regulars. The precariousness of the situation was not immediately apparent because of a new element introduced into the war — U.S. air power. In May 1964, the U.S. began bombing runs over enemy held positions. The plan was not only to limit the communists' ability to mount major offensives against Vang Pao's forces but also to shatter the social and economic infrastructure of enemy held territory. In plain language, the aim was to kill and terrorize civilians under communist control, forcing them to abandon their homes and leave the communists masters of depopulated zones; without farmers to feed their troops, coolies to transport their munitions, or laborers to construct their roads, the communists would be obliged to do more with less.

The deadly implications of this larger goal were not immediately apparent to either the enemy or the civilians living under their rule. The first bombing sorties were in propeller powered planes and numbered only a few per day. Only later, when the daily sorties were in the hundreds and fighter bombers guided by radar planes saturated villages and fields with napalm, antipersonnel bombs, and high explosives did the object of the air raids become brutally clear.

Even in the early, less murderous, stages of the bombing, major communist advances against positions held by Vang Pao's troops were few in number. Except for the Plain of Jars itself, where the communists held their ground with bulldog tenacity, Vang Pao's montagnard army controlled nearly all of Xieng Khouang and Sam Neua provinces.

COMMANDER OF THE 2ND MILITARY REGION

In December 1964, Vang Pao was called to Vientiane for a meeting with Souvanna Phouma. In an attempt to impress the Hmong commander with his patriotism the prime minister showed him a thick account ledger indicating the millions he had socked away in Parisian banks. And why wasn't he back in Paris spending this money and having a good time, the prime minister asked? It was because he was a dedicated patriot who placed the welfare of his nation above his own happiness. As Vang Pao later recalled, the first thing that crossed his mind when Souvanna Phouma finished answering his own question was how a true patriot was able to amass such a fortune on a prime minister's salary.

Souvanna Phouma appealed to Vang Pao's own patriotism. He must take command of the 2nd military region, encompassing Vientiane, Xieng Khouang and Sam Neua provinces, and save the country from the communists. It was, the prime minister reminded him, his duty to his country.

Actually, Vang Pao already controlled most of the 2nd military region. And as long as the Americans continued to be committed to a free Laos, their military support would remain solidly attached to his army. What the prime minister offered was the legitimation of fact. And, of course, for heeding the call to duty Vang Pao would at last receive the promotion that had so long eluded him. He would be made a general of the Royal Laotian Army.

Whether the reason for Vang Pao's slow advancement was due to Laotian prejudice against his race or, as reported, because of his attempted assassination of a Laotian commander who upbraided him for manhandling one of his recruits, or because he had meddled in politics by getting Touby to prevent a planned repression of some rebellious Sam Neua Hmong, the fact remained that he was held back and it cut him to the quick. The chance for promotion was therefore enticing.

Yet, it was the larger issue of long term Hmong interests that finally led Vang Pao to agree to the legitimation of his command. It meant a public recognition that the Hmong, as well as the other tribal minorities like the Yao and Kha who were now represented in significant numbers in Vang Pao's army, were bearing the full burden of the national defense. If they succeeded in saving the country from the communists they might at last be treated as equals by the Laotians.

Indeed, recent events highlighted how far the Hmong had yet to go to achieve this nominal equality. Just two months prior to Vang Pao's audience with Souvanna Phouma, the Laotian court system was brought to its knees by a general strike of the Royal Government's court officials. The strike was in response to the appointment of Touby's brother, Tougeu, to the post of General Director of the Justice Department. Tougeu had worked in the Justice Department for nearly four years before his promotion to General Director. Nor had he encountered anything approaching this level of hostility. But, of course, he was then only an official and not a director. It is likely many Laotian jurists conceded that the rising military importance of the Hmong necessitated a certain number of Hmong political appointees. That was politics. But to actually grant a Hmong authority over the Laotian court system was something else altogether. It implicitly acknowledged that the Hmong had a right to share real power over the lives of Laotians. The Hmong, the strikers complained, are too ignorant to be given authority over ethnic Lao. They are not real Laotians. They are foreigners. Even though Tougeu did not resign his position, and the strikers returned to work, the "Tougeu Affair" revealed the depth of Laotian racist feelings toward the Laotian Hmong.

After assuming formal command of the 2nd Military Region, Vang Pao established a forward headquarters at Na Khang on the edge of Sam Neua province. Happily for his soldiers, the fighting slowed to a snail's pace during 1965 because north Vietnam was preoccupied with other matters. The Joint operations of ARVN (Army of the Republic of Vietnam) and U.S. forces were causing problems for the Viet Cong and over ten thousand North Vietnamese regulars had to be diverted from other operations to be sent to the rescue. Even more troublesome, on February 13, the U.S. began operation Rolling Thunder. For the first time North Vietnam was subjected to saturation bombing, although at first the air attacks were restricted to strategic targets in unpopulated areas. The aim was not massive destruction but to provide an incentive for the communists to enter negotiations for a peace settlement. When this muzzled approach did not bring the desired effect, napalm and cluster bombs were included in the arsenal and more targets, some quite populated, were added to the list.

By late December 1965, President Johnson was persuaded to attempt a peace initiative and called a halt to all bombing in North Vietnam on Christmas day. The bombing pause lasted thirty-seven days, just long enough for the North Vietnamese to rush troops into Laos in an attempt to retake lost ground. Vang Pao's forward headquarters at Na Khang came under repeated attacks, and in one of them the General was shot in the left arm. The bullet from a Soviet AK47 shattered the humerus just below the shoulder. Vang Pao was flown to Honolulu for reconstructive surgery. After a brief recuperation and quick tour of Waikiki Beach, he was back in the field with his troops.

A TASTE OF MODERN LIFE

From 1966 to 1968, increased air support from U.S. fighter bombers enabled Vang Pao to hold on to the territory he had won, and even extend it. Of course, the intensive bombing made life in many areas precarious at best and thousands of residents chose migration to safer areas as the prudent course. They joined the swelling population in and around the two towns of Long Cheng and Sam Thong which had remained safe havens from enemy attacks. As early as 1964 the two towns had grown to 30,000 and 15,000 respectively with perhaps another 30,000 living in small villages in the surrounding hills. In the next two years thousands more were added to these numbers.

The congestion inevitably altered the traditional Hmong lifestyle. Because of the unsuitability of the available land, opium farming diminished in importance. On the other hand, corn and rice were in high demand in the crowded towns of Long Cheng and Sam Thong. For the first time, Hmong farmers were raising these staples as cash crops. The town people had the money to buy their produce because nearly every family had sons and brothers serving in Vang Pao's army receiving nearly four times the monthly pay of their Laotian counterparts in the regular army.

Vang Pao's soldiers were paid in Laotian kip rather than silver, which was traditional. Hmong reservations about the inflation prone kip were dispelled by the decision of the U.S. government to back the kip with dollars. Not only did this dramatically increase the money supply but, in comparison with silver bars, it was highly liquid. Money could now be used for small as well as large transactions, satisfying one very important condition for a commercial economy. In former times, Chinese or Vietnamese merchants would have rushed in to take advantage of the situation, but the war excluded them from the area. Hmong filled in the gap. Hundreds of tons of manufactured goods were transported each month on trucks and planes from Vientiane to Long Cheng where they were received by Hmong merchants who hawked their goods in the expanding markets of Long Cheng and Sam Thong or carted them by truck or jeep over the newly improved roads to surrounding villages.

Some of these merchants, like Vu Neng, enjoyed considerable prosperity. Vu Neng opened a general store at Long Cheng in 1967.

For ten years before his entry into the business world he worked in the Ministry of Information and Tourism in Vientiane. It was a good job, but his income did not increase fast enough to meet the needs of his growing family. The career change solved his financial problems. Within three years he had saved enough money to purchase a new family home in Vientiane.

Some enterprising Hmong built an ice factory at Long Cheng, while others opened restaurants. Hmong also took up new professions. There were Hmong photographers and Hmong dentists; Hmong became tailors, bakers, cobblers and radio repairmen. A new cottage industry, the fabrication of brooms, blossomed in the outlying villages giving employment to over 200 Hmong families.

Road traffic between Sam Thong and Long Cheng picked up as well, and not all of it consisted of trucks carrying goods to villages. A large proportion of the vehicles were military jeeps converted into taxis transporting Hmong over distances that would have taken days to travel by foot.

Not only was the economy growing, Hmong were sending their children to school in record numbers. The vast majority of these schools were built and run by Hmong and financed by the funds set aside by Edgar Buell from the U.S. refugee relief program. The schools were generally perceived by the Hmong as their first real chance to acquire the skills necessary to compete on an equal footing with the ethnic Lao. Despite the many lives lost in the war, the loss of their land and the crowded conditions of their new communities, the Hmong looked to the future with considerable optimism.

They were also developing the skills necessary to emerge as a political force in Laos. After the evacuation of the civil administration of the Royal Laotian government from Xieng Khouang and Sam Neua provinces during the communist offensive of 1961, Vang Pao assumed full responsibility for establishing an interim, and unofficial, civil bureaucracy that provided the Hmong with self-government for nearly fifteen years.

Hmong officials in the new refugee settlements took charge of coordinating the ongoing relief effort, maintaining law and order, and recruiting soldiers for induction into Vang Pao's army. With so many different clans thrown together, new skills were developed in conciliation and compromise. At Long Cheng, for example, to prevent charges of favoritism in the court no clan was allowed to have more than one representative on the panel of judges. The secrets of urban politics and the governing of large numbers of people were no longer the sole preserve of the ethnic Lao.

However, these remarkable gains would only translate into lasting improvements if the north Vietnamese were prevented from turning Laos into a puppet state. Should the Hmong fail to frustrate north Vietnamese imperialism not only would they lose their bargaining position with the dominant ethnic Lao, the Vietnamese might very well exact a terrible price for their persistent opposition. Indeed, the Hmong would be perfect scapegoats for the defeated Lao as well as the conquering Vietnamese and their Pathet Lao collaborators. Both sides could point a finger at the Hmong as the root cause for all the bloodshed. The Lao would be off the Hook for resisting the communist takeover, and the communists could employ terrorism against the Hmong as an object lesson to the Lao should they prove uncooperative citizens of their new police state.

THE FALL OF PHA THI

Such dark forebodings may have seemed out of place in early 1967 when Vietminh operations were at a standstill and their Pathet Lao allies nearly everywhere on the run. But by the end of that year pessimism once again seemed in order. The Vietminh put thousands of coolies to work constructing a road from Sam Neua city to Pha Thi. It was the first stage in the preparations for a major assault on the radar installation.

There was only one way for the enemy to get a sizeable force to the top of Pha Thi. Troops would have to work their way up a narrow pass and then use grappling hooks to negotiate a sheer cliff. In anticipation of this possibility the Hmong at Pha Thi placed land mines in the pass. Unfortunately, the north Vietnamese sent in teams of specialists who worked patiently for two months removing most of the mines.

The assault on the radar station followed a diversionary action. In January 1968, a combined Pathet Lao and Vietminh offensive was launched against Vang Pao's positions throughout Sam Neua province. With the Hmong in retreat and unable to mount a relief operation for their comrades at Pha Thi, the Vietminh began their assault on "The Rock" in early March. Heavy artillery bombarded the Hmong defenders and the thirteen American technicians who were dug in on the summit while the communists moved in force up the pass offering cover fire for suicide squads using ropes to scale the cliff. The Hmong picked them off, one by one until all the ropes dangled free in the wind. The artillery attack continued, however, and at one point it became so intense that the defenders dared not even raise their heads out of their trenches. Food and water was tossed from trench to trench. And there was little to go around. Helicopters attempting to drop in supplies were repeatedly driven off by enemy anti-aircraft guns. By early June, Vang Pao conceded the impossibility of his men holding out any longer. After blowing up what was left of the battered radar installation, the Hmong and the one surviving American technician abandoned the summit.

Three months later Vang Pao led five battalions in a vain effort to retake Pha Thi. The Hmong general faced two divisions of determined north Vietnamese regulars. After three weeks of heavy fighting only one company of Hmong had advanced far enough to secure a tenuous foothold on one of the mountain's main slopes. After another week of fighting and the loss of three hundred men, Vang Pao conceded that he had made the mistake of leading his guerrillas into a set piece battle where fire power and the ability to sustain high casualties determined the outcome.

In February 1969, Vang Pao's forward headquarters at Na Khang came under attack. Heavy cannon, rocket launchers, and mortars pounded the base. After three days the headquarters was reduced to rubble and the Hmong were dug into ground that resembled a moonscape. It was then that five thousand Viets advanced in waves against the Hmong trenches. Hundreds were cut down and still they came tumbling over the piles of their own dead. Vang Pao's losses were high, too, and it was not very long before his men began to run out of ammunition. He ordered a retreat and left Na Khang as a cemetery for the Viets.

The communists continued their advance, reoccupying territory that Vang Pao had wrested from them during his 1964-65 offensive. In April they captured the post at Phou Koum south of Vang Pao's former advance headquarters at Na Khang. The communists were moving down highway 6 toward the Plain of Jars and Vang Pao's redoubt at Long Cheng. The only Hmong outpost that blocked their route was the one at Bouam Long situated just off the main highway and, thus, an easy mark for the heavy artillery rolling down the road toward the plain.

Again, assault waves followed on the heels of a devastating artillery attack. Dead Vietnamese draped the barbed wire around Bouam Long's perimeter until the weight of the bodies caved in the fencing at places where fresh troops streamed through. Vang Pao directed his small Hmong air force of prop driven T-28s against the Viet waves. The post held out for twelve days before the enemy withdrew to lick their wounds. Vang Pao immediately dispatched an airborne battalion against Phou Koum and recaptured the fallen post. The liberated post held out against a last ditch effort by two communist battalions to dislodge the defenders.

Having momentarily halted the enemy's advance, Vang Pao began a counterattack. He loosed three battalions against the Viet Minh. One captured Dong Dane on highway 4, giving the Hmong control over the main route to the Plain of Jars from communist stronghold at Xieng Khouang city. A second battalion assaulted communist positions northeast of Xieng Khouang city, and a third marched on Xieng Khouang city itself. The fighting continued for two weeks.

Watching from the sidelines, and by now thoroughly disillusioned with the communists, an airborne battalion of Kong Le's neutralists suddenly switched sides and joined the Hmong assault just in time to share in the victory. The intense fighting had reduced the provincial capital to piles of shattered stones and masonry. Instead of establishing a base on the site, Vang Pao withdrew his forces to the surrounding hills. The loss of the city was a major setback in the communist offensive and Vang Pao's intelligence reports informed him that they were gathering for a counter attack. The intelligence was good news. The communists had let their pride rule their reason. By concentrating their forces in an assault on Xieng Khouang city they left the Plain of Jars unprotected. It was an ideal time to divert troops to the plain and dislodge the communists.

Leaving a portion of his troops dug in near Xieng Khouang city to keep the communists occupied once they began the campaign to retake it, Vang Pao prepared for a push against communist positions on the Plain of Jars. All through July and early August, American bombers blasted Vietminh positions on the plain. By the time Vang Pao's forces marched out to engage the communists the saturation bombing had driven most of the larger Vietminh units to the periphery of the plain where they were unable to offer quick assistance to the Pathet Lao who for the first time in years had to face the Hmong alone. Within a few weeks the fighting turned into a complete rout.

MASTER OF THE PLAIN OF JARS

In early October 1969, Vang Pao declared himself master of the Plain of Jars. He was also master of a huge cache of weapons the communists had stored on the plain to support a planned siege of Vang Pao's main headquarters at Long Cheng. There were enough weapons and ammunition to supply a good sized guerrilla force for ten years and Vang Pao stockpiled them for just that purpose.

Vang Pao's victory was not celebrated in Vientiane. Anti-war sentiment in the U.S. Congress resulted in the Cooper Amendment which barred the appropriation of additional funds for U.S. supported military action in Laos. Vang Pao was ordered to withdraw from the plain or face a cutoff of all supplies. The Hmong general ignored the order. If the U.S. cut off his supplies he would draw on those captured from the communists.

In late November the Vietminh threw three divisions at him and entered the plain with newly supplied Soviet heavy artillery and tanks. The Hmong held them at bay but at a high price. When orders were again sent from Vientiane to evacuate the plain Vang Pao complied. The Vietminh pursued him toward Long Cheng until the Hmong turned and forced them to retreat back to the plain.

186

With his army bottled up at Long Cheng, Vang Pao prepared for the inevitable assault on his headquarters. Three elite divisions plus four regiments and a battalion of Dac Cong (suicide forces) were devoted to the capture of Long Cheng. The incessant attacks forced the evacuation of most of the civilian population to Ban Son just a few miles south of Long Cheng.

The heaviest attacks on Long Cheng occurred between December 1971 and April 1972 when eleven thousand rounds of enemy artillery were fired into the city. By early 1972 the Vietminh had gained a foothold on the limestone mountains surrounding the base. Though three Hmong battalions were able to retake the mountains, they were soon dislodged by new Viet units. But instead of continuing their assault the Viets dug in. Vang Pao correctly presumed they were waiting for more reinforcements for the final push. Intelligence reports indicated they would come from the south in an attempted rear guard action. Vang Pao's soldiers encountered them less than a mile from Long Cheng in the Nam Ngum valley, close enough for the artillery at Long Cheng to decimate the surprised Vietminh regiment.

In early April 1972, after two attempts to drive the Vietminh off Long Cheng's protective mountain perimeter were beaten back by enemy artillery, Vang Pao ordered special units to infiltrate enemy positions. Their job was to identify the location of enemy artillery and direct air assaults against them by U.S. Phantom jets. Within two weeks most of the enemy's artillery was put out of commission. This time the Hmong were able to drive the Vietminh off the mountains.

One of Vang Pao's Hmong officers, Vue Seng, commanded a company of Hmong during one of the assaults. It was rough going through heavy underbrush up a steep trail. When his unit was within a few hundred yards of the summit it came under heavy fire and his men were forced to proceed at a snail's pace. Vang Pao was circling overhead in a helicopter at the time, checking the progress of the assault. He radioed Vue Seng to pick up the pace. As an incentive he informed him that if his men did not reach the top within 30 minutes, T-28's would be ordered in to bomb his position. Vue Seng argued with the general. He explained his circumstances and asked for more time. Vang Pao refused to reconsider. Vue Seng argued with him some more, and the more he argued the more enraged he became. He would show Vang Pao what he and his men were made of and rub the general's nose in it when he was through. This, of course, was exactly the effect Vang Pao intended. For within five minutes Vue Seng's men reached the summit and sent the Viets pell-mell down the other side. Vang Pao was ecstatic when Vue Seng informed him of the achievement.

Hmong Pilot

Unfortunately, another company attacking the dug in Viets on a different crest transmitted incorrect coordinates to the T-28s crisscrossing the mountains and assaulting enemy positions. Within a few minutes after his conversation with the general, Vue Seng's men were ducking for cover as a squadron of T-28s began to unload on them. The rocky soil at the summit was so hard packed that the shock waves of the exploding bombs lifted the Hmong several feet into the air. Luckily no one was killed, but Vue Seng concluded that the general had for some strange reason carried through with his threat to call in an air attack on his position. Once he had checked the condition of his troops he was back on the radio giving Vang Pao a piece of his mind. Vang Pao was shocked, and apologetic. "Any casualties?" he asked. Vue Seng paused and then reported: "There are many dead and wounded." Vang Pao was distraught and promised immediate aid to evacuate the wounded. When Vue Seng thought Vang Pao had suffered enough he told the relieved general the truth.

Having regained control of Long Cheng's mountain perimeter, Vang Pao's troops drove the Vietminh back to the plain. Civilians returned to the battered headquarters and rebuilt their homes and shops. The return would not be permanent.

BEGINNING OF THE END

In late 1972, Souvanna Phouma was informed by Henry Kissinger of U.S. intentions to withdraw all military support for the Royal Laotian Army once a peace settlement with the north Vietnamese was finalized. By February of the following year the Laotian prime minister concluded negotiations with the Pathet Lao to begin the process of forming a new coalition government. In honor of the settlement both sides agreed to a general cease fire.

As usual, fighting continued in the field as the Pathet Lao and the Vietminh hurried to claim more territory for their side. To help improve the position of the rightists and neutralists in the negotiations the U.S. air lifted in five thousand Thai troops to beef up Vang Pao's beleaguered forces. Some Hmong still remember the day when the first Thai units arrived at Long Cheng. Parading around in starched uniforms and shiny boots they boasted they would quickly route the Vietminh and end the war. A few weeks later, after being badly mauled by the Viets, the Thai soldiers were pulled in from the field and demoted to conducting local patrols where they were unlikely to make a mess of things and endanger the lives of Hmong veterans.

A new coalition government was finally formed in April 1974. Though Touby was appointed Deputy Minister for Post and Telecommunications and two other Hmong were placed on the National Political Consultative Council, Hmong influence over Vientiane politics was near its end. As events soon revealed, the communists had no intention of sharing power with anyone, especially Hmong who had supported Vang Pao. Typically, gestures of conciliation were followed with military actions designed to capture power by non-political means.

The fighting heated up in 1975 and by March of that year the communists mounted another major offensive south of the Plain of Jars. When Vang Pao's troops began to make headway against the communists the general was called back to Vientiane where a worried Souvanna Phouma ordered him to cease his attacks against the communists. Vang Pao inquired what orders he was to follow should his soldiers come under attack. Retreat was the answer. Retreat to where? To Vientiane. To Thailand, Vang Pao shouted, ripping off his general's stars and angrily tossing them on the prime minister's desk.

Souvanna Phouma was later reported to have described Vang Pao's response to the French Ambassador and remarked that "The Hmong have served me well, Vang Pao has fought well for me. The Hmong are good soldiers. It's a pity that peace may come only at the cost of their liquidation."

For Vang Pao the war was over. The Vietminh and Pathet Lao took advantage of the situation by advancing on Long Cheng where a general evacuation was already underway. At Phou Kang a few miles away several thousand Hmong refugees were huddled near a bluff. Those near the front raised their hands to protect their eyes from the dust and debris thrown up by the rotors of a landing helicopter. A dejected Vang Pao emerged and, in a voice choked with emotion, addressed his people for the last time. "My brothers it is with great sadness that I address you today. My greatest desire was to end my days among you. That has become impossible. The political situation has deteriorated so much that my presence is the cause of great damage. One day, if destiny favors me, humbly I will again serve the Hmong people."

Vang Pao surveyed the upturned faces and delivered his final orders. "After I leave, the Pathet Lao will accuse me of a thousand crimes, and ask you to concur. Do so. When in the presence of the communists never say anything good about me; never reveal what is in your heart. Rather, invent wrongs, charge me with all the crimes of the land. Understand me well; I do not say to you: 'have no confidence in the Pathet,' but only defy their methods and their hypocritical proceedings. They will want you to hand over your weapons. Give them to them, but not all. Hide the rest carefully because I fear that you will soon have need of them."

Tears now streamed down his face. "Farewell my brothers. I can do nothing more for you. I would only be a torment for you. Remain united, retain your solidarity. May heaven keep you."

The helicopter carried Vang Pao nineteen miles south to Muong Cha where a plane waited to carry him to the U.S. air base at Oudorn, Thailand. On the way he had a change of mind. Though he was no longer commander of the 2nd Military Region, no longer a general in the Royal Laotian Army, he was still a Hmong. And there were five thousand Hmong soldiers still willing to follow him. He would continue the struggle alone.

When Vang Pao stepped out of his helicopter he ordered the pilot of the waiting plane to fly to Thailand without him. He returned to Long Cheng and immediately set about distributing arms and ammunition to his troops. He was busily reorganizing them into guerrilla units when he received a piece of information that forced him to abandon the project.

The source of the information was Yang Dao, who had recently returned from a junket to East Germany and Moscow sponsored by the new coalition government. Any illusions Yang Dao may have had about future fair treatment of the Hmong by the communists were shattered when he attended an East German banquet held in honor of their Laotian visitors. One of the speakers paused during the mandatory encomium of the communist revolution in Laos to point a finger directly at Yang Dao and bellow: "It is because of the damned Hmong that it has taken so many years to achieve a communist revolution in Laos." Proof that this was not an aberration was provided by President Podgorny in Moscow when he informed the Laotians that for the good of international communism the Hmong would, of course, have to be liquidated.

There was more bad news when Yang Dao returned to Vientiane. He learned from friends that not only were the Pathet Lao and Vietminh preparing for a major assault on Long Cheng, no one, not even the rightists, would lift a finger to intercede. What was worse, sensing the end was near, neutralist and rightist troops were joining the communists in droves. Given the drift of events, it would soon be the Hmong against everyone else.

Yang Dao boarded a plane for Long Cheng to apprise Vang Pao of the situation. The general had no wish to needlessly sacrifice the lives of his men in a futile last stand. And he certainly wanted to avoid anything that might make the Hmong victims of a race war. He had no choice but to disband his army and leave for Thailand.

HIN HEUP

Shortly after Vang Pao's departure the communists took command of Long Cheng. Meanwhile, thousands of Hmong refugees crowded together in the sprawling tent city of Phou Kang, anxiously waiting to see what the communists had planned for them. Judging by the angry articles surfacing in the Vientiane newspapers it would not be pleasant. On May 9th the Pathet Lao paper, *Khao Xane Pathet Lao*, intimated the party's position: "It is necessary to extirpate, down to the root, the 'Hmong' minority."

Fearing for their lives, the residents of Phou Kang joined thousands of other Hmong refugees (nearly forty thousand in all) from nearby towns and villages in a long march toward Vientiane with the vague intention of somehow crossing the Mekong and joining their leader in Thailand. Like the great migrations of the past, they carried all their worldly goods on their backs, but this time they did not walk the crests but followed the dirt trails and roads that descended into the Vientiane plain.

At one point in the march the throng paused to watch a helicopter land at the head of the column. A Hmong emerged from the cockpit. It was Touby Lyfoung. "Return to your homes and villages," he pleaded. The former guerrilla commander was now sixty-one. The years of sedentary life in Vientiane had made him fat. When asked if he could guarantee their security if they returned home, Touby responded that they needed none. "Vang Pao is gone, you have committed no crimes. You will be safe." Unconvinced, the crowd announced their intention to push on to Vientiane. With the sad realization that his word no longer carried much weight among his own people, Touby climbed back in the helicopter and departed for Vientiane.

Touby returned the next day in the company of Pathet Lao soldiers in a last ditch effort to convince his people to abandon the march and return to their villages. Using the back of a jeep as a podium, he informed the crowd that he had recently talked to Vang Pao on the phone. Their leader was in the United States and wanted them to remain in Laos. Again Touby was asked if he could guarantee their security if they went home. "Will you come and live among us, Touby," one Hmong inquired. "You could protect us from the Pathet Lao. If you swear to join us we will remain." "I can't," Touby replied. He told them that he was in contact with Faydang, his former enemy and now a high official in the Pathet Lao. "Faydang," he assured them, "will come and guarantee your safety." When this information did not sway them Touby suddenly raised his hand. "All who will stay here in Laos with me raise your hand." He counted the hands. It did not take long, only four were raised. Not without a sense of humor, Touby observed there would be at least five Hmong left in Laos.

Before leaving, Touby promised he would return the next day with assurances from the Vientiane government that the Hmong would come to no harm if they remained in Laos. The marchers never saw him again. What they did see as they drew closer to Vientiane was more Pathet Lao soldiers who arbitrarily confiscated their food and valuables. When one exhausted Hmong tried to bargain for space for his family on a passing truck a Pathet Lao soldier forced him out of the vehicle at gun point and shouted "the war is over and the Hmong have nothing left to do but die!" It was a bad omen.

On the ninth day of the march the Hmong reached the outskirts of Hin Heup, a small town on the edge of highway 13 that led directly to Vientiane. The entrance to the town was barricaded. When some Hmong tried to remove the barriers Pathet Lao soldiers swarmed around them and blocked their path. Several Hmong tried to push through the soldiers and were knocked down. Shots rang out. An old woman fell to the ground. Other soldiers began to use their rifles, some as clubs on whomever was in easy range, while the rest shot indiscriminately into the crowd. Armored vehicles were used to herd the Hmong down the road to the narrow bridge that crossed the Nam Lik River. Many Hmong simply fell off the bridge into the water and drowned. Others were deliberately tossed into the river by soldiers. Thousands of Hmong sought refuge in the forest, others turned and ran back up the road. Soldiers chased them, shooting or bludgeoning the stragglers.

Most of the survivors of the Hin Heup massacre returned to their villages only to be subjected to repeated interrogations by Pathet Lao soldiers who routinely accused them of having fought with Vang Pao. Many were sent to reeducation camps. Few ever returned. Even Touby, living in Vientiane, was not immune. He was sent to a reeducation camp in Sam Neua province where he reportedly died from malaria in 1978.

Thousands of Hmong were forced into agricultural communes in the lowlands where they were stricken by tropical diseases. Others were given a bag of rice and a few tools and plopped down in the mountain wilderness where they were expected not only to survive but to become self-sufficient peasant farmers.

Some Hmong were permitted to return to their old villages in Sam Neua and Xieng Khouang provinces where much of the land was barren from the years of U.S. bombing and overgrown with imperata, a form of rugged grass with deep roots against which Hmong hoes are no match. The repatriated Hmong were barely able to produce enough to keep alive. Nor was it much consolation to realize that the ethnic Lao were not faring much better. Within a few years the inefficiencies of forced collectivization coupled with bouts of heavy flooding dramatically reduced the output of Laotian farmers. Not only did the Lao People's Democratic Republic (LPDR) have to rely on International aid to prevent famine, it lacked sufficient revenue to run the state. Desperate for funds, the government encouraged the Hmong to resume opium farming. Following the lead of the "French imperialists', the LPDR established its own opium monopoly, and required Hmong opium farmers to sell their harvests to the state at below market prices.

After thirty years of more or less continuous fighting and the loss of approximately one third of their population, the Laotian Hmong found themselves back where they started three generations earlier: poor, repressed, and longing for freedom.

CHAPTER
11

RESISTERS, REFUGEES, AND IMMIGRANTS

RESISTANCE

Not all of the Hmong who remained in Laos after the 1975 communist takeover sought accommodation with the new regime. Thousands took to the hills, dug up the rifles they had buried and organized a resistance. One of the leaders of the rebels was Yang Shua Sai. He was sent to a reeducation camp in the spring of 1975 and probably would have died there if he had not agreed to return to his village and organize a propaganda campaign highlighting the alleged crimes committed by Vang Pao and his U.S. supporters against the Laotian people. The day Yang Shua Sai was returned to his village he escaped into the forest and began recruiting Hmong guerrillas. Within a few months he returned to his old village and liberated it from the communists.

The major concentration of Hmong resisters was around Phu Bia mountain on the southern edge of the Plain of Jars. The area remained impregnable to the Viets and Pathet Lao until 1978 when four Vietnamese divisions backed by MIG-21s and heavy artillery conducted a protracted campaign against the Hmong rebels. While the MIGs and artillery inflicted heavy damage on the Hmong guerrillas, it was actually the chemical warfare and napalm that forced them into an early submission. Xiong Chong Neng commanded a unit of the Phu Bia rebels. His men enjoyed several victories over the Vietminh even after their massive troop buildup. Being outnumbered was hardly a new experience. What was new were the rockets fired from Soviet gunships. Xiong Chong Neng had seen rockets before, but they were different than the ones used against them now. Instead of white smoke, these rockets trailed red or yellow smoke and exploded above the ground spraying a fine powder over fields and villages. If the powder got on your skin, or you breathed it in, you got very sick. The major symptoms were bleeding from the nose and mouth, nausea and severe stomach cramps followed by diarrhea. If the powder got into a village stream it affected nearly everyone. The very old and very young often died, while adults remained sick for several weeks; and, of course, affected rebels were too ill to fight.

Just how many Hmong were killed by the chemicals is unknown, though if one can trust the testimony of Pathet Lao soldiers who participated in the chemical warfare, the number was high: nearly 50,000 killed between 1975 and 1978 in the Phu Bia region alone.

While the deadly effects of the"red"and"yellow"rain seriously weakened the resolve of the Hmong rebels, the napalm effectively broke the back of the Phu Bia rebellion. Though napalm bombs were sometimes dropped on villages, crops were the primary targets. The bombing often intensified just before harvest. In many villages the napalm completely destroyed the corn and rice crops, leaving thousands near starvation within a few months.

It was the mass starvation that crushed the rebellion and forced the rebels to leave their mountains and join the other Hmong refugees in Thailand. Many did not survive the trek. If they were not shot by Pathet Lao or Viet soldiers, they died of starvation or drowned when they tried to cross an unguarded (often unguarded because the river was presumed too dangerous to cross) section of the Mekong. One group of 2,500 Hmong arrived at the Hong Khai refugee camp in December 1977. The group had numbered almost 8,000 when the march began.

Not all of the rebels left for Thailand. Some Hmong retreated north into the mountain wilderness and continued the struggle. In 1980, China, feeling threatened by the partnership between its Soviet nemesis and its historical adversary, Vietnam, attempted to blunt the tip of the Vietnamese sword that at any moment might be pointed at its own underbelly by supplying Hmong rebels, as well as thousands of other Laotian hill tribesmen, arms and military advisors to support their guerrilla operations against Vietnamese and LPDR military forces. The fighting continues even today.

HMONG IN THAILAND

After Laos fell to the communists in 1975 thousands of Hmong crossed the Mekong river and sought asylum in Thailand. Perhaps an equal number who also attempted the crossing perished, either by drowning or from being shot by communist soldiers. At first, the government of Thailand allowed the immigrants to settle near established Hmong communities in the provinces of Nong Khai, Nan, and Chiang Rai. But, as the numbers began to swell, the Thai administration had second thoughts. With Laos now a puppet of bellicose Vietnam the Thai did not want to be open to the charge of harboring rebels who might use Thailand as a home base for guerrilla incursions into Laos. Nor did the Thai government find inviting the prospect of Hmong rebels living in close proximity to existing Hmong communities in Thailand. As recently as 1967, Thai military units had been used to suppress Hmong revolts in Chiang Rai, Nan, Phetchabun and Tak provinces. And while new aid programs had gone a long way to smooth relations with Hmong communities, worries over new rebellions remained.

To avoid these problems, Hmong refugees were isolated in border camps at Chang Khong, Chang Kham, Ban Nam Yao, Sob Tuang, and Ban Vinai. And to dissuade other Hmong from crossing the Mekong into Thailand, the government provided less than minimal assistance to the camp inmates. This did not prove to be an efficient deterrent, for by late 1978 the camps held over 50,000 Laotian Hmong.

Given the low level of government assistance, many camp inmates would have perished from malnutrition or disease had it not been for the help of private relief agencies and, later, funds from Hmong relatives who had immigrated to France and the U.S. While private aid kept the Hmong alive, it did not raise them out of poverty. For this they needed employment which, from the very start, has been difficult to find. The government has prohibited Hmong refugees from moving to urban centers where there are jobs, and there are few opportunities for work close to the camps. Outside of tending a garden plot to augment the family diet, many Hmong have remained unemployed for over a decade. To add to their problems, the Thai sometimes victimized camp inmates. At Ban Vinai, for example, Thai bandits regularly preyed on Hmong entering and leaving the camp. On occasion Hmong women working in their fields were attacked and raped by the same bandits. In 1982, Hmong from Ban Vinai armed themselves with axes, hoes, and knives and tracked down the criminals, killing nearly a hundred within a week.

Impoverished and sometimes persecuted, cooped up in camps and denied access to mountain land where they could at least become self-subsistent, many Hmong in the camps turned to messianism to lift their spirits. This was not something new. Dispirited Hmong in Laos had earlier embraced Hmong messianism as a way to cope with mass suffering and persistent uncertainty.

A large part of Pa Chay's appeal was due to his explicit messianism that carried the promise that heaven would intercede to make the Hmong victorious over their enemies. In the late 1920s, two shamans in Xieng Khouang province whipped the Laotian Hmong into a rebellious mood, using magic and appeals to heaven to build a small army. There was another outbreak of Hmong messianism in 1950

197

in Sam Neua and, in the late 1960s, a Hmong war refugee from that same province tried to generate a messianic movement at Long Cheng, the site of General Vang Pao's headquarters.

In August 1967, Yang Chong Leu announced to the war weary citizens of Long Cheng that salvation was near at hand. As proof of his authenticity as a messenger for heaven he had in his possession a Hmong script taught to him by the gods. And the message he carried was that the Hmong would be sent a king. Yang Chong Leu even specified the date of the messiah's arrival. It would be on September 15th.

When the promised king did not appear Yang Chong Leu tried to explain away the failed prophecy with the claim that the messiah had come but couldn't find any Hmong and left. He couldn't find them because the Hmong at Long Cheng had become indistinguishable from the ethnic Lao. Yang Chong Leu warned that salvation would never come until the Hmong rejected modern ways and honored the traditions of their ancestors.

The prophet's following was sufficiently large to be a matter of concern to Long Cheng authorities who eventually had him imprisoned and later executed. The movement did not end with his death. His disciples elevated Pa Chay to the status of a demigod and called themselves the Chao Fa, God's disciples. They chose the pig as a symbol of their movement, and new converts were taught to read the Chao Fa script, a version of Yang Chong Leu's Hmong alphabet. In fact, many of the Hmong rebels operating around Phu Bia after the communist takeover of Laos were Chao Fa disciples, and aping Pa Chay they engaged in magical ceremonies before battles and carried magic flags to deflect the communists' bullets.

After their defeat, large numbers of the Phu Bia rebels wound up in refugee camps in Thailand where they began recruiting other camp inmates into the Chao Fa. While no exact numbers are available, the Chao Fa in the camps are reported to have a sizeable following. Indeed, the Chao Fa sect at Ban Vinai exhibits all the signs of having become an established religion. Members do not just meet in village homes. They have their own temple replete with religious icons. In front of the temple stands a ten foot high statue of a Chao Fa patron saint referred to as Tzong Patheng. Another, smaller statue of another protector spirit, a two-headed clay incarnation of a creature from Hmong mythology, sits on an altar inside the temple. Off to one side of the temple inside the shelter of a gazebo stands a life sized statue of a boar. The temple courtyard also houses a youth center where children are taught the Hmong Chao Fa script and learn the traditions and recite the legends of their people, the catechism of the Hmong Chao Fa. The message preached by the Chao Fa at Ban Vinai is simple: only through the preservation of tradition can the Hmong hope for salvation, for a nation of their own.

Hmong Chao Fa priest

Hmong Chao Fa temple

HMONG IN THE U.S.

Many Hmong who fled Laos after the communist victory chose to migrate to western countries rather than remain closed up in Thai refugee camps. Several thousand settled in France, Australia, and Canada, but most chose the U.S. because it was now the home of Vang Pao.

Granted political asylum in 1975, Vang Pao settled on a 450 acre cattle ranch in the remote Bitter root mountains of Montana. Except for the winter snow, the coniferous forests of the Bitter roots were not much different from the mountain forests of Laos. But herding cattle was not the same as commanding men, and the general naturally became restless. His forced retirement did not last long. Hmong were migrating to the U.S. in large numbers and soon his phone was ringing off the hook with appeals for advice and aid.

In 1977, Vang Pao left his mountain ranch for southern California where he founded Lao Family Community, a self-help organization for Laotian refugees. Funding by the California Department of Social Services a year later enabled his organization to expand its operations into other states and qualify for federal grants. Eventually Lao Family Community established offices in nearly every Hmong community in America. Hmong received aid in finding jobs, obtaining vocational and language training and advice and representation in their dealings with the wider community.

Even with the support of Lao Family Community, many Hmong had problems adjusting to American society. In rural and sometimes not so rural areas Hmong unaccustomed to either fishing licenses or hunting seasons were arrested for taking game illegally. There have also been arrests for raising opium for personal consumption — usually for an elderly member of the family suffering from chronic pain associated with arthritis or some other degenerative disease.

The principal difficulty, however, has been the adjustment to American materialism and individualism. Though the Hmong are perfectly at home with the capitalist ethic and hold those who achieve wealth through hard work in high esteem, this exists in the context of their traditional culture which emphasizes communal over individual values. This has made it difficult for Hmong to take full advantage of economic opportunities. More often than not, place of residence has been determined by the number of Hmong already living in a locality than by the the availability of jobs. This has forced thousands of Hmong to accept welfare, which they find extremely distasteful.

Even when jobs are available, Hmong often do not have the necessary skills to land them. Except for their brief exposure to modern life at Long Cheng, the experience of most Hmong refugees is that of the peasant farmer. While more than a few Hmong dreamed of becoming successful American farmers and were

Beauty Contest

sometimes provided free or subsidized land by private and government agencies, most ventures have been economic failures due mostly to unfamiliarity with the complexities of marketing farm produce after it is harvested.

Even low skilled jobs have remained out of the reach of many Hmong because of the language barrier. And while most Hmong refugees eventually acquired some command of English, it is the young adults and especially the children who have done the best. This has created strains within Hmong communities. The difficulty is not that young adults often become the primary breadwinners for families. In Hmong society children are expected to take care of their parents. Nor does this tend to diminish the parents' authority when it occurs. The difficulty is that the young adults have been better able to manage relations between the Hmong family and community and the broader society and its institutions. Not only has this resulted in a loss of authority for some elders, it has caused many to feel superfluous. In a few instances this has led to suicide.

The bright spot on the horizon is the new generation of American Hmong. Encouraged to excel at school, and publicly praised at community gatherings for their academic achievements, large numbers of Hmong children will likely be successful competitors for high skilled jobs and the professions. Some Hmong are already working as engineers, computer programmers, social workers and university professors. What is uncertain is the extent to which this growing economic progress will weaken traditional Hmong culture and the solidarity of Hmong communities. To date, the effect appears to be negligible. True, Hmong women, traditionally independent spirited, have sometimes been quick to demand a more equal partnership in the housekeeping and the care of children; but most still see their role as wife and mother as central to their lives. And, overall, family and community solidarity remains strong, as does respect for tradition. Even Hmong shamanism continues to thrive, though mostly as an adjunct to modern medicine. Hmong still only marry other Hmong and most still observe the strict incest taboo that requires mates to be selected from different clans. And, if anything, the celebration of the New Year festival has gained in importance as a symbol of Hmong solidarity. Each year upwards of thirty thousand Hmong converge in central California to celebrate the New Year Festival. And while the addition of beauty contests and band competitions reflects the influence of American culture, the traditional sacrifices and ceremonies, as well as the courting rituals, remain as the central focus of the event.

If most Hmong have become American without ceasing to be Hmong, a sizeable minority nevertheless desire to return to Laos. At one time, this was the dream of vast majority of Hmong refugees in America. Then, ties to the Hmong in Thai refugee camps were still strong. Letters, and audio casettes, were exchanged with relatives in the camps on a regular basis. This guaranteed a steady flow of stories of the exploits of Hmong freedom fighters operating in Laos and rumors of the impending collapse of the LPDR. In the late seventies and early eighties, Hmong communities throughout the U.S. contributed huge sums to support Hmong guerrilla operations in Laos. Many American Hmong were even willing to travel to Thailand and organize a resistance army to invade Laos and attempt to bring down the communist regime so that Laotian Hmong scattered across the globe could be repatriated.

It is now over a decade since Laos went communist, and the LPDR and their Vietnamese sponsors still rule the country with an iron fist. Understandably, this hard fact has dampened the enthusiasm of American Hmong for grand plans to launch new guerrilla operations or organize resistance movements. Today, only the very old continue to cling to the dream of repatriation. For their children, many of whom now have families of their own, Laos is a fading image, still warm but no longer glowing.

It is nothing new for the Hmong to be driven from their homeland and to be forced to start life anew in a foreign country. The difference for American Hmong is that they chose the U.S., a nation of immigrants who shared one dream: to build a society where no one has to ever start over again. Noted for their love of freedom, and oppressed for centuries because of it, the Hmong are a welcome addition to the melting pot called America.

BIBLIOGRAPHY

Adams, Leonard."China: The Historical Setting of Asia's Profitable Plague." appendix to Alfred McCoy. *The Politics of Heroin in Southeast Asia*. New York: Harper & Row, 1972.

Allen, Nathan. *The Opium Trade*. 13 vols.; London: Longwood Press, 1978.

Beauclair, Inez. *Tribal Cultures of Southwest China*. Taipei: The Orient Cultural Service, 1972.

Bernatzik, Hugo Adlof. *Akha and Miao: Problems of Applied Ethnography in Farther India*. New Haven: Human Relations Area Files, 1970.

Bertrais, Yves. *The Traditional Marriage Among the White Hmong of Thailand and Laos*. Chiangmai, Thailand: Hmong Center, 1978.

Bessac, Suzanne and Jo Rainbolt. *Notes on Traditional Hmong Culture from Montana Hmong Recollections*. Missoula: University of Montana Press, 1978.

Bhikkhu, Dhammaraso and Virocano Bhikkhu. *The Historical Background and Tradition of the Meo*. Bangkok, Thailand: n.p., 1973.

Bliatout, Bruce Thowpaou. *Hmong Sudden Unexpected Nocturnal Death Syndrome: A Cultural Study*. Portland, Oregon: Sparkle Publishing Enterprises, 1982.

Bonifacy, Auguste. *Cours d'Ethnographie Indochinoise*. Hanoi-Haiphong: Imprimerie D'Extreme-Orient, 1919.

Bourotte, Bernard."Marriages et Funeralles Chez les Meos Blancs de la Region de Nong-Het (Tran Ninh)." *Institut Indochinois Pour l'Etude de l'Homme, Bulletins et Travaux*. vol. 6. 1943.

Branfman, Fred (ed.). *Voices from the Plain of Jars*. New York: Harper Colophon Books, 1972.

Bridgman, E.C."Sketches of the Miau-Tsze." *Royal Asiatic Society*. no. 3. 1859.

Burchette, Wilfred. *Mekong Upstream*. Berlin: Seven Seas Publishers, 1959.

"_____Pawns and Patriots: The U.S. Fight for Laos." in Nina Adams and Alfred McCoy. *Laos: War and Revolution*. New York: Harper & Row, 1971.

Burling, Robbins. *Hill Farms and Padi Fields*. Englewood Cliffs, New Jersey: Prentice-Hall, inc., 1965.

Chagnon, Jacqui and Roger Rumpf."Dignity, National Identity and Unity." *Southeast Asia Chronicle*. Vol. 73. June 1980.

Chard, Chester. *Man in Prehistory*. 2nd ed.; New York: McGraw-Hill Book Co., 1975.

Chindarsi, Nusit. *The Religion of the Hmong Njua*. Bangkok: The Siam Society, 1983.

Clark, Grahame. *World Prehistory in New Perspective*. 3rd ed.; Cambridge: Cambridge University Press, 1977.

Clarke, Judith."The Laotian Dilemma." *Asia Week*. February 2, 1986.

Clarke, Samuel R."The Miao and Chungchia Tribes of Kweichow Province." *East of Asia*. vol. 3. September 1904.

Coon, Carelton. *The Living Races of Man*. New York: Alfred A. Knopf, 1965.

Cooper, Robert."The Hmong of Laos: Economic Factors in the Refugee Exodus and Return." in Glen Hendricks, Bruce Downing and Amos Deinard (eds.). *The Hmong in Transition*. New York: Center for Migration Studies, 1986.

Coulborn, Rushton. *The Origin of Civilized Societies*. Princeton, New Jersey: Princeton University Press, 1959.

Daniel, Glyn. *The First Civilizations: The Archaeology of their Origins*. New York: Thomas Y. Crowell Co., 1968.

Dasse, Martial. *Montagnards, Revoltes et Guerres Revolutionairres en Asie du Sud-Est Continentale*. Bangkok: DK Book House, 1976.

De Lajonquiere, Etenne Lunet. *Ethnographie du Tonkin Septentrional*. Paris: Ernest Leroux, 1906.

Diguet, Edouard. *Les Montagnards du Tonkin*. Paris: Challamel, 1908.

Dommen, Arthur. *Laos: Keystone of Indochina*. Boulder, Colorado: Westview Press, 1985.

Doyle, Edward and Samuel Lipsman. *The Vietnam Experience: Setting the Stage*. Boston: Boston Publishing Co., 1981.

Durdin, Peggy."Soviet Imperialism: The Grim Lesson of Laos." in Harry Schwartz (ed.). *The Many Faces of Communism*. Berkeley: Berkeley Publishing, 1962.

Eberhard, Wolfram. *A History of China*. 2nd ed., Los Angeles: University Press, 1960.

China's Minorities: Yesterday and Today. Belmont Calif.: Wadsworth Publishing Co., 1982.

Ebihara, May."Mon-Khmer." in Frank Lebar, et. al. *Ethnic Groups of Mainland Southeast Asia*. New Haven: Human Relations Area Files Press, 1964.

Everingham, John."One Family's Oddyssey to America." *National Geographic*.Vol. 157. No. 5. May 1980.

Fagan, Brian. *Men of the Earth: An Introduction to World Prehistory*. Boston: Little, Brown and Co., 1974.

Fall, Bernard. *The Two Viet-Nams: A Political and Military Analysis*. rev. ed.; New York: Frederick Praeger, 1964.

_____*Hell in a Very Small Place: The Siege of Dien Bien Phu*. Philadelphia: J.B. Lippincott Co., 1967.

Fass, Simon M."Economic Development and Employment Projects." in Glen Hendricks, Bruce Downing and Amos Deinard (eds.). *The Hmong in Transition*. New York: Center for Migration Studies, 1986.

Feldman, Orna."A New Life for the Hmong." *Boston Magazine*. Vol. 75. April 1983.

Feng, H.Y. and J.K. Shryock."The Black Magic in China Known as 'Ku'." *American Oriental Society Journal*. vol. 55. 1935.

Fink, John."Secondary Migration to California's Central Valley." in Glen Hendricks, Bruce Downing and Amos Deinard (eds.). *The Hmong in Transition*.New York: Center for Migration Studies, 1986.

Foisie, Jack."U.S.-Backed Laotian General Scorned by Other Army Leaders." *Los Angeles Times*. March 12, 1970.

Franke, Wolfgang. *A Century of Chinese Revolution: 1851-1949*. New York, Harper Torchbooks, 1970.

Garrett, W.E."The Hmong of Laos: No Place to Run." *National Geographic*. Vol.145. No. 1. January 1974.

Geddes, William. *Migrants of the Mountains: The Cultural Ecology of the Blue Miao (Hmong Njua) of Thailand*. Oxford: Clarendon Press, 1976.

Girard, Henry. *Les Tribus Suavages du Haut-Tonkin: Man et Meos*. Paris: Imprimerie Nationale, 1903.

Graham, David Crockett. *Songs and Stories of the Ch'uan Miao*. Washington D.C.: Smithsonian Institution, 1954.

Grandstaff, Terry."The Hmong, Opium and the Haw: Speculations on the Origin of their Association." *Siam Society Journal*. vol. 67, no. 2. 1979.

Gryaznov, Mikhail. *The Ancient Civilizations of Southern Siberia*. translated by from the Russian by James Hogarth. New York: Cowles Publishing Co., 1969.

Gua, Bo."Opium, Bombs and Trees: The Future of the Hmong Tribesmen in Northern Thailand." *Journal of Contemporary Asia*. Vol. 5. No. 1. 1975.

Her, Thao. *Interview*. Visalia, California. June 15, 1985

International Narcotics Control, Hearings. Committee on Foreign Affairs. House of Representatives. 87th Cong. 2nd Sess. 1982.

Jackson, Larry."The Vietnamese Revolution and the Montagnards." *Asian Survey*. Vol. 9. No. 5. May 1969.

Karnow, Stanley. *Vietnam: A History*. New York: The Viking Press, 1983.

_____"Free No More: The Allies America Forgot." *Geo*. Vol. 2. 1980.

Keen, F.G.B. *The Meo of Northwest Thailand*. Wellington, New Zealand: R.E.Owen, Government Printer, 1966.

Knoll, Tricia. *Becoming Americans: Asian Sojourners, Immigrants, and Refugees in the Western United States*. Portland, Or.: Coast to Coast Books, 1982.

Lancaster, Donald. *The Emancipation of French Indochina*. London: Oxford University Press, 1961.

Langer, Paul and Joseph Zasloff. *North Vietnam and the Pathet Lao*. Cambridge, Mass.: Harvard University Press, 1970.

_____"Laos Under the Gun." *Asia Week*. October 5, 1979.

Larteguy, Jean. *La Fabuleuse Aventure du Peuple du l'Opium*. Paris: Presses de la Cite, 1979.

Lee, Bliacher. *Interview*. Merced, California. June 18, 1985.

Lee, Gary Yia."Culture and Adaptation: Hmong Refugees in Austrialia 1976-83." *Hmong-Australia Society Newsletter*. vol. 6, no. 2. June 1984.

_____."Minority Policies and the Hmong." in Martin Stuart-Fox (ed.). *Contemporary Laos*. New York: St. Martin's Press, 1982.

Lemoine, Jacques. *Un Village Hmong Vert Du Haut Laos*. Paris: Editions du Centre National de la Recherche Scientifique, 1972.

_____."Les Ecritures du Hmong." *Bulletin des Amis du Royaume Lao*. nos. 7 & 8. 1972.

Lyman, Thomas Amis."Green Miao (Meo) Spirit-Ceremonies." *Ethnologica*. Vol.4. 1960.

Mason, Linda and Roger Brown. *Rice, Rivalry, and Politics: Managing Cambodian Relief*. London: University of Notre Dame Press, 1983.

McAlister, John."Mountain Minorities and the Viet Minh: A Key to the Indochina War." in of Peter Kunstadter (ed.) *Southeast Asian Tribes, Minorioties, and Nations*. 2 vols.; Princeton, New Jersey: Princeton University Press, 1967.II.

McCoy, Alfred. *The Politics of Heroin in Southeast Asia*. New York: Harper & Row, 1972.

_____."French Colonialism in Laos, 1893-1945." in Nina Adams and Alfred McCoy. *Laos: War and Revolution*. New York: Harper & Row, 1971.

Mickey, Margaret Porcia."The Cowrie Shell Miao of Kweichow," *Papers of the Peabody Museum of American Archaeology and Ethnology*, XXXII, no. 1. 1947.

Morechand, Guy."Notes Demographiques Sur un Canton Meo Blanc du Pays Tai." *Bulletin de la Societe des Etudes Indochinoises de Saigon*. vol. 27. 1952.

Mottin, Jean. *The History of the Hmong (Meo)*. Bangkok: Odeon Store Ltd., 1980.

_____*Elements de Grammaire Hmong Blanc*. Khek Noy: Don Bosco Press, 1978.

_____*Allons Faire Le Tour du Ciel et de la Terre: Le Chamanisme des Hmong Vu dans les Textes*. Sap Samothot, Thailand: n.p., 1981.

_____55 Chants D'Amour Hmong Blanc. Bangkok: Siam Society, 1980.

_____Fetes Du Nouvel An Chez Les Hmong Blanc De Thailande. Bangkok, Thailand: Don Bosco Press, 1979.

Moua, Yao Naotou. *Interview*. Spokane, Washington. 1985.

Norindr, Chou. "Political Institutions of the Lao People's Democratic Republic." in Martin Stuart-Fox (ed.). *Contemporary Laos*. New York: St.Martin's Press, 1982.

Olney, Douglas."Population Trends." in Glen Hendricks, Bruce Downing and Amos Deinard (eds.). *The Hmong in Transition*. New York: Center for Migration Studies, 1986.

_____"Opium Found in St Paul; Woman Held." *Minneapolis Star and Tribune*. August 12, 1982.

Papa, Mary Bader."Waking up to the American Dream." *Twin Cities Magazine*.May 1982.

_____"Police Pounce on Poppy Patch." *The Spokesman-Review*. July 30, 1982.

Richburg, Keith."Cambodia is Turning Out to be Vietnam's Vietnam." *The Washington Post National Weekly Edition*. December 1, 1986.

Rocher, Emile. *La Province Chinoise Du Yun-Nan*. 2 vols.; Paris: Ernest Leroux, 1879.

Roux, Henri and Tran Van Chu."Quelques Minorites Ethniques du Nord Indochine." *France-Asie*. Vol. 10. 1954.

Roy, Jules. *The Battle of Dienbienphu*. translated by Robert Baldick; New York: Harper & Row, 1965.

Savina, F.M. *Histoire Des Miao*. Paris: Societe des Missions-Etrangeres, 1924.

Schanche, Don. *Mr. Pop*. New York: David McKay Co., 1967.

Schein, Louis. "The Miao in Contemporary China: A Preliminary Overview." in Glen Hendricks, Bruce Downing and Amos Deinard (eds.). *The Hmong in Transition*. New York: Center for Migration Studies, 1986.

Shaplen, Robert. *Time out of Hand: Revolution and Reaction in Southeast Asia*. New York: Harper & Row, 1969.

_____A Turning Wheel. New York: Random House, 1973.

"A Reporter at Large: Survivors." *New Yorker*. September 5, 1977.

Shrock, Joanne, et. al. *Minority Groups in Thailand*. Washington D.C.: Department of the Army, 1970.

____*Minority Groups in North Vietnam*. Washington D.C.: U.S. Government Printing Office, 1972.

Smalley, William A."Stages of Hmong Cultural Adaptation." in Glen Hendricks, Bruce Downing and Amos Deinard (eds.). *The Hmong in Transition*. New York: Center for Migration Studies, 1986.

____."Khmu." in Frank Lebar, et. al. *Ethnic Groups of Mainland Southeast Asia*.New Haven: Human Relations Area Files Press, 1964.

St. Cartmail, Keith. *Exodus Indochina*. Auckland: Heinemann, 1983.

Stover, Leon and Takeko Stover. *China: An Anthropological Perspective*. Pacific Palisades: Goodyear Publishing Co., 1976.

Terry, Charles and Mildred Pellens. *The Opium Problem*. reprint of 1928 edition; Montclair, New Jersey: Patterson Smith, 1970.

_____."The Agony of the Hmong." *Asia Week*. Dec 15, 1978.

The Global Connection: Heroin Entrepreneurs, Hearings. Subcommittee to Investigate Juvenile Delinquency. U.S. Senate. 94th Cong. 2nd Sess. 1976.

The Hill Tribes of Thailand. Chiang Mai, Thailand: Technical Service Club Tribal Research Institute, 1986.

The Hmong in St. Paul: A Culture in Transition. St. Paul, Minnesota: Community Planning Organization, 1980.

Trinquier, Roger. *Les Maquis d'Indochine*. Paris: Albatros, n.d.

____."Temoignage: Les Maquis d'Indochine." *Revue Historique des Armees*. Vol.2. 1979.

Vreeland, Susan."Through the Looking Glass with the Hmong of Laos." *The Christian Science Monitor*. March 30, 1981.

____."Future of Laotian Folk Art Hangs by a Thread." *The Christian Science Monitor*. November 19, 1981.

Vu, Fu. *Interview*. Spokane, Washington. 1984.

____*Interview*. Spokane, Washington. 1987.

Vu, Tou. *Interview*. Spokane, Washington. 1984.

___*Interview*. Spokane, Washington. 1985.

Vue, Cher Sue. *Interview*. Sacramento, California. 1985.

Vue, Nao Yang. *Interview*. Spokane, Washington. 1985.

___*Interview*. Sacramento, California. 1985.

Vue, Neng. *Interview*. Spokane, Washington. 1985.

Vue, Seng. *Interview*. Visalia, California. 1985.

Vue, Shue Long. *Interview*. Sacramento, California. 1985.

Vue, Tong Leng. *Interview*. Spokane, Washington. 1985.

Vue, Xia Ying. *Interview*. Sacramento, California. 1985.

Wekkin, Gary."The Rewards of Revolution: Pathet Lao Policy Toward the Hill Tribes Since 1975." in Martin Stuart-Fox (ed.). *Contemporary Laos*. New York: St. Martin's Press, 1982.

Westermeyer, Joseph. *Poppies, Pipes, and People: Opium and Its Use in Laos*. Los Angeles: University of California Press, 1982.

Whitaker, Donald et. al. *Area Handbook for Laos*. Washington D.C.: U.S.Government Printing Office, 1972.

Wiens, Herold. *China's March Toward the Tropics*. Hamnden Conn.: The Shoe String Press, 1954.

Xiong, Katoua (formerly known as Xiong Chong Neng). *Interview*. Spokane, Washington. 1985.

Yang, Dao. *Les Hmong du Laos Face au Developpement*. Vientiane, Laos: Edition Siaosavath, 1975.

___"Guerre Des Gaz: Solution Communiste Des Problemes Des Minorities Au Laos?" *Temps Modernes*. Vol. 30. No. 402. January 1980.

___"Why Did the Hmong Leave Laos?" in Bruce Downing and Douglas Olney (eds.). *The Hmong in the West: Observations and Reports*. Minneapolis, St. Paul: University of Minnesota Press, 1982.

Yang, Nao Ying. *Interview*. Spokane, Washington. 1984.

___*Interview*. Spokane, Washington. 1987.

Yang, Cher Cha. *Communication*. Fresno, California. 1985.

Yie-Fu, Ruey."The Miao: Their Origin and Southward Migration." *Proceedings: International Association of Historians of Asia*. October 1962.

Yun, Lu."Miao Woman Pioneers Reform." *Beijing Review*. vol. 29, no. 38.September 22, 1986.

Zacher, Mark W. and R. Stephen Milne (eds.). *Conflict and Stability in Southeast Asia*. New York: Anchor Books, 1974

INDEX